EFL GUID

Fifth Edition

Managing Editor
Daniel Ward

Consultant Editor
Barry Tomalin

Design
George Ajayi

Illustrations
Chris Duggan

Advertising
Liz Pannell

Production
Sheldon Pink

Publishers
John Gorner and Daniel Ward

Written and researched by
Gillian Campbell, Matthew Hancock, Andrew Scales, Barry Tomalin, Daniel Ward

Additional research by
Paula McLaughlin, Liz Pannell, Richard West

Acknowledgements
The publishers would like to thank the following for their invaluable help
Manju Aggarwal, Oxford Delegacy; Christine Nuttall, John Wheeler, John Whitehead of the
British Council and British Councils worldwide; Kate Naameh & Michelle Watson, International
House; Charlotte Boyle, Trinity College; Lynette Murphy O'Dwyer, UCLES; Simon Learmount,
Saxoncourt; Brenda Towsend, ARELS; Bill Reed, Canning School; Vincent o'Neill, Siemens;
David Cervi, KDC Consulting, Stuart Rose, NZEIL; Duncan Baker, Lydbury English Centre; Vera
Wojna, University of the Cariboo; Hilary MacElwain & Mary Large, RELSA; Dr. Kevin McGinley,
ATT; David Young, New European Bookshops; Richard West, Manchester University; Geraldine
Egan, Irish Tourist Board; Dominic Gallagher, Dept. of Education, Dublin.
Cover Illustration by Richard Caldicott.

ISBN 0 951 4576 4 0

Published by EFL Ltd.,
9 Hope Street, Douglas, Isle of Man IM1 1AQ, British Isles.

Printed by Mannin Printing, 28-30 Spring Valley Industrial Estate, Braddan, IOM, British Isles

ECS Limited

ECS Limited, the largest employer of English Language teachers in the United Arab Emirates, has vacancies for EFL teachers throughout the year for projects in the UAE and elsewhere, teaching children and adults. We would like to hear from young professionals seeking opportunities for career development.

PROFESSIONAL OPTIONS

- ❏ Aston University MSc in ESP
- ❏ Trinity College London Licentiate Diploma in TESOL
- ❏ Trinity College London Certificate in TESOL

CAREER ENHANCEMENT

- ❏ Teacher Training
- ❏ Curriculum/Materials Development
- ❏ ELT Management
- ❏ ESP Course Design

Interested? Then contact ECS Cyprus on:

Tel: Int. Code + 357 (5) 340103
Fax: Int. Code + 357 (5) 340691

Or, write to: ECS Limited, PO Box 3032,
Limassol, Cyprus

Educational Consulting Services   Toronto, Limassol, Abu Dhabi, Dubai

PREFACE

How the EFL Guide will help you:

The Guide is for anyone considering or already involved in English Language Training; prospective teachers, teachers, training/personnel managers, publishers, consultants, etc., but different sections will naturally be more relevant to some groups than others.

●Training/Personnel Managers, or Consultants

Start with **Section One - English in Business**, which examines the commercial benefits of language training and English, in particular. It is especially relevant for the training manager of small to medium-sized companies, who is considering investing in language training, but wants to make sure that the company gets value for money.

For local information and schools, consult your country's section of **World English.**

To get a real understanding of what you can expect from teachers, read through **Sections Two and Five,** which will show you what teaching qualifications actually enable teachers to do. You can now produce a specification for any language training provider with authority.

●Prospective Teachers

Turn straight to **Section Two - Becoming a Teacher -** for anyone considering EFL/ESL teaching as a career, or as a short-term means of working while you travel, this section maps out a route for you by providing clear advice and information on basic teaching courses and qualifications. Once you have read this, go to **Section Four - World English**, to find out what opportunities there are for you in the countries of your choice.

If you are relatively sure that EFL is the career for you, **Section Three** shows you how to go about getting a job and **Section Five** will help you to plan a long-term career strategy.

●Teachers/EFL Professionals

If you do not have a qualification, go to **Section Two.**
If you want to improve your career prospects, **Section Five** explains how further qualifications will help.

For ideas about teaching and associated jobs, turn to **Section Three.**

Section One will give you an insight into the hugely important Business English market, which can provide some of the most exciting career options.

AND, if you are looking for a new job, anywhere in the world, **Section Four** has opportunities in over 100 countries.

As the UK still dominates the world EFL market, the Guide naturally emphasises the opportunities and programmes in Britain, but most information should be relevant to the profession worldwide. It is the EFL Guide's policy to be international in its outlook, so any suggestions/information from any source in any country would be appreciated.

English Language Training, Banbury

CONTENTS

Preparing For The TOEFL® Test?

Give Your Students An Official Head Start.

Help your students prepare for the TOEFL test with these official study materials from the developers of the test itself!

Understanding TOEFL provides a thorough overview of all three TOEFL test sections. *Listening to TOEFL* provides extra practice on Listening Comprehension, the most difficult section for many students. And *Reading for TOEFL* focuses on the Vocabulary and Reading Comprehension section.

Your students will hear both male and female North American voices. They'll hear spoken English without seeing the speakers' face and lip movements. And they'll practice taking a multiple-choice format test—with *authentic* test questions from previous TOEFL tests.

For economy, student workbooks are also available in classroom packs of 10. For more information about these and other TOEFL materials, return the coupon today.

INTRODUCTION

The 'English 2000' initiative is a major research project which will affect all teachers of English. Ian Stewart, Assistant Director of the British Council in Manchester, is a key figure in its implementation. He describes the challenges and opportunities facing the industry as it moves towards the millenium.

Political and economic changes in the last five years have dramatically altered our world; countries and systems that appeared to be permanent features have disappeared or become substantially different. Change is the only constant and this is true in virtually all aspects of life, including language. The present overwhelming position of English as the world's medium of business and commerce looks unassailable; more and more students are learning English and the number of international publications in English is testimony to its power and influence. But the language and this industry it fuels will face exciting challenges in the years ahead. Forces are at work which may cause significant change in the demand for English and the way it is taught in a relatively short period of time.

What are these forces that may affect the position of English in the world? One is undoubtedly the growing importance of other languages, such as German in Eastern Europe and Spanish in the United States. If China continues to develop economically as rapidly as now, Chinese will be a force in the next century. Linked to this is the rise of nationalism and the increased role of language in defining a nation's identity.

Another major influence is the development of electronics, probably the one area affecting us all where most dramatic changes are likely to occur. As machines talk to machines and it becomes possible to access the vast information banks of the world from the comfort of one's own language, so the means of acquiring English and the way teaching is delivered may change. Electronic publishing will continue to grow and the demands of English learners will become increasingly sophisticated.

Changes such as these offer exciting challenges both to EFL teachers entering the profession and to experienced teachers who need to continue to advance their professional development. To help teachers meet these challenges, the British Council, one of the world's leading teaching and training bodies, has initiated English 2000 with the aim of helping teachers improve their skills and to enhance the status of EFL, ESL and ESOL as a profession.

English 2000 is an initiative which seeks to research, predict and organise in order to meet new patterns of demand. For 30 years English as a Foreign Language led the way in new ideas on methodology and educational technology; what many British teachers of French and German now regard as innovative their EFL colleagues were doing many years ago. But are English language teachers continuing to respond quickly to change? We need to exchange information on changes in demand, to forge new partnerships and develop new methodologies based on what the market is demanding. We need to listen to learners to see what they need. We need to be constantly concerned to develop and expand our professional skills. We need to seek out ways of pooling resources to build a common strategy.

The first step is to define more clearly where we are - to establish how and where English is taught around the world. Much of this research will come from teachers involved in classroom research of their own. E2000 also recognises that it would be wrong to generalise globally from one region alone. There are differences in demand and expectation from country to country, so there will be a strong regional focus in the project. This year of research will help us form a strategy to enable the industry to identify and respond to new patterns of demand and to enhance the development of the teaching of English as a profession. This strategy will be implemented over the four years to the end of the century.

By the year 2000, partly as a result of this initiative, we hope that ELT worldwide will remain as thriving, fit and innovative an industry as it has been for the last 40 years. Its success will depend on the enthusiasm and creativity of English teachers in seeking to build on what they and their predecessors have achieved for the language over the last few years and ensure that change when it comes is grasped as an opportunity and not a threat. The British philosopher Edmund Burke said "you can never plan the future by the past", but what you can do is establish strategies and develop skills so that you remain able to adapt quickly to changing circumstances.

More and more students are learning English and the number of international publications in English is testimony to its power and influence.

What many British teachers of French and German now regard as innovative their EFL colleagues were doing many years ago.

University of Oxford
Delegacy of Local Examinations

▶ Oxford International Business English at

- First Level

- Executive Level

▶ Tourism English Proficiency

For further details, please write to:-

M. Aggarwal,
UODLE
Ewert House,
Summertown,
Oxford,
OX2 7BZ
U.K.

ENGLISH IN BUSINESS

For training/personnel managers, consultants, school managers or business English teachers, this section assesses the trends in the market. It shows you how to determine the language needs of your staff, how to decide which is the most cost-efficient training option for your needs and how to assess the proficiency of English speaking employees. The section ends with two case studies: one from a German multinational and one from a specialist language school, after which we explain how, with some help from the experts, your computer system can provide translation and language support.

BUSINESS ENGLISH: WHY BUY NOW?

Business English training is now within the reach of smaller companies. As professional opportunities grow, English language training is attracting more and better qualified instructors.

While individuals see English as a means of career progression, organisations invest in training to realise a financial advantage.

By its very nature, the business of English language training tends to be presented in an academic rather than a commercial light, which detracts from the majority of consumers' reasons for learning English. While individuals see English as a means of career progression, organisations invest in training to realise an advantage, be it in terms of efficiency or sales. There are those who learn English for more ethereal reasons, but they are only a small minority. Teachers embarking on a career in EFL must consider the development of the market in which they intend to work. There are also many potential consumers who require hard evidence of the benefit of English language training in order to justify the expenditure.

In order to profile consumers within the language training market, the general employment and training market must be examined. The world recession has taken its toll on the employment market, but this does not necessarily reflect on the training market. Traditionally, this market stands up well during recession, because individuals turn to training in order to increase their chances of employment. Demand for teacher training courses in EFL has been huge during the economic recession of the early 1990s. The result of this is that there is a larger pool of better specialist teachers, which, in turn, has led to more specific and cost effective training - in fact, a better deal for the purchaser.

English has become a practical necessity for employees at different levels of seniority in companies of all sizes.

So for those who have opted for such a career, who will they be teaching over the next few years? Over the last ten years, there has been a recognition within Europe that employment growth will be generated by small to medium sized enterprises (SMEs, firms with less than 500 employees), rather than through the expansion of larger multinational firms. This theory is based upon the experience of the US market and reflects developments within Europe.

That is not to say that the traditional large-scale consumers of training, the multinationals, are no longer an important market, but personnel or training managers within smaller companies are being encouraged to learn from the example set by firms with the resources to implement comprehensive language training programmes. The most fundamental question to be considered by any firm, small or large, when undertaking language training is whether or not the cost justifies the perceived return. This question is particularly pertinent for smaller companies without substantial training budgets operating under harsh economic conditions, so many governments have adopted policies to assist SMEs in their training programmes.

In Europe, the EC's Task Force on Human Resources has set up a number of funding programmes to assist smaller businesses to overcome the financial strain of training, so it is a good idea to examine the financial assistance available before finalising a training policy. Many schemes have rigorous qualification criteria, which make it difficult to adapt a programme for eligibility once it is in place.

One example of national commitment is that of the French government which has made it a legal requirement that all companies spend 1.4% of their gross profits on training. Many companies use these funds for English language training. The globalisation of commerce is a development resulting largely from improved communications, which has been accelerated by the signing of international cooperation agreements, such as NAFTA (the North American Free Trade Area), EEA (the European Economic Area, incorporating EFTA, the European Free Trade Area and the EU) and ASEAN (the Association of South-East Asian Nations). Its effect on most businesses is that international trade is the route to expansion, so language training is no longer just a perk for multinational executives, but an integral part of corporate staff training.

English has become a practical necessity for employees at different levels of seniority in companies of all sizes. Through a balance between different training methods and by capitalising on assistance available, most companies can now benefit from having staff capable of communicating with expanding markets without an enormous budget. This is good news for teachers of EFL, who are entering an evolving but exciting career.

DEMAND FOR BUSINESS ENGLISH

The recession has led to geographical changes in demand. along with new courses, methods and materials.

The key feature of 1994 is the continuing recession in Europe and Japan, and its effect on the demand for the teaching of business English. One of the earliest casualties of the recession is cutbacks in company training programmes and the onus being placed on executives to seek their own training, perhaps at their own cost. Training has to yield immediate results.

Information suggests that the business EFL industry has been reduced by as much as 30% over the four years since the the mid to late eighties with corresponding effects both on the size and structure of suppliers. It is believed that recovery will be slow in 1994 to 1995, and there will then be great opportunities for a more efficient business EFL sector.

Changes in structure

Japan has been notable for the withdrawal of some of the key corporate training companies, releasing a significant number of experienced business English teachers on to the language market. Japan has built up a corpus of experienced Japanese speaking 'gaijin' residents of American, Canadian, Australian or British origin, which makes the market resistant to newcomers. Nevertheless, for the committed teacher, working in Japan will be a rewarding experience.

In the European sector a number of countries are effectively closed to the UK and other trainers seeking contracts, either because the need is filled by existing suppliers, or the market is saturated and not expanding. They are Scandinavia, Italy and Spain.

Germany and France, two of the traditionally strongest business English training markets, are still open to contracts, but the structure and nature of these contracts is changing. The German market is traditionally one where a trainer or trainers are absorbed into a company to provide their business EFL training. The companies where business English training is likely to survive are ones where language training has been absorbed into general business education. The language trainer is now expected to be a company specialist, if not a business specialist in his or her own right.

The French market has traditionally been inspired by the practice of "formation continue",

the law that demands that 1.4% of gross company profits must be used for in-service training. This has kept the French training market reasonably buoyant in the face of recession, although little expansion has taken place.

In the UK market where suppliers are seeking contracts either to attract company personnel or to send teachers into companies, there is a clear change discernible both in the size and structure of the industry. First, a shake-out. Schools who felt that an executive centre could be established with a plush reception and general English courses dressed up with business terminology are not doing well. Schools that have dedicated executive centres with specialist teachers and resources are keeping their heads above water, despite the investment and overhead required.

There is also a change in the type of demand. Executives are coming over for shorter courses, usually of a maximum duration of two weeks. They are also looking for highly targeted courses, often involving business specialists as well as language trainers. This has suited established business language trainers, and especially those who can call on retired businessmen to share their expertise with foreign executives on training courses.

The cost of courses has also stabilised. Whereas the cost of a day's training in other disciplines in the UK can vary between £300 and £900 a day, EFL business training is now relatively reasonable with two week courses costing about £1000 a person for group training. Language training prices have remained stable during the three years of contraction. Paradoxically, for companies that can afford it, there has never been a better time to buy economical language training.

An expanding area of the market is the sole trainer. This is the situation of a business executive who provides language training, accommodation and a family atmosphere in his or her own home. The trainer, usually a retired or redundant business person, maybe with several years' service in a major corporation, can provide a week or two's accommodation, conversation and business contact at very low cost compared to the Executive Training Centres.

EFL business training is now relatively reasonable with two week courses costing about £1000 a person for group training.

For companies that can afford it, there has never been a better time to buy economical language training.

The other side of this market is the sole trainer servicing say 6-8 corporate clients on site. Once again by using the employer's location, the trainer maintains low overheads, while providing a personalised, targeted executive training service.

Associations and organisations
In British and American ELT the most popular Special Interest Groups (SIGs) in IATEFL (the International Association of Teachers of English as a Foreign Language) and TESOL are the Business SIG and MUESLI - the Computer Aided Language Learning SIG. Training managers and teachers interested in buying or selling language training services would be well advised to make contact. Each SIG has a newsletter and holds a variety of seminars both in the UK and on the continent of Europe. To contact either of these SIGs, go through the IATEFL secretariat (See p.168).

Other organisations coordinating and promoting British suppliers of Business English training are the British Council and ARELS (The Association of Recognised Language Schools). The British Council has produced a short video (in collaboration with the British Tourist Authority) about business english teaching centres in the UK. ARELS runs regional seminars, sometimes in collaboration with local Chambers of Commerce, on new products and methods.

Under the auspices of the British Council English Language Promotion Unit, the Council's office in Austria will host a major Business English seminar for teachers and training managers from Central Europe and the Eastern Lander of Germany. Once again the aim is to raise awareness of the methods, quality and availability of EFL business training.

Materials
Notwithstanding the recession, publishers have come out with a range of new business English materials, especially at elementary and lower intermediate levels. The *Macmillan Business English Course* is audio led with a video supplement forthcoming. Longman has 'English Works', an audio-led elementary course by Robert O'Neill. The BBC has brought out a new elementary level video based course called 'Starting Business English' and Thomas Nelson have courses at intermediate level. OUP have released the video 'Meeting Objectives' for OUP at intermediate level and, in an interesting new initiative, Prentice Hall International has collected business reports from ABC news network in a video and book package called 'Focus on Business'.

Interactive developments
Probably the most interesting development in the Business English materials field is the quantity and sophistication of interactive video. A range of materials has been developed by companies in the UK, on the continent, in the USA and Japan. One of the most comprehensive lists has been developed by Vektor Ltd in the UK, who, working in collaboration with the BBC, have produced a range of bilingual courses from elementary to upper intermediate level.

The newest software contains a vastly increased range of options, including on-screen tutorials, visual indices of exponents of language functions, grammar, lexis explanations, and much more.

In California, the DYNED Corporation, an American company using Japanese technology allied to Microsoft's DOS system, has developed a compelling elementary course, called 'Dynamic English', for interactive video and CD ROM.

The spread of interactive video is inhibited both by cost and by the uncertainty about technical standards. All producers are united in the recognition that CD ROM technology is the basis for all development in Interactive Media, and that for language learning, full screen video animation is the key to successful motivation and usage. For the next two to three years the 12-inch laser disk is likely to be the delivery mechanism for the corporate market, moving into CD ROM when it is capable of full screen animation.

A further uncertainty concerns the role of interactive media in relation to classroom teaching. Manufacturers insist that the function of interactive video is to free teacher contact hours for more creative work and is certainly no replacement for them. Large corporations use interactive video in this way, but some companies have invested in interactive video training without teachers for corporate students.

Although not excessive, the cost of setting up interactive video has tended to inhibit language schools and colleges from investing. Although we are now seeing a rapid change in policy, interactive video is likely to remain based in the corporate market, where it will be a major feature of business language teaching in large international corporations over the next five years. In the longer term, there can be no doubt that interactive technology will play a part in all training.

Probably the most interesting development in the Business English materials field is the quantity and sophistication of interactive video.

Manufacturers insist that the function of interactive video is to free teacher contact hours for more creative work

ASSESSING THE LANGUAGE NEEDS OF YOUR COMPANY

Why do your staff need English? The key question before you buy training. This is how you find out.

The language audit

Most smaller companies appear to have only a vague idea of how language ability can improve their chances of success. Meanwhile, larger firms with transnational operations and markets have had the time and resources to analyse the contribution that languages can make to their profitability. To avoid losing out to the large firms, smaller firms should take advantage of the groundwork already done by large companies, in particular, the language audit.

The language audit is merely a term used to refer to any means of assessing language needs and the subsequent training required. Its purpose is to determine the precise language skills needed to carry out specific jobs, assess the language skills presently available and predict future language training requirements. It is usually applied when language needs have become apparent in a company, either as a result of internal factors or external events, such as the advent of the Single European Market. Ideally, the audit should be implemented as part of the planning for long-term objectives.

In most cases, a language audit is carried out by a consultant (the 'auditor') in cooperation with the firm's training/personnel manager. There are examples of language audits freely available, however, such as the model developed by CILT (Centre for Information on Language Teaching and Research), which is divided into four stages:
1/ A survey of available skills.
2/ Identification of training needs.
3/ Selection of training options.
4/ Evaluation of the language audit and provision of a maintenance programme.

1. The first stage commences with an in-house survey of existing skills, including the ability and/or willingness of employees to use and improve these skills. Once collated, this is handed to the auditor as 'input' information. The auditor then designs a timetable.

2. During the second stage, the employer puts forward their plans regarding foreign languages, from which the auditor draws up a preliminary report on the levels of ability required by specific employees. It is at this stage that the employer must link language training to the objectives of the company in the long term, so that an integrated language training policy will be implemented. In devising this policy, the following questions must be asked:
a) Who will be trained?
b) How will the trainees be chosen?
c) When will training take place?
d) Will trainees be offered incentives to learn?
e) How will skills learned be kept 'up to scratch'?
f) What is the budget for language training?
g) How will employees be encouraged to use foreign languages?
h) How will language needs affect recruitment?

Refinements to the needs report are made as a result of this and the auditor now specifies the skills needed by groups or individuals.

3. The third stage involves the auditor examining and evaluating training options. According to the budget allocation, the employer has to establish priorities as to who should be trained, in what languages and to what level. The auditor can now begin to contact relevant language training providers.

4. The final stage involves the monitoring and assessment of the training programme. The auditor should have a continuing role, as language needs change as quickly as the marketplace, so training schemes may need to be adapted or tuned. For this reason it is a good idea to keep an updated record of the language ability of all employees. A language audit should yield the following information:
a) An up-to-date profile of your staff's language competence.
b) A 'target profile of language skills' - the predicted needs according to job function.
c) A specification of the training programme required to bridge the gap between a) and b), which is tailored to the working patterns of employees.

The language audit is an involved process, in which the employer should take an active part. The experience of large multinational companies has shown that the acquisition of language skills must form part of the overall strategy of the firm if it is to be of real long-term value.

Smaller firms should take advantage of the groundwork already done by large companies.

The experience of large multinational companies has shown that the acquisition of language skills must form part of the overall strategy of the firm.

TRAINING OPTIONS

You have decided to invest in language training for your staff. You are now confronted with the choice of which type of training. Which one is right for you?

Local language schools

In some cases, local schools can be a very good option. They are convenient and costs are relative to the local economy. If you are unsure which school to choose, ask about the qualifications/experience of their teachers (See Sections Two and Five) and for references from previous clients. If there is a local recognition scheme (see p106) and the school is not recognised, find out why. Check that the school has a history of teaching business English, or it may lack the necessary business materials. Make sure that the classes are not too big - 15 students or under is acceptable - and that all the students in the class have the same language requirements. One-to-one classes are best avoided for beginners, and avoid the embarrassing situation of having mixed levels, such as a fluent secretary in the same class as a struggling director. See Section Four for language schools in your area.

Avoid the embarrassing situation of having mixed levels, such as a fluent secretary in the same class as a struggling director.

Getting a teacher to work in-house

Some businesses prefer the teacher to come to them rather than sending employees out of company premises. If you choose this option, make sure you can provide facilities, at least a blackboard.

Give the teacher a good idea of what you expect your employees to come away with.

Whether you choose a teacher from the local language school or a freelance teacher, ask to see a list of his or her former clients and check his or her qualifications. You could ask to see a sample lesson. Say if you want the teacher to have a specialist knowledge, in law, for example, before you take him or her on. Give the teacher a good idea of what you expect your employees to come away with; if they have a presentation in a month, tell the teacher this, but do not expect miracles!

Using a recruitment agency

Like employment agencies, recruitment agencies attempt to find a suitable teacher for your needs. Check that the agency has experience in your field of business, and compare their rates with local schools. Their commission may seem high, but take into account the amount of time and expense that they can save you in the long term.

Using an ESP consultancy

ESP (English for Specific Purposes) consultancies can offer a mixture of specialist training and consultancy services to businesses. There are a limited number of such agencies around, and they may offer a narrow range of services. The consultancy should be able to provide a detailed language audit (see previous page). To find an ESP consultancy, ask reputable recruitment agencies. (See p.65)

Tailor made courses

When you have chosen your language trainer, you could be offered a customised course for your specific needs. This sounds ideal, but ensure you get what you pay for. A language audit is essential for a customised course. As a rule, expect the trainer to spend a day preparing for each week of a tailor made course. If you are offered such a course starting the next day, it is not properly prepared.

Remember that there is a lot of commercially available material in some fields, such as English for air traffic controllers, so it is not worth paying extra for a tailor made course if this is the case. Only do so if you have a very specialised need.

Cross-cultural training

Some companies find that their staff speak perfect English, but that communications are still breaking down when they are doing business with people from another culture even if they, too, seem to be fluent in English. Cross cultural training seeks to avoid these misunderstandings by explaining how to react in problematic situations.

Cross-cultural training has taken off in recent years with the growth in international trade. In the UK, there is no organisation to monitor such courses and cross-cultural training tends to be a component of general business English. Farnham Castle Centre for International Briefing, Farnham, Surrey is the leading UK centre in this field. Language Training Services in Bath also run a systematic course.

The Society of International English Cultural Training and Research (SIETAR) runs teaching courses in cross-cultural training. The society can also provide advice and recommends other training organisations, which may be more suitable for you. Contact: SIETAR International, 733 15th Street NW, Suite 900, Washington DC 20005 USA. Tel: 202 7375000.

RECRUITING ENGLISH SPEAKERS

The staff you hire will show you their language qualifications, but do you know what they mean?

Having established that your organisation would benefit from an improved level of English, you may decide to recruit staff with language skills. However, in addition to the standard difficulties recruitment presents to most organisations, assessment of language capability must also be taken into account. Depending on your budget and the importance of the position, you may choose to engage a specialist agency with the capability to determine candidates' language level, or trust in your own selection procedure. In either case, there are a number of key questions which will influence your recruitment decision.

The position
The level and type of language ability required are dependent upon the role that the prospective employee will play in your organisation. Although this may seem obvious, it is essential to keep this in mind throughout the recruitment process. A receptionist must be able to answer telephone queries in another language, but it is of little significance to you if he or she can translate Shakespeare. Should you wish to test candidate's language skills, devise a practical scenario which reflects what the position will involve on a daily basis. Remember that linguistic ability is a tool with which someone can improve the way in which

they do a job; it is no substitute for the ability to do the job in the first place.

Qualifications
Unless your own English is impeccable, the most reliable way of judging a candidate's skills is by their qualifications and matching those qualifications to your needs. A Master's degree in English Literature may look very impressive on paper, but it is no proof of its owner's ability to sell your latest technological advance to a Canadian purchasing manager.

There is now a selection of internationally recognised English qualifications (and so many confusing acronyms) that some sort of a guide to what the qualifications actually mean is essential. The following table gives a brief summary of the main examinations, but the amount of information is naturally restricted. It is worth noting that new specialist qualifications, such as LCCI's new English for Tourism and Cambridge's CBET, are always being developed, so you can be quite specific in your demands.

For fuller details of all examinations, see The Longman Guide to English Language Examinations (Longman 1989).

Key To Coverage
W = Writing
R = Reading
L = Listening
S = Speaking

NOTES
These indicate aims and status. For more details, see English Language Entrance Requirements in British Educational Institutions (HMSO 1991).

NB. This table is not intended to be a comprehensive list of EFL examinations available.

Board	Examination	Coverage	LEVEL: elementary int. adv. ESU 1-2 3 4 5 6 7 8-9 ALTE I II III IV V	Notes
ARELS	Diploma.	general LS	pass = ESU 8	Spoken English exams conducted in a language lab or with radio equipment. Oral counterparts of the Oxford EFL exams.
	Higher Certificate.		pass = ESU 6	
	Preliminary Certificate.		pass = ESU 4	
Educational Testing Service	TOEFL.	general LR	550 = int.	TOEFL 550 accepted by most US universities. UK institutions may demand evidence of writing and speaking. EuroCert = TOEFL + TSE + TWE.
	TSE.	general S		
	TWE.	general W		
International Baccalaureate	English as a Second Language.	general RWS	not available	Higher: college entrance exam for English majors. Subsidiary: college entrance exam for non-English majors.
International Certificate Conference	Language Certificate System - English.	general R (W) L S	not available	German-based exams available on demand. Business, Hotel & Catering, Technical English exams also available.

BOARD	EXAMINATION	COVERAG	LEVEL: elementary int. adv. ESU 1-2 3 4 5 6 7 8-9 ALTE I II III IV V	NOTES
London Chamber of Commerce	English for Commerce.	business RWS	1st = ESU3 2nd = ESU5 3rd = ESU7.	Traditional business-English exam.
	English for Business.	business RWS	1st = ESU3 2nd = ESU5 3rd = ESU7.	More recent business-English exam.
	SEFIC.	business LS	Thresh. = ESU 5 Int. = ESU 6 Adv. = ESU 7.	= Spoken English for Industry & Commerce.
	English for Tourism.	business LS	1st = ESU 3 2nd = ESU 5	Business English for the tourism industry.
Michigan	MELAB.	general R W L (S)	75 = intermediate.	Accepted by most US universities. Oral rating is optional.
NEAB (formerly JMB)	University Entrance Test.	academic R W L S	pass = ESU 6.	Academic English examination widely accepted by UK universities.
Pitman	ESOL & spoken ESOL.	general L R W & L S	Int. = ESU 5 Higher Int = ESU 6 Adv. = ESU 7.	Five-stage exams available on demand. Higher Int accepted by some UK universities.
	English for Business Communication.	business L R W	Elementary = ESU 5 Int. = ESU 6 Adv. = ESU 7.	Three-stage business exams available on demand.
Trinity College London	Spoken English Grades.	general L S + R W at higher levels	Initial (1-3) = ESU 1/2 Element. (4-6) = ESU 3/4. Int.(7-9) =ESU 4/5 Adv. (10-12) = ESU 6/8.	A series of 12 graded tests in spoken English with examiners from the UK.
University of Cambridge (UCLES)	Proficiency (CPE).	general R W L S	ALTE V.	Established exam. accepted by most UK universities.
	Cert. in Advanced English (CAE).	general R W L S	ALTE IV.	Newer exam. accepted by most UK universities.
	1st Certificate (FCE).	general R W L S	ALTE III.	Established exam. widely accepted by employers.
	Preliminary English Test (PET).	general R W L S	ALTE II.	Elementary test to encourage further learning.
	Key English Test (KET).	general R W L S	ALTE I.	Lower-level exam. introduced in 1994.
	Cert. in Communicative Skills in English (CCSE).	general R W L S	1 = ALTE II, II = ALTE III, III = ALTE IV, IV = ALTE V.	Formerly RSA CUEFL: skills available separately.
	IELTS.	academic R W L S	3 = ALTE I, 4 = ALTE II, 5 = ALTE III, 6 = ALTE IV, 7 = ALTE V.	Bands 6/7 accepted by UK universities.
	CEIBT.	business R W L S	pass = ALTE IV.	Cert. in English for International Business & Trade.
University of London (ULEAC)	GCE O Level (Syllabus B).	general R W	pass = ESU 6	Grade C accepted by most UK universities.
	Certificates of Attainment.	general R W L (S)	1 = ESU 3, 2 = ESU 4, 3 = ESU 5, 4 = ESU 6, 5 = ESU 7, 6 = ESU 8.	Six-stage graded tests with optional oral.
University of Oxford (UODLE)	Higher Certificate.	general R W	pass = ESU 6.	Higher (credit) + ARELS Higher accepted by some universities.
	Preliminary Certificate.	general R W	pass = ESU 3.	Higher (credit) + ARELS Higher accepted by some universities.
	International Business English Certificate.	business R W L S	First = ESU 4/5 Executive = ESU 6/7.	Counterparts of ARELS exams.
	Tourism English Proficiency.	business R W L S	First = ESU 4/5.	Business & Tourism exams based on authentic situations.

BUSINESS CASE STUDY: THE MULTINATIONAL

How do other companies organise their language training?
Siemens A.G. provides us with their solution.

Siemens is a large international corporation, specialising in electronics. It places a high priority on training, especially since it has companies operating in some forty countries. *Vincent O'Neill* is Head of its Inter-Cultural Co-operation and Projects in International Communications Department based in Munich. His department employs eight core trainers and up to eighty freelancers depending on demand. His own Research and Development department produces special materials to meet the demands of different courses. The International Co-operation department acts as an independent business unit within Siemens, offering its services to different departments within Siemens. Most training is carried out within the Siemens department - approximately 10% of the work is contracted out to outside language specialists.

Siemens employs 400,000 people world-wide of which 136,000 work in Germany. Of the total workforce, some 250,000 are Germans and 150,000 are non-Germans. Vincent O'Neill's training division trains about 2000 employees a year. Training concentrates on three main areas, Language and Communication, Culture and Business Issues. Managers of different nationalities in Siemens will have different ideas of what constitutes R&D or contractual negotiation. One of the functions of Siemens training is to harmonise these different conceptions. Another is to introduce English as a vehicular language where a third international language is needed. An example is the new Siemens company in Kazakhstan where Turkmenish is spoken. Only English will serve in this territory as a vehicular language where German is not spoken and neither Turkish nor Russian is accepted.

International communication is heavily dependent on English. The *Encyclopaedia Britannica* (1987) notes that one in seven of the world population speaks 'survival English'. 90% of all technical and scientific publications appear in English, 70% of the world's mail and computer interaction, 60% of all radio and TV broadcasting is in English.

The problem is that our staff and teams have their hands full just dealing with new situations; jobs, tasks and people - whether colleagues, customers or international partners. There just isn't that much time to work on developing the communication skills they need or will need...and that's where we come in!

- Our intensive, total exposure courses are time efficient in two ways:

1. We provide a complete training package that includes a pre-course module for either individual preparation or group preparation (21 hours in a two-week period) and a follow-up module to maintain communication skills and transfer.

2. Our courses run from a Friday evening over two weekends, entailing only five days out of work time, but nine days training time.

- Our intensive, total exposure courses are learner efficient in two ways:

1. We work with trainer teams from (almost) all English-speaking countries, with clear trainer roles. You work alternately in small groups of six, pairs and plenary groups. Your group trainer changes every three days, and your course leader too. The complex of changing trainer teams, changing learning situations and changing groups maintains optimal concentration and variety.

2. A range of training methods and feedback loops caters for both the variety of learner types and individual consultation with our team of 5-7 trainers on any given course day.

- Our intensive, total-exposure courses are training efficient in two ways:

1. We diagnose your present level of communication skills beforehand, recommend the right level in our 5 intensive training levels and give you a diagnosis of your progress at the end of the course, together with concrete advice on how to proceed afterwards.

2. The programme is structured to cover general and individual needs, to get the most out of your

Training concentrates on three main areas, Language and Communication, Culture and Business Issues.

There just isn't that much time to work on developing the communication skills they need or will need.

time, (a day = 8am to 10pm), and is held at several venues accordingly to level and needs. To expect people, no matter how excellent their professional competence is, to be able to cope effectively with international change demanding a high degree of social and intercultural competence is both too simplistic, and worse, counterproductive. Professional competence is rarely the problem in international business situations. What is at stake is the competence required to assess and react to the complex, interwoven patterns of communication and interaction involving

a) *individuals and their personalities,*
b) *business situations and issues* (negotiation, project team, staff dialogue, meeting, marketing presentation, etc),
c) *corporate cultures and their impact on behaviour* (mission statement, corporate values, ethical codes),
d) *national and regional culture impacts* (on attitudes, value systems, assumptions, expectations, communication, behaviour),
e) *random factors* (market changes, reorganisations, image loss or enhancement, impact of social and political change). Any one of these can attain dominance at any time. Some, however, like underground rivers, rarely change their course suddenly, and as a result, are more predictable, and therefore easier to grasp, understand and cope with.

Coping strategies in intercultural training depend in the first place on understanding cultural differences and their effect on the way people think and behave. So the first step in dealing with our own and others' cultural baggage is to appreciate *why things are done differently* in our own culture as opposed to another culture. There are always good reasons for the difference, perfectly sensible, natural reasons, which are as cogent as the climatic reasons for different forms of vegetation in different parts of the world. Caught in the cocoon of our own culture, we are too often *simply not aware of the reasons.*

That is why the initial level of intercultural training concentrates on *charting the differences and discovering their influence on thinking and behaviour.* We help you to recognise the differences and accept them, and to avoid putting on a judge's wig and falling into the trap of classing your way as 'better' than the other.

The next level of training focuses on situation related *communication and interaction.* Theoretical recognition and acceptance of cultural differences is one thing, communicating and interacting appropriately in 'live' business situations quite another skill altogether. Keeping

Professional competence is rarely the problem in international business situations.

The first step in dealing with our own and others' cultural baggage is to appreciate why things are done differently.

in mind the pitfalls of the 'common' business language, let alone body language, the complex task of concentrated effort to solve the business issues, cope well with the social aspects and establish a balance of power in the varying corporate, departmental, group and personal interests demands a *high level of international communicative and interactive competence.*

The last type of intercultural training tackles head-on the area of *integrating people in international teams and supporting them in finding a framework of co-operation* that will produce better business results for all of them. Increasingly, people are sucked into a whirlpool of change, and feel, as in present day politics, that they no longer have any control, either over the course of events or over their own future. This is difficult enough within one culture or company, but infinitely more serious when different national groups and corporate cultures are concerned. It is possible to match the strengths of divergent business cultures, but it has to be worked on and people have to be trained to do it in their own backyards, unfortunately, often when they are already feeling pain.

It cannot be done overnight, and grandiose phrases like 'the challenge of global markets' are worse than useless. This is why our intercultural training run on two tracks. One track is aimed at long-term human resources development, to ensure that the company builds on its potential of intercultural skills for future business developments. The other track is dedicated to providing consulting and training in international teams and situations in which problems are breaking through the surface like wayward icebergs cast afloat by the heat of international competition. The seven-eighths beneath the surface can easily sink the best endeavour in terms of business, professional and personal success.

BUSINESS CASE STUDY:
THE LANGUAGE SCHOOL

The Canning School trains business executives to teach English to other executives.
How have they adapted to changes in the business market?

As European economies recover, the likely expansion is going to come in 'people services'

This school specialises in business English. It has four centres in the UK and schools in Japan and Italy. It employs eighty staff, of which half are involved in teaching.

Changes in demand

Demand for business English in the UK has altered as the market has contracted due to recession. In Southern Europe particularly, the devaluation of the Spanish and Italian currencies against the pound has worked against the advantage of stable prices for UK-based training over the last three years, thus reversing the situation of the eighties when the pound was weak.

Training budgets have been reduced and managers are wary of spending money on new training. However, there are other factors affecting demand. In the seventies, huge proportions of training budgets were devoted to language training, but now it is balancing out with other types of training. Corporate restructuring has meant that hierarchies are flattening out, so there are fewer people to train, but those that remain will be working in cross-border teams, so the long-term demand for language is likely to be greater.

In addition to this, demand has switched from month-long courses to short two-week intensive courses. Whereas managers used to attend courses as an incentive or reward, now all courses are tightly 'needs-based'; to allow an executive to perform a particular function for a particular job in English. The stress is as much on effective communication techniques as language training using English.

Going to the school site offers the advantage of being in an English speaking environment and the opportunity of working with other international managers.

Industry demand is also changing. The large contracts from the oil industry are gone. Manufacturing industry is wary of language training. The computer industry is going through its own difficulties and a large part of its training has to be technical rather than communicative. However, the pharmaceutical and financial services sectors still provide a strong client base. As European economies recover, the likely expansion is going to come in 'people services', such as insurance, accounting, retailing and catering.

Types of courses

Canning runs courses both in-company and at its own centres. The main reasons for in-house training are economies of scale - the opportunity to train large numbers of people at lower cost, minimal absence from the office and the chance to be very specific about the type of training required. Going to the school site offers the advantage of being in an English speaking environment and the opportunity of working with other international managers.

In common with other training providers, the school offers three types of courses. Open courses with small groups of 4-6 managers, one-to-one courses and more recently introduced, combination courses in which group courses are combined with one-to-one training.

When course members gather, levels are usually already known and groups ready formed. On the first day, the needs of the group are analysed and the course programme finalised using in-house materials. In this way, each course is tailor-made to suit the needs of its participants. The schools's own R&D department is responsible for researching and producing new materials, incorporating new methods.

Student recruitment

The tailor-made course is an important feature in successful recruitment. For an established business language centre core recommendation is word of mouth. Bill Reed, a partner in the school, feels that the most important thing is to keep in close touch with clients and listen to them. That way you can respond to their needs and stay ahead of the market. In building the business market personal contact with clients is all-important. There is no substitute for going to see a potential client to make that first presentation.

In summary

The key to successful training over the next few years will depend on listening carefully to existing and new clients and tailoring courses to their specific needs. It will involve the recruitment of business specialists who can train managers in a broad range of communication skills.

USING TECHNOLOGY

How new devices can turn your computer or your telephone into a translation bureau or even a self-access language training centre.

The most effective answer to learning English is still classes. However, increasingly sophisticated business translation packages have come onto the market this year. The telecoms industry is beginning to offer new alternatives that, while still expensive, can deal with an increasing number of foreign language business requirements.

Company language training

Over the past year the ELT industry has exploited the facilities that multimedia has made available. BBC/Vektor have pioneered development of multimedia business language training on laservision (laser disks are basically 12-inch CDs). Standard 5-inch CD ROMs are still dominating the market, because it is far less expensive to buy the equipment to run them (a CD ROM drive, Soundblaster card and associated software costs about 30% of the price of a standard PC), but they lack the enormous animation capabilities of laser disks.

A year ago there was not much choice in the range of CD ROMs for language learning. Today there are packages available in a selection of languages for children and adults studying general English, but the widest range caters for business English. With few exceptions, current business English packages cater for the low to mid-intermediate levels complemented by more general packages for beginners.

The low cost of providing basic business language training through multimedia has positive implications for staff training budgets. It may be worth considering the provision of multimedia training on in-company computers before sending staff abroad. The multimedia learning environment of sight and sound is a highly motivating form of total immersion and is ideal preparation for a short course of study abroad. Furthermore, although most people want to take trips abroad, many simply cannot afford more than a week away from their jobs, and do not like being away from their families. Finally, the facility is available to all staff whenever they have the time or inclination to study.

That most CD ROM titles cater for lower levels may be the strength and weakness of current multimedia. The strength is in the preparatory work that motivates people to want to learn more and to go on to classes; the weakness is that current CD ROM technology cannot provide the interactive communication of classes.

Translation devices and packages

There are a number of new business correspondence translation packages, ranging from bilingual dictionaries with verb conjugations and grammar help to packages that facilitate first draft translations. These work by selecting standard business letter topics and browsing through alternative phrases. The problem with these packages is knowing which alternative to choose, which presupposes the user is already conversant in both languages, thus diminishing its value. For a company sending a large amount of business correspondence the advantage of translation packages is their ability to save time by preparing rough drafts.

Telecom translation services

For companies that do not have their own translator and/or interpreter, most telecom companies have been operating translation services for some time now, but they are expensive and the service needs to be booked well in advance. Several telecom giants have attempted to turn one language into a code recognised by a computer that could then translate it back into another language. Some of the major problems have been regional dialects, stress and intonation patterns, which when varied can alter meaning.

One of the most interesting projects is a translation machine based on video-conferencing. Its first language objective is the translation of English - Japanese - English. The video telephone facility will show both parties on the video screen, as well as the words they are speaking. The computer first transcribes Japanese as Romaji (Japanese with English spelling, e.g. sayonara) which is then translated into English. Voice activated translation machines already exist, but language is limited to a specific range of words and phrases, which must be spoken slowly and clearly.

Further rapid advances in technology and the continuing convergence of television, computers and the telephone are changing automated foreign language communication products and services. The speed of these developments is likely to require a more frequent revision of strategies for staff language training.

The low cost of providing basic business language training through multimedia has positive implications for staff training budgets.

The computer first transcribes Japanese as Romaji which is then translated into English.

OXFORD HOUSE COLLEGE
(CENTRAL LONDON)

RECOGNISED
by the
BRITISH COUNCIL

A R E L S
ENGLISH IN BRITAIN

Professional Trinity College London Teaching Qualifications. Accepted by the British Council, open to native and non-native speakers of English.

TRINITY COLLEGE CERTIFICATE IN TESOL
For those with no or little experience of teaching English

✓ 4 Week Intensive Courses throughout the year

✓ 13 week Part-Time Courses with regular start dates

✓ Extensive Supervised Teaching Practice in Small Groups

✓ Resource Centre

✓ Central London Location

✓ Personal, friendly service and guidance

✓ Job Counselling Service

TRINITY COLLEGE LONDON LICENTIATE DIPLOMA IN TESOL
For experienced teachers who wish to further their career

✓ Unique distance-learning + 2 week "London Block" scheme

✓ Study anywhere at your own pace

✓ Constant guidance

✓ UK-based "telephone tutor"

✓ Continual contact with other trainees

✓ All areas of syllabus covered in a systematic, challenging way

FOR FULL DETAILS OF CERTIFICATE AND DIPLOMA COURSES CONTACT US ON:
071-734 3889 (phone) / 071-287 1623 (fax) or write to:

**Teacher Training Department, Oxford House College,
3 Oxford Street, London W1R 1RF**

BATQI

The British Association of TESOL Qualifying Institutions

BECOMING A TEACHER

You can start teaching English if you are fresh out of college, seeking a new career, newly retired or even if you have no qualifications or experience. This section explains all the options, shows you what qualifications to get, where to get them and even guides you through your first class.

SO, YOU WANT TO TEACH ENGLISH?

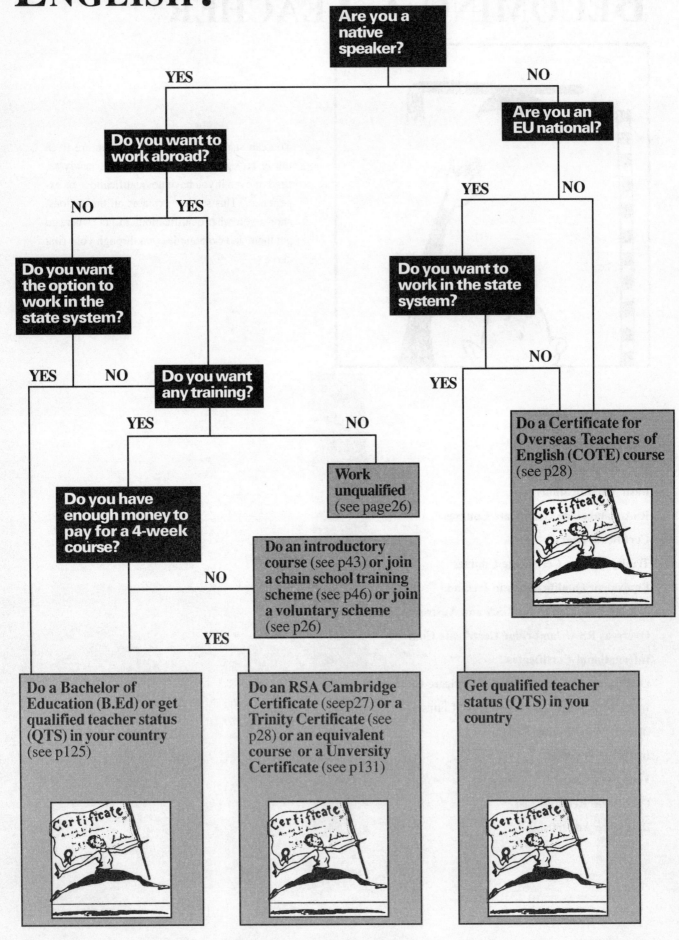

Are you a native speaker?

YES — **Do you want to work abroad?**

NO — **Do you want the option to work in the state system?**

YES

NO

YES — **Do you want any training?**

YES

NO — **Work unqualified** (see page26)

Do you have enough money to pay for a 4-week course?

NO — **Do an introductory course** (see p43) **or join a chain school training scheme** (see p46) **or join a voluntary scheme** (see p26)

YES

Do a Bachelor of Education (B.Ed) or get qualified teacher status (QTS) in your country (see p125)

Do an RSA Cambridge Certificate (seep27) **or a Trinity Certificate** (see p28) **or an equivalent course or a Unversity Certificate** (see p131)

NO — **Are you an EU national?**

YES — **Do you want to work in the state system?**

NO — **Do a Certificate for Overseas Teachers of English (COTE) course** (see p28)

YES — **Get qualified teacher status (QTS) in you country**

CAN I TEACH EFL?

Do I have to get a qualification?
No. There are some countries, where you can teach English unqualified (see p26). Remember that schools will pay more and generally treat you better if you are qualified.

Is it better to look for a job once I reach my destination?
It is often easier to get a job if you are already in the country where you want to work. Check in the local English language newspaper for job adverts or approach individual schools (see p81 -121). Note that some countries will only offer work permits to teachers who have been offered work before they enter the country.

I am already a teacher. Can I teach EFL?
If you want to teach in the state educational system, you must achieve QTS (Qualified Teacher Status). Unless you have a PGCE in EFL or ESL or hold another EFL qualification, a PGCE does not automatically qualify you to teach EFL.

What is an EFL qualification?
At present there are no standard international EFL qualifications. In the UK recognized schools are only permitted to employ teachers with at least a certificate. These are widely recognized overseas and the courses last about a month. If you are unable to take one of these courses, there are plenty of alternatives, some of which will be regarded highly by employers.

Are there shorter courses in EFL?
There are various introductory courses in EFL which give you an EFL grounding even if not a formal qualification. They are worth considering if you do not want to commit yourself to a long time in EFL. They also tend to be cheaper. Some schools run their own courses for unqualified teachers which train you in the methods of that particular school - which is worthwhile if you wish to work for that organisation (see p46). It may also be worth considering a course which combines distance learning with a short course.

Where can I train?
You can take TEFL courses throughout the world (see p35 - 42). The price generally reflects the economy - and/or the popularity - of the country or destination.

Do I have to have teaching experience to do an EFL course?
No, although many people do teach first before doing a course.

Do I need to be a graduate to get on a course?
Most courses demand some sort of further education qualification, not necessarily a degree. Non-graduates may be required to do an introductory course. Remember that some countries demand a degree before issuing work permits (see p81 - 121).

I want to go to university before I teach EFL. Where should I go?
In the USA there are various courses that train teachers of EFL at undergraduate level. There is not an undergraduate qualification in the UK for teaching EFL, although the modern languages degree at East Anglia University has an RSA in TEFL as part of the course.

How can I pay for my course?
In the UK you cannot get a grant to do a teacher training course at a private institution, although there are further education colleges that offer subsidised courses. However, you may be eligible for a Career Development Loan, which is a government-backed scheme, whereby banks make unsecured loans at preferential rates to students - call 0800-585505 for details. In the US and Australia there are also government loan schemes available.

Am I too old for EFL?
If you are under about 50, it is not too late to start teaching EFL. Indeed if you have had a career in a specialist field such as with the police, you may have the expertise to teach ESP (English for Special Purposes - teaching Spanish policemen useful

English terminology, for example. (See p148). EFL could therefore be a part-time job during your retirement.

Can I be an EFL teacher if English isn't my mother tongue?
Yes, although most of the job opportunities will be within your own country unless you are completely fluent. See information of COTE courses (p42).

Can I train by post?
Some courses are offered partly by correspondence, partly with on-site training involving teaching practice. Courses which are totally correspondence courses are not usually recognised by employers (see p43).

Will the place I train at find me a job?
Most establishments will give you advice on finding a job, and some may offer you employment especially if you have a good grade (see p46).

How much can I expect to earn?
This will vary greatly from country to country and school to school (see p81 -121).

How do I know a school is reputable?
There are organisations that have been set up to monitor schools. It is often useful to contact the local British Council. If you are working in the UK or for British schools abroad, contact ILTB. Elsewhere, contact the local teaching union or relevant association (see p171 - 177 for addresses).

If I get a job abroad, will I get my airfare paid for?
This will depend on the employer. Many employers will pay at least a proportion of your fare, but some will not, or will only do so on completion of your contract.

What will be my career prospects if I go into EFL?
There are various further qualifications which can lead to specialist jobs related to EFL (see p125). There are also various spin-off careers such as publishing (see p75).

WORKING UNQUALIFIED

How to find work without training.

As a native English speaker, you should be able to find work, at a school, giving lessons privately or through a local agency, virtually anywhere in the world, but some places and specific programmes offer the best opportunities for the complete novice.

There is a huge demand for English outside the state system in Hong Kong.

A report by the Centre for British Teachers showed that many EFL teachers get their first job as unqualified teachers, and around half of those who do training courses have never worked in EFL before. However, it is becoming harder to work without qualifications. There are good reasons to become qualified, especially if you plan to teach for more than about a year:-
1/ The better paid jobs, as well as those with better conditions and legal rights, are given to qualified teachers.
2/ A course will give you invaluable grounding in materials and teaching techniques.

If you want to try out EFL to earn some money, before getting qualified, or just for the experience, there are plenty of opportunities. Summer schools occasionally take on unqualified teachers (see p67), but you will have to be very persistent. It is also possible to work unqualified in many countries if you want to earn money while travelling or living abroad, although remember that you may be technically working illegally and open to exploitation.

Eastern Europe
There are unqualified possibilities in both state and private language schools, especially in the Czech Republic and Poland. Conditions are still not easy, especially outside the major cities. There is a huge demand for English, and private schools are opening up particularly in the Baltic states and the Ukraine. As a result of the area's dire economic situation, teachers often earn a local salary, tiny by western standards.

Primary English is one area which is growing, especially in France and southern Europe.

Western Europe
If you do not have any personal contacts, finding steady work without a qualification can be difficult. Standards of English teaching have greatly improved in both the private and state sectors in recent years, which has restricted opportunities for unqualified teachers. Primary English is one area which is growing, especially in France and southern Europe. If you can get a work permit, Finland and Norway are possibilities for adult education. Greece has thousands of private language schools to approach. If you have a knowledge of business and speak their language, France and Germany (especially former East Germany) also may be good bets.

The Far East
Despite fierce competition for jobs, there is a huge demand for English outside the state system in Hong Kong. Unqualified teachers should be able to find employment, but there is rarely recruitment from outside the country. The same applies to Thailand, where most schools rely on native English speakers 'passing through' on their travels. Indonesia has a large number of private schools, but unqualified teachers get half the amount that qualified teachers earn. Japan, Korea and Taiwan have traditionally been very lucrative markets for native English speakers, but their governments have been clamping down on illegal workers. Schools are now more wary of employing unqualified staff. If you have some business experience, you stand a better chance.

Elsewhere
If you are prepared to turn up and look for work, you will probably find teaching work in Turkey, Egypt, Morocco and many of the larger Latin American countries.

GOVERNMENT PROGRAMMES

Many countries run government programmes that offer good conditions of work and job security, although in developing countries the salaries could be low. Finally, there are voluntary organisations that may be prepared to recruit unqualified teachers, though a degree might be required (see p79).

Eastern Europe
There are government-run schemes recruiting teachers for the state sector in many Central and Eastern European countries. In the UK, contact the Central Bureau or the East European Partnership (see p79).

Japan
The Japan Exchange and Teaching Programme (JET): Around 400 native English speakers are recruited each year to work as Assistant English Teachers in Japanese secondary schools. No previous teaching experience or TEFL qualification is required, but some experience of living and working overseas and/ or of working with children is an advantage. Candidates should be graduates under 35, with a real interest in Japan. Teachers are paid their return air fare and around 3,760,000 yen a year. Apply through your local Japanese Embassy.

BASIC QUALIFICATIONS

If you want to be reasonably confident of securing of employment with a good salary and legal rights, a qualification in teaching EFL is invaluable. However, there is not one standard qualification, and some qualifications are more useful than others.

Although anyone can teach English once their proficiency in the language reaches a high level, and it is often said that those who have learned English themselves are better placed to teach it, native speakers have a natural advantage, and, indeed, a certain 'cachet' when it comes to looking for employment. Therefore, this section is aimed mainly at Americans, Britons, Australians and the Irish.

Probably as a result of the recession, more and more people have been trying to find work in the 'boom' area of EFL. Most centres offering teacher training courses agree that demand is still rising, and, interestingly, report that the percentage of applications from more mature candidates with experience - such as engineers, bankers or mothers going back to work, as opposed to young graduates, has increased dramatically. The objective of nearly all of these people from different backgrounds is to find the quickest and cheapest route to a well-paid teaching job in the country of their choice.

Beginners' courses can vary from a few days to a few years with corresponding variances in coverage and cost, but most employers consider certificates resulting from courses lasting at least four weeks full-time to be the minimum qualification.

The important thing to remember is that most schools throughout the world only recognise certain qualifications depending on their status and location. Most American teachers will have completed an MA course (see p135), which will obviously cover considerably more than a four-week course, but it may not involve teaching practice, which is of fundamental importance to employers and is an important component of most certificate courses. The most commonly accepted qualifications in Europe are the RSA Cambridge and Trinity certificates or state Qualified Teacher Status (QTS), preferably with a TEFL component (although such courses are being cut back on). These are generally seen as a minimum qualification.

This does not necessarily mean that alternative courses are not very good. A qualification of some sort will certainly be considered preferable to no qualification at all. Make sure, though, that your course has a practical element.

At present there is no set policy in European countries towards other TEFL qualifications obtained in the United States, Canada, Ireland, New Zealand or Australia. This does not mean they are not recognised, but the policy of recruitment is to take each case as it comes. A teacher with such a qualification will be expected to have completed a course containing a balance of theory and practice. Remember that teaching practice is particularly valued - a course that only involved theory would not normally be considered adequate.

Larger organisations such as the British Council, ELS, International House and the Bell Educational Trust would normally require a diploma or QTS in TEFL. The RSA or Trinity certificate may be accepted, but only in certain centres, such as in the Middle East where there are relatively few locally qualified teachers. However, teachers already in a particular country should not be put off applying to such organisations if they only have the RSA or Trinity certificate, as recruitment often depends on local management. Unfortunately, local contracts may be less lucrative.

Non-EU nationals who hold an RSA or Trinity certificate or QTS should not assume this is an automatic means to getting a job teaching in Europe - they will still need to obtain a work permit.

The British Association of TEFL Qualifying Institutions was set up in 1991 to look at teacher qualifications across the European Union, and it is possible that certain aspects of teacher training will change as part of EU policy.

RSA/Cambridge Certificate

The RSA Cambridge Certificate (also known as the RSA CTEFLA or the RSA Preparatory certificate) is a four-week intensive course. As it has been running for so long, it is widely recognised and respected as a minimum TEFL requirement internationally. Although the majority of their centres are in the UK, there are centres throughout the world which run RSA Cambridge courses (see p37), for example, one of their newest centres is Georgetown University, Washington D.C. It can sometimes be cheaper to take the certificate course overseas than in the UK.

Most employers consider certificates resulting from courses lasting at least four weeks full-time to be the minimum qualification.

Most schools throughout the world only recognise certain qualifications depending on their status and location.

The RSA Certificate is probably most suitable for trainees who have either had some sort of teaching experience or are very committed.

The course is aimed at training teachers to teach adults from beginners to Cambridge First Certificate (upper intermediate) level, and is highly practical. Lecture and seminar sessions dealing with language teaching techniques are followed up by observed teacher practice. The course is very intensive, and if you have no teaching experience, some sort of background reading is recommended before you embark on it (see p50). If you are not familiar with basic grammatical terms, find out about the tense system and common terminology first.

The RSA Certificate is probably most suitable for trainees who have either had some sort of teaching experience or are very committed. However, if you have a lot of teaching experience, you may find your established teaching methods have given you 'bad' habits. Experienced teachers sometimes complain that the RSA certificate expects you to conform too rigidly to their methods and ideals. It certainly helps if you are outgoing, but sensitivity to students' difficulties is also appreciated.

Trinity Certificate in TESOL
Trinity College London run the Certificate in TESOL (Teaching English to Speakers of Other Languages), which has been running for over ten years. The number of validated centres offering this course has been growing rapidly in recent years, and, like the RSA, there are centres outside the UK and the qualification is now recognised worldwide.

The Trinity course is also open to people under the age of 20.

The Trinity syllabus has a basic set of requirements that all its validated centres must meet. However, the course designer in each centre is free to submit his or her own course design to supplement these requirements. This means that individual centres may give a different weighting to certain elements. For example, one course may focus more on phonetics, another on discourse analysis. This degree of flexibility has proven popular with trainees and teacher trainers alike, but check that the focus of the course meets your requirements.

Most Trinity centres also offer pre-sessionals before the one-month or six-week intensive course begins, giving the trainee some basic grounding. The Trinity course is also open to people under the age of 20, unlike some other courses. Most centres emphasise the importance of actually teaching foreign students, however, ensure that the course you choose offers sufficient teaching practice, as the criteria

for the number of hours offered in this is unclear. A complaint that has been made about the RSA Certificate is that it does not prepare teachers for the teaching of younger children, which is a growing requirement especially in France and southern Europe. The Trinity syllabus may include teaching practice at centres with young learners, and covers the use and design of materials for children.

Trinity students also do a student profile, with a detailed study of the background, linguistic difficulties encountered by a particular student and a plan for their progress to make teachers aware of individual needs.

Trinity College is now hoping to increase its centres overseas. In addition to the Associate Diploma courses for non-native teachers in Singapore, Dubai and Uruguay, Trinity plans to offer TESOL certificate courses in Spain and Malaysia. The college has also developed a non-native teacher scheme to teach young learners, called CertTeyl (Certificate in Teaching English to Young Learners). Trinity College hope overseas centres will be able to offer this course shortly. See page 32.

International certificates
There are a number of other certificate courses of roughly the same level as the RSA and Trinity, which are listed on page 40. They may not be as well known on a global level, but they are often very well respected within their own geographical sphere.

University courses
In addition to their degree and diploma courses (see Section Five), there are also cerificate EFL courses run by universities. Make sure they contain teaching practice with foreign students, not just with other teachers (see p131).

COTE/DOTE
COTE (Certificate for Overseas Teachers of English) and DOTE (Diploma for Overseas Teachers of English, for more advanced English speakers) are non-native English speaker courses. The courses take regional conditions into account and use local classrooms for teacher training. COTE requires that teachers are roughly at the standard of Cambridge First Certificate. The course is popular in Spain, Turkey, Egypt and South America, and is being developed to suit Eastern Europe.

See page 42 (COTE) and page 129 (DOTE) for detailed information on these courses.

RSA/Cambridge Certificate - CTEFLA

College	Course length	FT/PT	Fees	Start dates	Entry requirements	Contact	Comments	Max no. of students
Anglia Polytechnic Univ., Cambridge	4 wks	FT	£750 + exam fee	July	University entrance level	Mary O'Leary		15
Anglo-Continental, Bournemouth	4 wks	FT	£787	Feb, May, Sep	University entrance level	Miss J Haine		12
Anglo School, London	4 wks	FT	£775	Throughout year	University entrance level; Min age 20; Native speaker comp	John Shepherd		12
Basil Paterson, Edinburgh	4 wks 6 mths	FT PT	£825	Throughout year	University entrance level; Degree pref	Mary Beresford-Peirse		15
Bedford College of Higher Education	8 mths	PT	£650 + exam fee	Sep	University entrance level; Degree pref	Ken Wilford		12
Bell Language School, Cambridge	4 wks 30 wks	FT PT	£860 + exam fee	Throughout year	University entrance level; Min age 20	Sue Sheerin	Intensive	15
Bell Language School, Norwich	4 wks	FT	£840 + exam fee	Throughout year	University entrance level; Min age 20	Sarah Knights	Intensive	15
Bournemouth & Poole College of Further Ed	24 wks	PT	on appl	Sep	University entrance level; Interview	TEFL Coordinator	Apply early	12
Brasshouse Centre, Birmingham with Handsworth College	18 wks	PT	£750 + exam fee	Oct	As per UCLES	Deborah Cobbett Claudia Jolly		12
Brooklands College, Surrey	8 mths	PT	£300	Sep	University entrance level	Janet Drysdale		12
Brunel College, Bristol	5 wks	FT	£700	Feb, Oct	By interview	David Hughes		12
CILC, Cheltenham	5 wks	FT	£775 + exam fee	Jan, Feb, Apr, May	University entrance level	Gillian James	Apply early	15
City of Liverpool Comm College	9 wks	PT	£950	Oct, Jan	As per UCLES	Diane Lane		12
Clarendon College, Nottingham	16 wks	PT	£300	Sep, Feb	Interview	Neil Pearson		12
Concorde Intl, Folkestone	4 wks	FT	£792	Throughout year	University entrance level; Foreign lang pref	David Riddell		12
Devon School of English, Paignton	4 wks	FT	£800	Throughout year	University entrance level; Degree pref	Joan Hawthorne		10
Eastbourne College of Arts & Tech	2 terms	PT	£183	Sep	As per UCLES	Mrs B A Barber	Write for leaflet	12
Eastbourne School of English	4 wks	FT	£840	Throughout year	Degree or equiv pref	Dorothy Rippon	Apply early	12

See pages **54-58** for reference advertising

and pages **172-177** for addresses

College	Course length	FT/ PT	Fees	Start dates	Entry requirements	Contact	Comments	Max no. of students
Edinburgh Language Foundation	5 wks	FT	£825	Jan, Apr, Nov	University entrance level	Anne Rowe		15
ELT Banbury, Oxford	4 wks	FT	£837	Throughout year	Good Higher Ed; Native speaker comp; Min age 20	Mike Sayer	Apply early	10
Filton College, Bristol	9 mths	PT	£595	Sep	University entrance level; Degree pref	Helen Bowen		12
Frances King School of English, London	4 wks	FT	£699	Throughout yearl	High standard of education	Nathalie Ivemy	Entry by interview	12
GEOS English Academy, Hove	4 wks	FT	£807	Throughout year	University entrance level; Native speaker comp; Min age 20	Dir of TT	Accomm avail	15
GLOSCAT, Cheltenham	7 wks 36 wks	FT PT	£695 + £550 + exam fee	Sep, Jan, Apr	On appl	Audrey Wilton	FT course incl a study week	16
Greenhill College, Harrow	7 mths	PT	£450	Jan	University entrance level; Native speaker comp	Melanie Faulmann		10
Hammersmith & West London College	4 wks 20 wks	FT PT	£695	Throughout year	University entrance level; Native speaker comp	CTEFLA Course Director	Candidates with no higher education may be considered	15
Handsworth College, Birmingham	20 wks	PT	£750	Oct		Brigid Bird		12
Harrow House, Dorset	4 wks	FT	£725	Throughout year	University entrance level; Native speaker comp; Min age 20	Gaynor Wells	Fully residential; Accomm avail	8
Hendon College, London	9 mths	PT	£620	Sep	As per UCLES	Dina Brook		12
Hilderstone College, Broadstairs	4 wks	FT	£767 + exam fee	Throughout year	Good education; Native speaker comp; Min age 20	Valerie Horne	Accomm avail	12
International House, Hastings	4 wks	FT	£652 + exam fee	Throughout year	Interview	Adrian Underhill	Accomm service	18
International House, London	4 wks 12 wks	FT PT	£775 + £910 + exam fee	Throughout year		TT Dept	Apply early	-
International Language Institute, Leeds	4 wks	FT	£780	Regularly		Steven Procter	Accomm & job counselling	10
ITTC, Bournemouth	4 wks 8 mths	FT PT	£776 + exam fee	Monthly Oct	University entrance level	Louise Garel-Jones		18

See pages **54-58** for reference advertising and pages **172-177** for addresses

RSA/CAMBRIDGE CERTIFICATE - CTEFLA

College	Course length	FT/ PT	Fees	Start dates	Entry requirements	Contact	Comments	Max no. of students
Leeds Metropolitan University	4 wks	FT	£757	Throughout year	As per UCLES	Language Centre		18
Loughborough College	15 wks	PT	£320	Sep, Feb	Degree or equiv	Jan Sanders		15
Newnham Language Centre, Cambridge	4 wks	FT	£760-£800	Jan, Feb, May, Jul, Aug, Oct	University entrance level or Degree; Good standard English	Melanie Dunnico	Pre-selection Interview	16
University of Northumbria at Newcastle	1 yr	PT	£590 + exam fee	Oct	Degree; Teaching Qual or equiv	Dept Office Hist & Crit Studies	Flexible entry & exit points	15
Oxford Brookes University	1-2 terms	PT	£860	Sep, Apr	University entrance level; Min age 20	ICELS Secretary		12
Oxford School of English (Godmer House)	4 wks	FT	£950	Monthly	Pre-selection Interview	Katherine Tustain		14
Pilgrims, Canterbury	1 mnth	FT	£960 + exam fee	Throughout year	Language awareness & people skills	Simon Marshall	Intensive & thorough	12
Regent Language Training, London	4 wks	FT	£750 + exam fee	Monthly	University entrance level; Min age 20; Native speaker comp	Heather Qualtrough	Central London location; Advice on job hunting	12
St Giles College, Brighton	4 wks	FT	£840	Monthly	University entrance level; Min age 20	Sue Laker		15
St Giles College, London	4 wks	FT	£840	Monthly	Degree or University matriculation	Sarah Rapetti	Interview	15
Skola Teacher Training, Marble Arch	4 wks	FT	£800-£830	Throughout year	Min University entry level	Lyndel Sayle		15
SOAS, London	4 wks	FT	£830	July		Fiona English	Access to University facilities	16
Stanton Teacher Training, London	4 wks	FT	£692	Monthly	University matriculation level	David Garrett	Language-learning exp preferred	6
Stoke-on-Trent College	13 wks	PT	£450	Sep, Jan	University matriculation level, Degree pref	R Cowan	Reduced fees possible	13
Thames Valley University, London	6 wks 15 wks	FT PT	£800	Feb, Jun	Degree or equiv; Min age 20	Sophia Davis		18
University College of Ripon & York St John, York	4 wks 2 terms	FT PT	£750 + exam fee	Jan, May	Degree pref	J Moody		12
University of Glamorgan	4 wks 6 mths	FT PT	£720 + exam fee	Apr, Jun Sep	Degree + TEFL exp pref	Maggy McNorton		12
University of Hull	4 wks 20 wks	FT PT	£740 + exam fee	Jun Oct		Debra Marsh		12
Westminster College, London	4 wks	FT	£820	Mar, Apr, Jun, Sep		Georgie Raman		-
Wigston College of Further Education	9 mths	PT	£600 + exam fee	Sep	University entrance level	D E Harris	Apply early	14

See pages **54-58** for reference advertising and pages **172-177** for addresses

CERTIFICATE DIARY

Zarmine Sarfaraz decided that she needed a change from her life as a City broker. Did the Trinity Certificate in TESOL provide the answer?

About seven years ago, I promised myself that one day I would go to the Maldives, having jealously listened to some friends tell stories of their trip there. However, it seemed a long way to go for just a short holiday, so I put the idea on hold for a few years until I heard someone talking about TEFL courses and decided that teaching English would be my ticket to paradise.

It is unbelievable how much you learn in such a short space of time; enough to actually stand up in front of a class of 15 students and believe in yourself.

I applied to Oxford House College in central London, because of its location and reputation. Candidates usually need to have a university degree, although exceptions can be made, in addition to which there is a fairly stringent selection process, comprising of an interview and an 'on-the-spot' test, which initially seemed basic, but soon caused me problems. Although we speak English every day, it is still difficult to suddenly confront the mechanics of the language.

I was convinced that I had failed, but three days later I received notification of my acceptance and was told to expect a package within the next few days - little did I now that it would contain pre-course reading and an assignment that took me two whole weeks to complete.

By the end of the first day I was sorry that I had started the course, but it was too late to back out. When you are told that it is an intensive course, take it seriously, forget about your social, love and family life for a month, because every spare hour out of school is spent on preparation or assignments. You are expected to attend classes from 9.15am to 5.30pm Monday to Friday, and to give you an idea of how busy you will be, here is an example of a typical day during Week 2:

When you are told that it is an intensive course, take it seriously.

9.15-10.15	Peer Teaching
10.30-11.30	Preparing for teaching today
12.00-13.00	Teaching complete 'ppp' lesson
13.00-14.00	Feedback on teaching and teaching point for tomorrow
14.30-15.30	Teaching Reading 1
15.30-16.30	Teaching Reading 2
16.30-17.30	Self-Access and CALL

Classes are shared between the course director/ tutor and at least four other teachers. The course director monitors your progress, lends a sympathetic ear when needed, and constantly provides encouragement, which you will need! The other teachers specialise in your main subjects: gram-

mar, phonology, communication techniques and your foreign language - in our case, Greek! The reason behind two weeks of Greek lessons is to put you in the same position as the students you will be teaching, so, hopefully, you will be more understanding.

My class of 15 trainees was divided into four groups. You work within your group for teaching practice and preparation, but the whole class attends lectures. My group worked well together at preparing lessons for the following day - at first we each taught for about 15 minutes at a time, but in the final week this had somehow become a full 60 minutes!

The course is made up of 12 hours of teaching practice and just over 50 hours of theory and input lessons, plus four assignments:
An analysis of your Greek lessons,
A profile of a student, his or her needs, difficulties and a lesson plan designed for him or her,
The working project: a detailed examination of your ability to come up with original and interesting ideas for lessons, and,
A day-by-day log of your own teaching and an analysis of it, which tests your capacity for self-assessment.

After this you have an hour-long written exam on grammar and phonology and 15 minutes with the external moderator, who decides your final grade. The teaching practice makes up 40% of your final grade, so you have to pass it.

So what do you actually learn? Most schools in the private sector use the 'communicative' method of teaching English, whereby you only teach in English, so you are taught to communicate with students even if they cannot speak a word of English, but you also have to be able to teach up to the level of Cambridge Proficiency, so your grammar has to be good. It is unbelievable how much you learn in such a short space of time; enough to actually stand up in front of a class of 15 students and believe in yourself.

The emphasis may be different at another s····ol, but I enjoyed my course. However, the ·····n point of the course is to find a job, and, although the school does help with opportunities, there are no guaranteed positions. As for me, I have just been offered a year's contract teaching in Male in - you guessed it! - The Maldives, which I found through the *EFL Guide*.

TRINITY COLLEGE CERTIFICATE IN TESOL

College	Course length	FT/PT	Fees	Start dates	Entry requirements	Contact	Comments	Max no. of student
Abbey College, Malvern Wells	5 wks	FT	£748	Oct, Feb, Apr	Degree + Practising teacher	Stewart Griffiths	Also 4 wk summer course	12
Aberdeen College	7 mnths	PT	£169	Sep, May	Degree or equiv	Anne Bain		10
Blackpool & Fylde College	36 wks	PT	£330	Sep	Higher Ed qual or equiv	Tony Foster	1 eve p.w + 6 hrs home-study	18
Bracknell College, Wokingham	32 wks	PT	£536	Sep	Good standard of Ed	Colette Galloway	2 eves per week	14
Bradford & Ilkley Comm. College	4 wks 1 yr	FT PT	£680	Throughout year	University entrance level	Elaine Thurtle	Large EFL dept.	12
Cicero Lang Intl, Tunbridge Wells	4 wks	FT	£725 + exam fee	Throughout year	University entrance level + enthusiasm	Dr John Brown	Accomm. avail.	10
Class Teaching, London	13 wks	FT PT	£575	Throughout year	University entrance level; Degree pref	Ray De Witt/ Dina Serra	Knowledge of foreign lang pref	16
Colchester Institute,	10 wks 30 wks	FT PT	£450 + £400 + exam fee	Sep	Degree or equiv	Simon Haines		10
Coventry TESOL Centre	4 wks	FT DL	£695	Throughout year	Good English; Min age 18	Christopher Fry	Incl Teaching practice + 1:1	12
Croydon Coombe Cliff Service	3 wks 6 mnths	FT PT	£760	Jan, Sep	Course Director's discretion	Tessa Bates/ Janet Ott	Pre-course study pack	14
East Berkshire College, Langley	23 wks	PT	£475	Sep	University entrance level	Mr C Hammonds		15
Surrey Adult Ed, Esher	20 wks	PT	TBA	Jan	Interview	Carole Kinsey	1 day per week	18
Farnborough College of Technology	1 yr	PT	£460 + exam fee	Sep	negotiable	A Ashwell	Non-native teachers welcome	16
Grimsby College	30 wks	PT	£250	Jan	Degree + teaching exp	Faculty of Continuing Ed	4 hrs per week	15
Grove House, Dartford	4 wks	FT	£695	Throughout year	Course Director's discretion	Heather Jeynes	Accomm avail + help with jobs	12
Hart Villages, Odiham	9 mnths	PT	£350	Sep	Flexible entry	Margaret Mitchell	Incl teaching practice placements	16
Hopwood Hall, Rochdale	5 wks 22 wks	FT PT	£640 £580	Jan Apr	University entrance level; Min age 20	Arnold Spencer		16
Hull College	8 wks 32 wks	FT PT	£215 EC £800 non EC	Jan, Sep, Oct	University entrance level	Tina Cole/ Richard Hart	Degree or teaching exp an advantage	12
inlingua, Cheltenham	5 wks	FT	£725 + moderation fee	Throughout year	University entrance level	Dagmar Lewis	Poss posts overseas on completion	10
ITS English School, Hastings	4 wks	FT	£720	Feb, Jul		John Palim		12

See pages **54-58** for reference advertising and pages **172-177** for addresses

TRINITY COLLEGE CERTIFICATE IN TESOL

College	Cours length	FT/ PT	Fees	Start dates	Entry requirements	Contact	Comments	Max no. of studen
Language Link, London	4 wks	FT	£620 + exam fee	Every 5 wks	'A' level English min	Robyn Bowman Zayade		10
London Study Centre	5 wks 15 wks	FT PT	£700	Throughout year	Interview	Kevin McNicholas		16
University of Luton	2 sems	FT PT	£110	Oct	Good standard educ	Vicki Vidal	Part of modular B.A degree	20
Oaklands College, Borehamwood	12 wks	PT	£550	Jan, Sep	Higher Ed background pref	Johnathan Brook		12
Oxford House College, London	4 wks 13 wks	FT PT	£690	Monthly	Degree pref Min age 20	Jan Brindle	Central London	16
Polyglot Lang. Services, London	4 wks 21 wks	FT PT	£695	Throughout year	University entrance level	Secretary		8
Regency School of English, Ramsgate	4 wks	FT	£650	Jan, Apr, Oct	Good educ background	Director of Teacher Training	Intensive Course; Accom avail	12
Richmond Adult Comm College	33 wks	PT	£750	Sep	Degree or equiv	Barbara Beaumont	Day course; Apply early	16
St Brelade's College, Jersey	4 wks	FT	£620 + exam fee	Feb, Mar, Sep	Degree or appropriate training	Mr Brown/ Miss Pastorelli		12
St George's School of English, London	4 wks 16 wks	FT PT	£595	Throughout year	Min age 21	Max Loach	Accomm avail; Apply early	10
Sace-Waverley Area, Godalming	28 wks	PT	£400	Sep	Degree or equiv	Mrs Sieglinde Ward	Day & Evening courses	18
Sandwell College, West Midlands	12-16 wks	PT	On appl	Oct, Feb	Degree or teaching exp; Min age 25	Central Enquiries		15
Scot-Ed Courses, Edinburgh	5 wks 14 wks	FT PT	£783	All year	University entrance level	Joanne Gunnion		10
Sheffield College, Stradbroke Centre	35 wks	PT	£425	Sep	Good ed background	Alison Rost		12
Sheffield Hallam University	4 wks 16 wks	FT DL	£800	All year	Degree	Gill King	DL incl 4 wks FT	20
South East Essex College	1 yr	PT	£290	Sep	Degree or equiv; Native speakers	Marketing	Informal interview	20
Southwark College, London	4 wks	FT	£695	Jan, Jun	Degree or equiv	P Jakes		12
Surrey Lang. Training	1 mnth	FT	£750	Feb, May, Sep, Nov		Mr Ronald Micallef		12
Thurrock College, Essex	16 wks	DL	£550	Feb, Aug, Nov, Dec	Degree or teaching qual.	Beryl Andrews	Incl 4 wks FT; Accom avail	14
Waltham Forest College, London	2 terms	PT	£500	Sep	University entrance level; Native speakers; Min age 21	Course Tutor	Interview	12

EQUIVALENT QUALIFICATIONS IN IRELAND

How to get basic qualifications in Ireland.

In the past the qualification system in Ireland was rather loose. Although a large number of Irish teachers have always worked overseas, there has frequently been a problem with their qualifications. To teach in Ireland, a degree is required, but in the past Irish Tourist Board regulations allowed recognised language schools to employ anyone with a TEFL qualification, and that included a huge variety of short course certificates. Many of these short courses are run within Irish colleges. With the growth in demand for EFL in Ireland, fuelled by dissatisfaction with certain aspects of British schools and the devaluation of the Irish Punt, such short courses proliferated.

The problem with such short courses is that foreign students generally go to Ireland in the summer months (although this too is changing towards all year courses), so that outside this time trainee teachers simply do not have enough students to practise on.

Language schools in Ireland are now trying to find common ground to ensure there is more consistency in their qualification system.

RELSA The Recognised English Language Schools Association are introducing a course that aims to control the number of TEFL courses available. The RELSA training course, the Preparatory Certificate in TEFL, lasts 70 hours and involves teaching practice, observation and a project. At present there are six schools that are licensed to run such courses should ease out the less reputable schools offering courses lasting under 20 hours. The RELSA certificate is already considered an acceptable qualification in some schools overseas who were previously baffled by the diverse range of certificates Irish teachers presented them with. However, the RELSA course is still shorter and less well known than the RSA certificate.

Association of Teacher Trainers (ATT)
The Association of Teacher Trainers (ATT) is an association of seven schools that are concerned with improving teacher training in Ireland. They run a Preliminary Certificate and an International Certificate in TEFL. The

In the past Irish Tourist Board regulations allowed recognised language schools to employ anyone with a TEFL qualification.

Preliminary Certificate lasts just 40 hours and is designed to persuade trainee teachers away from less reputable short courses. The International Certificate lasts over 100 hours and comprises teacher training and practice. ATT hope that this certificate will soon be seen as comparable to the RSA and Trinity Certificates. Any institution can run the ATT Certificates once they have been approved. Courses will cost around Ir£500, not including exam fees.

RSA Cambridge and Trinity Certificate
The RSA and Trinity certificates are respected in Irish schools, and there are a growing number of centres running RSA courses, and some colleges offering the Trinity certificate (see p37).

State sector qualifications
The state EFL sector is fairly small in Ireland, although the Universities of Dublin and Cork do a teacher training course the College Certificate in EFL, which runs in conjunction with the Higher Diploma in Education over two years. This is considered as an equivalent to the RSA certificate.

For details of working in Ireland, see p66.

The RELSA certificate is already considered an acceptable qualification in some schools overseas

GETTING QUALIFIED IN AUSTRALIA AND THE USA

English speaking countries share the same language, but not as yet the same EFL qualification systems. So if you want to train in TEFL in Australia, the United States, what courses are available?

Australia

EFL teachers in Australia are generally required to have a degree and a certificate the same qualifications as in Britain (see p27). The National ELICOS Accreditation Scheme (NEAS) state that all teaching staff in their recognised schools must have either:

EFL teachers in Australia are generally required to have a degree and a certificate.

a) a degree and formal postgraduate teaching qualification (such as the RSA Cambridge certificate),

b) a formal teaching qualification which includes a significant TEFL/TESL component,

c) a degree or formal teaching training qualification plus a full-time certificate in TESOL (Teaching English to Speakers of Other Languages),

d) a TESOL diploma, plus at least 1,200 hours recent general teaching experience,

e) a degree or formal teacher training qualification plus at least 1,200 hours EFL/ESL experience. For further information, contact: NEAS, Locked Bag 2, Post Office, PYRMONT, NSW 2009.

The Australian Centre for Languages runs a 4 week intensive or 10 week course in TESOL, open to graduates. For details, contact: 02 742 5277. The University of Sydney run a one year full time diploma in TEFL, open to graduates with at least two years' relevant teaching experience. For more information, contact: University of Sydney, Sydney, NSW 2006.

You do not need any previous experience of teaching to take an MA in the US.

The Australian TESOL Training Centre run an intensive one week introductory course in TEFL from July to October aimed at people wishing to teach to supplement their income as they travel overseas. They also run courses for non-native speakers of English - the Certificate for Overseas Teachers of English and the Observation for Overseas Teachers of RSA Certificate in TEFLA. Both are for one month. The latter involves participating in the native speakers of English course combined with peer teaching. Both courses require a level of English equivalent to Cambridge First Certificate.

Contact: The Australian TESOL Training Centre, PO Box 82, Bondi Junction, NSW 2022. Tel: (02) 389 0249. For more information about Australian courses, see the grid on p40 and p145.

The United States

As yet the States have no equivalent to the RSA certificate, which has caused problems when American teachers have wished to teach in Europe.

The minimum qualification is generally a Master of Arts (MA) in TESL or Applied Linguistics (see p69). Courses vary widely, and many are mostly theoretical and have very little practical content hence the suspicion with which they are sometimes treated in countries which prefer more practical qualifications such as the RSA certificate.

You do not need any previous experience of teaching to take an MA in the US. This is again unlike the situation, for example, in Britain. However, there are voluntary ESL programmes in most American cities which offer the possibility of gaining some teaching experience.

The recent decision by Georgetown University, Washington, to run RSA/Cambridge Certificate courses is testimony to their increasing significance, but there are still only a handful of centres in the US. There are also one month courses run to a similar format as the RSA certificate in centres throughout the States, such as IH New York and St Giles Educational Trust, San Francisco (see p37 - 41 for details of these and other certificate courses in the USA).

Many institutions in the States do recognise the RSA Cambridge Diploma as an equivalent to an MA, so if you have a diploma, it is a valid qualification to teach there.

Because the USA expects teachers to have an MA, this can have a knock-on effect in countries which employ a lot of American teachers. For example, many organisations in the Gulf, such as those in Kuwait, prefer teachers to have an MA before they will consider employing them. This can be a disadvantage to British, Irish and Australian teachers, as in these countries an MA is essentially a higher academic qualification (see Section Five - Professional Development) for more detailed information about taking MAs around the world.

College	Course length	FT/PT	Fees	Start dates	Entry requirements	Contact	Comments	Max no. of students
Academia Lacunza, San Sebastian	110 hrs	FT	127500 PTS	Aug	As per UCLES	Head of TT		15
American University in Cairo	4 wks	FT	US$ 850	Throughout year	Native speaker English	Christine Zamer/ Magda Lawrence		10
Australian Centre for Languages, New South Wales	4 wks 12 wks	FT PT	A$ 21000 A$ 2230	Throughout year	As per UCLES	Oonagh Woods		12
Australian TESOL Training Centre, New South Wales	4 wks 12 wks	FT PT	A$ 1990	Throughout year	University entrance level; Min age 20	Gloria Smith		12
British Council, Abu Dhabi	12-14 wks	PT	DhS 7000	Feb	As per UCLES	Centre Manager	UAE residents only	12
British Council, Athens	5 mnths	PT	on appl	Jan	Degree	Martha Cavoura		12
British Council, Berlin	1 mnth	FT	DM 1150	Jul, Aug	Educated, Native speaker	Bill Dean	Pre-course interview	12
British Council, Cairo	5 wks	FT	2200 LE	June	Pre-course task + interview	Charles Napier		10
British Council, Caracas	5 wks	FT	US$ 1500	April	Pre-course task	Stuart Gale		12
British Council, Doha	10-16 wks	PT	on appl	Nov	UK Education	Chris Gibson		12
British Council, Hong Kong	140 hrs	PT	HK$ 14,500	Jan, Apr, Sep	Uni entrance level; Native speaker comp; Min age 20	Nick Florent	Incl intensive 1st week	-
British Council, Kuala Lumpur	5 wks 10 wks	FT PT	RM 3300	Jan, Apr, Jul, Oct	University standard education	Patricia Thorley		15
British Council, Lisbon	8 mnths	PT	P$ 180000	Oct	As per UCLES	Julie Tice		15
British Council, Milan	4 wks 6 mnths	FT PT	2.2m ITL	Jun, Sep Jan	Standard reqs	Andy Quin/ Amanda Bourdillon	Help with accomm	12
British Council, Muscat	10-16 wks	PT	RO 575	Throughout year	University entrance level	Melanie Pender		12
British Council, Naples	4 wks	FT	2.4m ITL	June	Uni entrance level; Native speaker comp	F C de la Motte	Min age 20	16
British Council, Parede, Portugal	4 wks 20 wks	FT PT	ESC 180000	Jun, Nov	As per UCLES	Ingrid Calhau		12
British Council, Singapore	40 wks	PT DL	S$ 2100	Jan, Apr, Sep	Native speaker level of English	Rose		18
British Council, Thessaloniki	135 hrs	PT	On appl	Oct	University entrance level	Camilla Ralls		16
British Council, Tokyo	12-14 wks	PT	Y 300000	Throughout year	Interviews	Asst Dir of Studs	Appls to check VISA status	16

See pages **59-61** for reference advertising

and pages **172-177** for addresses

College	Course length	FT/PT	Fees	Start dates	Entry requirements	Contact	Comments	Max no. of students
British Institute of Florence	1 mnth	FT	2.2m ITL	Jun, Jul	As per UCLES	Director	Some help with accom	9
British Institute, Indonesia	4 wks	FT	$1486	Nov, Feb, Jul	University entrance level	Gary O'Neill		15
British Language Centre, Madrid	4 wks 15 wks	FT PT	£600	Throughou year		Alastair Dickinson	Help with accomm	18
British School of Milan	4 wks 15 wks	FT PT	2.1m ITL	Throughou year	Gd education; Native speaker English	Rafaela Aldinucci	Pre-course interview (tel poss)	12
Cambridge School, Lisbon	4 wks	FT	£750	Jul, Aug	Interviews poss in UK	Jeffrey Kapkes	Help with accomm;	12
Cambridge School, Verona	4 wks 6 mnths	FT PT	2.1m ITL	Jun-Sep Jan	Gd education; native speaker English	Anne Parry	Help with accomm	12
Capital Language Academy, Wellington, NZ	4 wks	FT	NZ$ 2550	Jan, May, Oct	On appl	Eliss Hope		12
Dominion English School, Auckland	1 mnth	FT	A$2500	On appl	Prev exp helpful	Andrew Williams		-
Elcra-Bell, Geneva	4-12 wks	PT	SFR 3400	Throughou year	As per UCLES	Sean Power	Also in Zurich	12
English International, San Francisco	4 wks	FT	US$ 1975	Monthly	Degree + knowledge of foreign language	Deanne Manwaring	Professional job guidance	12
ETC Shane, Madrid	4 wks	FT	£675	July	Uni entrance level; Native speaker comp;Min age 20	Shane School, London	Job guaranteed on achieving grades A or B	12
Georgetown University, Washington DC	5 wks	FT	US$ 3000	May, Jul, Aug	Degree + 2nd Language	F Mary Marggraf		18
ILA South Pacific, New Zealand	4½ wks	FT	NZ$ 2800	May, Oct, Nov	Degree; 2nd language; Min age 20	Susan McAllister		12
ILC Paris	4 wks	FT	9400 FFR	Throughou year	Uni entrance level; Native speaker comp	TT Dept	Pre-selection task	18
International House, Barcelona	4 wks 4 mnths	FT PT	127000 PTS	Throughou year	University entrance level	Jenny Johnson	Help with accomm	18
International House, Budapest	4 wks 3 mnths	FT PT	£650	Jan, Feb, May, Jul	Degree pref; Min age 21	Head of TT		12
International House, Lisbon	4 wks	FT	£560	Throughou year	Pre-course interview & task	Kathryn Gordon		15
International House, Madrid	4 wks 16 wks	FT PT	127500 PTS	Jun, Jul, Sep, Oct	Higher ed pref; Native speaker comp;Min age 20	Steven Haysham		15
International House, Palma de Mallorca	4 wks 5 mnths	FT PT	120000 PTS	July Feb	Degree or equiv; Min age 20	Jan Wright		12

See pages **59-61** for reference advertising

and pages **172-177** for addresses

College	Course length	FT/ PT	Fees	Start dates	Entry requirements	Contact	Comments	Max no of students
International House, Rome	4 wks 8 mnths	FT PT	2.3m ITL	May, Jul Aug, Oct	As per UCLES	Director		12
International House, Sabadell	4 wks	FT	120000 PTS	July	University entrance level	Lilius Adam		18
International House, Valencia	4 wks 8 wks	FT PT	127000 PTS	Apr, Jul	Degree preferred	Seamus Campbell		15
International House, Vienna	4 wks 10 wks	FT PT	ATS 15900	Feb, Aug	Native speaker competence	Head of Training		12
International Language Institute, Cairo	4 wks	FT	£460	Throughout year	Degree preferred	Paul Mason	Accomm on request	12
ITTC, Melbourne	4 wks 20 wks	FT PT	$1820	Throughout year	Native speaker competence; Min age 20	Beatrice Taylor	Help with accomm	18
Language Centre of Ireland, Dublin	4 wks 9 wks	FT PT	IR £750	Jan, Jun, Jul, Sep, Oct	Pre-course interview	Tom Doyle		14
Language Institute, Athens	1 mnth 3 mnths	FT PT	£868	Jan, May, Jun, Sep	Personal Interview	Clare O'Donoghue/ Jennifer Smith	Poss jobs on completion	15
Languages International, Auckland	4 wks	FT	NZ$ 2750	Apr, Jun, Aug, Nov	University entrance level	John McMahon		12
Language Resources Ltd, Japan	17 wks	PT	Y 270000	Apr, Oct	As per UCLES	Bill Stanford		10
La Trobe University, Victoria	4 wks	FT	A$1800	Throughout year	As per UCLES	Maggie Mortreux		-
Milner Intl Coll of Eng, Perth	4 wks	FT	A$ 1890	Feb, May, Jul, Oct	Tertiary education	Warren Milner	Accomm avail	12
St Giles College, San Francisco	4 wks 3 mnths	FT PT	$1700	Throughout year	Higher ed; Knowledge of foreign lang & exp pref	Conrad Heyns	Course was first CTEFLA in US	15
Saxoncourt, Madrid	4 wks	FT	£700	Jul, Sep		Saxoncourt		12
School House, Goiania, Brazil	1 mnth	FT	$500 approx	Jul, Jan	Pre-selection test & interview	Maria Brown		15
University College Cork, Ireland	4 wks	FT	IR £700	Feb	University entrance level	Goodith White		12
York House, Barcelona	1 mnth	FT	125000 PTS	Jul, Sep	University entrance level; Native speaker	Montserrat Solé	Help with accomm	12

See pages **59-61** for reference advertising and pages **172-177** for addresses

INTERNATIONAL CERTIFICATES

College	Course Title	Course length	FT/ PT	Start dates	Entry requirements	Contact	Commen	Max no of students
Australia								
University of Canberra	Grad Cert TESOL	on appl	on appl	on appl	on appl	Gary Zeiler		-
University of Queensland	Grad Cert	on appl	on appl	on appl	on appl	Dr Ed Burke		-
Brazil								
The School House, Goiania	ITTI Cert	1 mnth	FT	Jul, Jan	Test & Interview	Maria Brown	Intensive	15
Egypt								
American University, Cairo	Prelim Cert in TE to Adults	6 wks	PT	May, Sep	Degree + excellent Eng	Jude Travers		6
France								
British Inst in Paris	Certificate Course	30 wks	PT	Oct	Normally degree	Eng Dept Sec	Incl Teaching Practice	18
Ireland								
Blue Feather School of Langs, Dublin	ATT Prelim Cert	2-3wks	FT PT	All year	Good standard of education	Gregory Rosenstock	Help with accomm	10
	ATT Intl Cert	106 hrs	FT PT	May, Nov	Degree or equiv + 2 yrs exp	Gregory Rosenstock	Help with accomm	10
Centre of English Studies, Dublin	RELSA Prep Cert	4 wks 2 wks	FT PT	Feb, May, Jun	Degree or equiv; min age 21	Rosemary Quinn		15
Cork Language Centre	RELSA Prep Cert	2 wks 3 wks	FT PT	Mar, Jun Feb, Sep	Degree; Min age 20	Niamh Morgan	Job advice given	12
Dublin School of English	RELSA Intro Cert	4 wks	PT	All year		Ernie Crossen		
English Language Ed Centre, Co Kerry	RELSA Prep	2 wks 10 wks	FT PT	Apr Sep	Higher Ed; Min age 20; Good Eng	John Kennedy	Help with accomm	15
English Language Inst, Dublin	RELSA Cert	2 wks	FT	Mar, May, Sep	Degree pref	Louise Byrne		15
Galway Lang Centre	TEFL Intro Course	4 wks	PT	All year	Degree or equiv			12
Grafton Tuition Centre, Dublin	ATT Prelim Cert	4 wks	PT	All year	Gd standard of education	Denis O'Donoghue	Career & accom help	12
	ATT Intl Cert	1 mnth	FT	June-Sep	Gd standard of education	Denis O'Donoghue	Career & accom help	12
Institute of Education, Dublin	Cert Prim/ Sec School Teachers	3 wks	FT	July	None	Michael David	Fee incl accomm	15

See pages **59-61** for reference advertising and pages **172-177** for addresses

College	Course Title	Course length	FT/ PT	Start dates	Entry requirement	Contact	Comment	Max no. of students
Ireland								
International Study Centre, Dublin	RELSA Prep Cert	2 wks	FT	Jan, Mar, Oct	Degree; Min age 21	Tim Connolly		10
Irish College of English, Dublin	ATT Prelim Cert	1 wk	FT PT	on appl	Uni entrance level; Min age 18	Francis Leavey	Summer work on completion	15
TEFL Training Inst, Dublin	ATT Prelim Cert	40 hrs	FT PT	All year	School level education	Angela Sweeney		10
	ATT Intl Cert	106 hrs	FT PT	Sep, Jan, Apr, Jul	Degree or equiv	Kevin McGinley	Incl teaching practice	12
University College Dublin	Cert TEFL	1 yr	PT	Aug	Degree or equiv; Native speakers only	Mary Ruane	Funding poss	18
University of Ulster	PGDip TEFL	9 mnths	FT	Sep	Degree or Teaching Cert or equiv	Dr Pritchard	Incl 6 wks teaching in Hungary	18
Westlingua Lang School, Galway	RELSA Cert	70 hrs	PT	All year	3rd level	Sandra Bunting		10
Words Language Service, Dublin	ATT Prelim Cert	6 days 3 wks	FT PT	All year	University entrance level	Director	Career advice	10
	ATT Intl Cert	4 wks 18 wks	FT PT	Jun, Oct	Degree or equiv	Director	Career & accom help	8
YES Lang Inst, Cork	ATT Prelim Cert	3 wks	PT	All year	Gd level of educ	Geraldine Marlborough	Careers advice	10
New Zealand								
Auckland College of Educ	Cert TESOL	6 mnths	PT	on appl	On appl	Roly Golding		-
Auckland Inst of Tech	Cert in Lang Teaching to Adults	on appl	on appl	on appl	No exp necessary	Alison Kirkness		-
Carrington Polytechnic, Auckland	Adv Cert in Lang Teaching to Adults	on appl	on appl	on appl	CLTA or equiv	Ross Currie		-
Christchurch College of Educ	Cert TESOL	varies	FT	on appl	On appl	Geoff Ormandy		-
Victoria Uni of Wellington	PG Dip in Teaching ESL	1 yr	FT	March	On appl	Helen Middleton		-
United States								
St Michael's College, Vermont	Inst in TESL	9 credits	FT	Jun	On appl	Dir of Studies		-
	Advanced Cert in TESL	18 credits	FT PT	Jan, Jun, Sep	On appl	Dir of Studs		-
Transworld Teachers, San Francisco	TT Certificate	4 wks 11-15 wks	FT PT	All year	On appl	Secretary		-

See pages **59-61** for reference advertising and pages **172-177** for addresses

OVERSEAS TRINITY CERTIFICATE IN TESOL

College	Course length	FT/ PT	Fees	Start dates	Contact	Comments
ECS, Abu Dhabi	4 wks	FT	7000 UAE Dirhams	Throughout year	Kate MacFarlane	Intensive; Incl Teaching Young Learner components
ECS, Dubai	4 wks 22 wks	FT PT	7000 UAE Dirhams	Throughout year	Charles Boyle	Intensive; Incl Teaching Young Learner components
Grafton Tuition, Dublin	4 wks 6 mths	FT PT	IR £625	Throughout year	Denis O'Donoghue	Help with accomm given; Careers advice; help with employment
Saxoncourt Teacher Training, Japan	TBA	TBA	TBA	TBA	Saxoncourt Teacher Training	First Trinity Cert run in Japan

RSA/CAMBRIDGE COTE

College	Course length	FT/ PT	Fees	Start dates	Entry requirements	Contact	Comments	Max no. of students
American University in Cairo	14 wks	PT	EG £1500	Sep, Dec	Adult Educational experience	Magda Lawrence/ Christine Zaher		12
Bilkent University, Turkey	10 mths	PT	TBA	Oct	Teaching Qual or 300 hrs ELT	Head of TT Unit	Practising EFL teachers	12
British Council, Lisbon	9 mths	PT	TBA	Oct	As per UCLES	Julie Tice		12
British Council, Mexico	1-2 yrs	PT DL	N/A	varied	Good English + 300 hrs exp			25
British Council, Thessaloniki	1 yr	PT	N/A	Oct	CPE + 300 hrs teaching exp	Camilla Ralls		16
Centro Anglo Paraguayo	9 mths	PT	US $600	Oct	Degree + 300 hrs teaching exp	Maureen Finn	Incl 1 mth intensive block	10
Eastern Mediterranean University, Turkey	1 yr	PT	N/A	Sep	Degree + 1 yr teaching exp	Edward Casassa	In-house & external candidates	20
ESADE, Barcelona	1 yr	PT	300000 PTS	Oct	Degree + 300 hrs exp + CPE English	David Block		20
Language Institute, Athens	3-5 mths	PT	£906	Jan	Personal Interview	Clare O'Donoghue/ Jennifer Smith		15
The School House, Goiania, Brazil	10 mths	PT	$500	Aug	Post-SCE	Maria Brown		12
Study Space, Thessaloniki	9 mths	PT	varies	Sep, Oct	1 yr exp; Interview	Chrissie Taylor	Help with jobs given	8

INTRODUCTORY AND CORRESPONDENCE COURSES

A good way to get an idea of what teaching EFL is all about without committing yourself to the time and expense of a full training course is to take an introductory or correspondence course.

If you are unwilling or unable to commit yourself to the time and expense involved in the RSA Cambridge or Trinity College Certificates, but are keen to have some sort of training in EFL, there are a wide range of introductory courses on offer. Most of these courses are about one week long. As they are inevitably limited in what they can teach you in this time, they are not generally considered as sufficient to enable you to go straight in to the classroom, but they have provided plenty of teachers with their first jobs.

Many centres who offer such courses will help you find permanent jobs, even if their range of posts may be limited. Such courses are also useful if you are interested in vacation work. In the summer in the UK and Ireland there are hundreds of EFL jobs (see p67), and there are also plenty of vacancies in Australia and New Zealand in the Christmas period (their summer). Due to the demand for teachers during these periods, an introductory course certificate may be looked on as a good enough qualification.

It may also be worth doing an introductory course to see if you would be interested in moving on to a full training course. Some UK centres offer introductory training courses linked to certificates that are also useful if you do not hold a degree, usually required for the RSA Certificate, such as Marble Arch Teacher Training, which offers direct entry for successful students to their RSA Cambridge course and Coventry Technical College does a one-week course, which counts as stage one of the Trinity College Certificate. Stage two must be done within a year. (See grid on following pages for details.)

Other courses inevitably vary in quality. Try to ensure that the courses have a balance between theory and practice and that you have practice with foreign students, not just peer groups, i.e. other trainee teachers. Some schools run classes in their own teaching method. For example, the Butler School of Languages offer the Butler Question Method. Teachers are trained in 'significant question techniques'. Butler School recruit from their course for their associate schools in Europe.

Distance learning/correspondence courses

Particularly in the UK, there are many courses that claim to 'teach' you how to teach EFL. Some of these are purely correspondence courses, others are a combination of self-study and a short intensive course, often a long weekend. If you are short of time or money, they may seem an attractive option, but choose the course carefully. Ask to speak to former students and avoid companies that do not advertise a telephone number and that operate from a PO Box or a business mailing address, rather than an actual school.

Courses that are totally correspondence may seem very good value, but they are not recognised by most employers. Avoid them unless you already have teaching experience - learning to teach without having teaching practice is like learning to swim without going near water.

Despite these warnings, certain courses seem to be achieving their objective of providing worthwhile, convenient training at an affordable price, as has been shown by the The College of Preceptors' recent accreditation under Royal Charter of the distance learning courses administered by Eurolink in Sheffield and Language 2 Associates in London.

Another interesting development is the growth of courses that combine distance learning with a two or three-day, intensive (often residential) course. These courses manage to cram an enormous number of training hours in to a short space of time, so you have to make sure that you have prepared very well. As with most courses, their quality is variable, but some programmes, such as those run by TEFL Training in Oxfordshire, are led by experienced teacher trainers, who certainly understand the business.

Taking in to account the time and money you have available, choose your course very carefully. Remember that the acid test of any vocational course is its success or failure in impressing prospective employers and securing a job for you.

Some UK centres offer introductory training courses linked to certificates that are also useful if you do not hold a degree.

Avoid companies that do not advertise a telephone number.

College	Course Length	FT/ PT	Fees	Starting Dates	Entry Requirements	Contact	Comments	Max no. of students
Aberdeen College	30 hrs	FT PT	£141	Various		Anne Bain		15
Abon Language School, Bristol	1 wk 10 wks	FT PT	£125	Throughout year		Heather Crispin		10
Aston University	4 wks	FT	£695	Jul, Aug	Degree	Sec, Lang Studs	No exp required	25
Bedford CHE	11 wks	PT	£80	Sep, Jan, Apr	Degree pref	Ken Wilford	College Cert awarded	16
BEET Language Centre, Bournemouth	2 wks	FT	£501	June	Eng prof	Lindsay Ross	Interview	14
Brasshouse Centre, Birmingham	1 wk	FT	£100	Throughout year		Deborah Cobbett		15
British Council, Hong Kong	30 hrs	PT	HK $3,150	Throughout year	Eng prof	Rebecca Ho		-
British Council, Singapore	20 hrs	PT	S$565	Jan, Apr, Jul, Sep	Good Eng	Rose	To Pre-school Children or Adults or Young Learners	18
CILC, Cheltenham	1 wk	FT	£175	Feb, May, Jul		Gillian James	Intensive & practical	15
Uni Coll of Ripon & York St John, York	1 wk	FT	£140	Jan, Apr, Jun	Degree pref	J Moody		12
Concorde Intl, Canterbury	1 wk	FT	£138	June	Degree pref; Min age 20	Course Director	For summer course teachers	12
Coventry TESOL Centre	1 wk	FT	£125	May		Christopher Fry	Feeder for RSA Certs	15
Diamond College, London	2-8 wks	PT	£411	Throughout year		Marc Diamond		8
Filton College, Bristol	1 weekend	FT	on appl	June		Helen Bowen	For summer school teachers	-
GEOS, Hove	1 wk	FT	N/A	Mar, Jun, Dec	Uni entrance level; Min age 20	Dir of TT	Help with accomm	15
University of Glamorgan	10 wks	FT PT	£120	Easter Sep		Maggy McNorton	Intensive Easter courses	15
Globe English Centre, Exeter	1 wk	FT	£130	Apr, May	Degree pref	Dir of Studs	Help with accom & summer work	10
Goldsmith's College, London	1 wk	FT	on appl	June		Laure Arthur	Apply early	20
Greenhill College, Harrow	1 wk	FT	£150	Throughout year		Judith Haigh		16
Grimsby College	10 hrs	PT	£115	Jan	Degree pref	Fac of Cont Ed	Some exp usual	20
Grove House, Dartford	1 wk 2 days + home	FT PT	£175 £145	Throughout year		Heather Jeynes	Accomm avail	12
Harrow House, Swanage	1 wk	FT	£150	Throughout year	Min age 18	Gaynor Wells	Fully residential	8

INTRODUCTORY COURSES

College	Course Length	FT/PT	Fees	Starting Dates	Entry Requirements	Contact	Comments	Max no of students
Hilderstone Coll, Broadstairs	1 wk	FT	£175	Apr, May, Oct, Nov	Good education; Min age 20	Valerie Horne	Accomm avail	12
Inlingua, Cheltenham	2 wks	FT	£285	Throughout year	Degree or equiv	Dagmar Lewis	Poss posts abroad	10
Intl Language Institute, Leeds	1 wk	FT	£155	Throughout year		Steven Proctor	Help with jobs & accomm	10
Klubschule Migros, Switz	20 wks	PT	660 Sw Frs	Oct	Eng prof	Peter Holland	Special prospectus	15
Language Institute, Athens	2 mnths	PT	£415	Feb, Sep	Interview	Clare O'Donoghue		15
Linguarama, Birmingham	1 wk	FT	£190	Throughout year				-
University of Luton	1 wk / ½ sem	FT / PT	£95	Aug Oct	University entrance level	Vicky Vidal	Informal interview	20
Lydbury English Centre, Shropshire	1 wk	FT	£250	Weekly	Degree or equiv	R A & D J Baker	Suitable for individuals	-
Multi Lingua, Guildford	1 wk / 5 Sats	FT / PT	£215	Throughout year		Dr G Connolly		12
Oxford Brookes Univ, Oxford	1 wk / 10 eves	FT / PT	£130	Throughout year		Pam Simpson		16
Pilgrims, Canterbury	1 wk	FT	£195	Throughout year	Interest in TEFL	Isabelle Cross	Practical & thorough	15
Polyglot Language Services, London	1 wk	FT	£165	Feb, Jun		Secretary		8
University of Portsmouth	1 wk	FT / PT	£150 £94	Throughout year		Mrs A Bailey		30
Richard Language Coll, Bournemouth	6 wks	PT	N/A	on appl		Lynda Edwards		14
Saxoncourt, London	1 wk	FT	£140	Apr, May			Also involved in recruitment	12
Skola Teacher Training, London	1 wk	FT	£175	Throughout year	Interview	Lyndel Sayle		15
South Trafford College	15 wks	PT	£100	Sep, Jan		Patrick Bennett	1 eve per week	-
Stoke on Trent College	1 wk	FT	£120	on appl			Interview	-
University of Strathclyde	1 wk	FT	£170	Throughout year	Uni entrance level; Eng prof	Paul Curtis		17
Surrey Language Training, Farnham	1 wk	FT	£170	Monthly		Ronald Micullef		12
University of Sussex, Brighton	1 wk	FT	£90	Dec, Mar, Jun		Margaret Khidhayir		20
TEFL Training, London	weekend + home study	FT DL	on appl	Throughout year		Tony Crofts	Various locations in UK	18
Waltham Forest College, London	1 wk	FT	£120	Jun, Jul, Oct, Jan	Good educ; Min age 21; Eng prof	Course Tutor	Counselling for work abroad	10
Westminster College, London	1 wk / 6 wks	FT / PT	£150	Throughout year		Georgie Raman		-

IN-HOUSE TRAINING

Some organisations own chains of schools, and run their own short courses to prepare people to teach in them. Schools within the chain normally either run their own courses or recruit directly from courses run by their headquarters. If you do not have the time or money to study for a certificate, they may be a good route to your first teaching job.

Generally, the stricter their teaching method is, the less useful it will be outside that organisation.

Certain schools concentrate on a particular teaching method peculiar to that group of schools, which may be a disadvantage if you want to work outside that chain. Generally, the stricter their teaching method is, the less useful it will be outside that organisation. However, some employers may be impressed by the certificate that is awarded at the end of these courses.

The following schools are some of the major chains:

BERLITZ (250 + schools worldwide)
Berlitz run introductory courses in EFL, but only for teachers who have already been taken on by a particular school in their organisation. For that reason, if you want to train in one of their schools in Spain, for example, you must apply directly to that particular school in writing. You will then be interviewed by them.

Berlitz prefer experienced teachers, preferably with a TEFL qualification. However, they will consider people who have worked abroad before, are language graduates or have been trained in a specific field, such as law or accountancy. They will only employ native English speakers. Their initial training course involves a method unique to the Berlitz schools, which lasts 1-2 weeks. Outside the UK, you may be paid a modest fee to see you through the course. Supplementary training is given during working hours for employed teachers in skills such as Business English and English for Children, again using their own methods.

The Salisbury School recruit EFL teachers for Sweden on behalf of the British Centre.

To get the addresses of Berlitz schools, contact **Berlitz International Inc.,** Research Park. 293 Wall Street, Princeton NJO8540 USA or **Berlitz School,** Wells House, 79 Wells Street, London WIA 3BZ. All apllications should be made in writing.

GEOS
Geos run introductory courses for teachers recruited for their schools in Japan.
Contact: **Geos Corporation,** PO Box 512, Ark Mori Building, 33rd Floor, 1-12-32 Akasaka, Minato-Ku, Tokyo 107, Japan.

Geos also run teaching courses for non-native English speaker teachers in January and June in the United Kingdom.
Contact: **Geos English Academy,** Teacher Training Department, 55-61 Portland Road, Hove, Sussex BN3 5DQ. Tel: 0273 73975.

inlingua (250 schools worldwide)
The inlingua method is a direct method in which the lessons are conducted orally. Teacher training courses in this method last two weeks and are tailor-made to qualify teachers to work for inlingua schools. One-to-one lessons, ESP and teaching children are areas that can be focused on. inlingua use their own coursebooks and prefer graduates of British or Irish nationality.
Contact: **inlingua Pedagogical Dept.,** UK Branch, Essex House, 27 Temple Street, Birmingham B2 5DB Tel: 021 643 3472 or: **inlingua,** Weisenhausplatz 28, 3011 Berne, Switzerland.

LINGUARAMA (35 + school worldwide)
Linguarama hold introductory teacher training courses in TEFL in the UK. The courses consist of five and a half days' intensive training made up of 40 hours' theory and teaching practice. They frequently recruit teachers from such courses for their schools, which are often business orientated. They do not accept non-native English speakers, and require people to have a degree or teaching qualification. Linguarama also run in-service training programmes for their staff.
Contact: **Linguarama,** Queen's House, 8 Queen Street, London EC4N ISP. Tel: 071 236 1992.

SALISBURY SCHOOL
Though not part of a language school chain, the Salisbury School recruit EFL teachers for Sweden on behalf of the British Centre, which is run by Folk University in Stockholm. The British Centre recruit for January and September, and Salisbury School run introductory courses for ten days immediately before teachers go to Sweden. These courses are free for successful candidates.
Contact: **The Salisbury School of English,** 36 Fowlers Road, Salisbury, Wiltshire SP1 2QU, UK. Tel: (0722) 331011.

YOUR FIRST CLASS

You've got the job. It's Monday morning, your first class. Your class might be children, adult beginners, elementary or advanced. Here's some advice to help you get through your first hour.

Read the teacher's book

You can carbon date teachers by which teacher's book they learned to teach from. For teachers in the sixties, it was probably *First Things First* and *Kernel Lessons*; in the seventies, *Strategies*, and in the eighties; *Cambridge English Course* and *Headway*. The point is that all teachers, even if they have a certificate, find their feet in the classroom by following a teacher's book. So find a course book and read the teacher's book before you start.

Learn their names

Learn your pupils' names and start using them. Use charts on your desk or United Nations style name cards propped up in front of the student - but learn them. After a couple of weeks it becomes embarrassing to ask a student's name and you may risk ignoring them as a result - to their detriment.

Get them talking

It's important for the class to talk, not you. Try and minimise TTT (Teacher Talking Time). Ask questions to elicit information rather than explain at length. Ask questions that elicit short answers: 'yes, he did'/ 'no, he didn't', questions that elicit simple sentences: 'where do you work?', 'At the Post Office', and open questions: 'what are you doing?'.

As soon as possible get the class talking to each other. If the class are elementary level or thereabouts get them to work in pairs, finding out each other's name, nationality and maybe job, and get them to introduce their partner to you. You can initiate the process by writing clues on the board - name, country, town, job - and then by engaging one student in a dialogue as a model. For example:

What's your name?	My name's...
	I am...
Where are you from?	I'm from...
Where do you live?	I live in...
What's your job?	I'm a...(student)

Try to get students to practice talking to each other, preferably in small groups, as much as possible.

Find out what they know

By getting your class talking, you will know what their real level is (their ability to communicate may be well below or well above their test scores or their grammar level) and be able to identify their most common mistakes. Have a pad of paper by you to take notes.

Error correction

New teachers are unsure if they should stop students and correct them every time they make a mistake. The tendency now is to concentrate on fluency and only to correct mistakes that can be corrected without interrupting the speaker's train of thought. Make a note of major errors and come back to them when the student has stopped speaking or for major points of grammar, as part of a grammar presentation later on.

Translation?

Time was when translation into the learner's mother tongue was anathema in the classroom. This view has changed. Most teachers now believe that all a learner's resources are important in helping them to learn a language and that translation is one of those resources. The aim should be to encourage students to speak in English as much as possible, but, if translation helps the teacher to briefly explain a word or concept, then translation should be used. In any event, try not to rely upon translation.

Answering questions

A source of terror for new teachers is being asked the meaning of a word, or the difference between two words or tenses, when you don't know the answer. The worst thing to do is to try and answer when you are unclear yourself. You'll end up talking too much and confusing the student. The best thing to do is to say you'll deal with the answer in the next class - and make sure that you do! Arm yourself with a couple of survival manuals, a good learner's dictionary - the *Longman Dictionary of Contemporary English*, the *Oxford Advanced Learners Dictionary* or the *Collins Cobuild Dictionary* - and a good grammar - *Practical English Usage*

The aim should be to encourage students to speak in English as much as possible.

The worst thing to do is to try and answer when you are unclear yourself.

(Oxford University Press) or *English Grammar in Use (Cambridge University Press)* and go to work.

Pronunciation

New teachers worry, 'Which accent shall I use?'. The answer is, if you are a native speaker of English, your own. It's the best model for the student. If you are not a native speaker of English, then your model is still the best for the students, but you may want to supplement it by using tapes of native speakers from ELT courses.

The stages of a lesson

Most lessons progress through stages - from controlled presentation and practice of language to spontaneous use of that language in the student's own situations.

The three stages are:
PRESENTATION IN SITUATION
(pre-presentation of key vocabulary and language patterns followed by comprehension of a short dialogue on tape or video or in the textbook)

CONTROLLED PRACTICE
(identification of key language to be learned, followed by repetition or drill practice, or practising and acting out the dialogue)

FREE STAGE
(students' own opportunity to use the new language through discussion, role-play reading and writing)

Planning your lesson

For a 45 minute or one hour lesson you should always have a written plan to serve as an 'aide memoire', not only in case you get distracted, but also to help you pace the lesson and to make sure you cover the points you intended to make. Keep successful plans, as they can be the basis of new lessons later on.

A lesson plan should contain the following:
-the aim of the lesson
-the texts or aids you expect to use (reading comprehension, tape, video or objects)
-the key vocabulary you expect to teach
-key comprehension points and questions you need to ask
-the key practice activities you will carry out
-the free stage activities you will carry out

It's worth spending time on it as it will help you feel more confident in the classroom. For a one hour class, plan three to five activities. These

may be different activities based on a single text or grammar point to provide better cohesion for the lesson.

Activities may include the following:

Lesson Plan

1 A warm up
   Saying hello, leaning people's names
2 Vocabulary work
   Teach and practice
3 New Language
   Presentation and practice of some new grammar through a text.
4 Free stage
   Role playing similar dialogues, understanding information in an advertisement or notice or writing a short note to someone else in the class.
   For example:
   Hello, I'm Juan. I'm from Spain
   Hello, I'm Fatima. I'm from Turkey.
5 Summary/Skills work
   Taking students through examples of homework activity or a lighthearted game or song.

A game such as Hangman to revise vocabulary is a good idea.

Put the first letter of a word on the board and put dashes for the other letters
eg L _ _ _ _ _
The class suggest the other letters. If they are right, write in the appropriate space. If they are wrong, begin drawing a gallows, like this:-

Can the class guess the word before the man is hanged? They have ten guesses.
When the class have the idea they can think of words and draw the hangman.

In Conclusion

Be friendly, smile, encourage your class ("Good"), don't criticise, keep eye contact (not too much, if they're Japanese), learn and use their names and you'll do fine. Have fun!!

For a 45 minute or one hour lesson you should always have a written plan to serve as an 'aide memoire'.

Keep successful plans, as they can be the basis of new lessons later on..

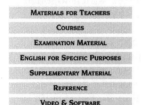

READING LIST

The following books feature on the RSA/Cambridge Cerificate reading list:

Alexander, LG - **Longman English Grammar** *(Longman)* This book looks at the problems and difficulties with which language learners are confronted.

Allsop, J - **Student English Grammar** *(Cassell)* A series of grammar explanations and theory with exercises. A good introduction to English grammar rules.

Bolitho, R and Tomlinson, B - **Discover English** *(Heinemann)* A book of exploratory exercises which together with the comments in the key will make you more aware of the language that you use everyday without thinking or analysing.

Byrne, D - **Teaching Oral English** *(Longman)* Techniques and procedures for teaching oral skills.

Byrne, D - **Teaching Writing Skills** *(Longman)* How to integrate writing with other language skills.

Gairns, R and Redman, S - **Working with Words** *(CUP)* A solid, thorough book on how to select, organise and teach vocabulary. Combines readable theory with realistic problems.

Gower, R and Walters, S - **Teaching Practice Handbook** *(Heinemann)* If you are attending a course with a teaching practice component, then this book will be a handy companion to help you structure and gain from this experience.

Hadfield, J - **Communication Games** *(Nelson)* A series of three photocopiable books offering functional games, activities and teacher's notes.

Harmer, J - **The Practice of English Language Teaching** *(Longman)* A reference book covering the theory of ELT including lesson planning and classroom management.

Haycraft, J - **An Introduction to English Language Teaching** *(Longman)* Based on material used on teacher training courses at IH London, the book is valuable for inexperienced teachers.

Holden, S - **Visual Aids for Classroom Interaction** *(MEP)*

Kenworthy, J - **Teaching English Pronunciation** *(Longman)* Teaching strategies for dealing with specific problems experienced by speakers of particular languages.

Klippel, F - **Keep Talking** *(CUP)* A practical guide to conununication activities for the classroom, including photocopiable material.

Leech, G and Svartik, J - **A Communicative Grammar of English** *(Longman)* A communicative approach to grammar.

Lewis, M - **The English Verb** *(LTP)* The book explains the main issues of the English verb and suggests that they are more regular than often believed.

Longman Keys to Language Teaching Series Practical advice on techniques and approaches in the classroom.

Maley, A and Duff, A - **Drama Techniques in Language Learning** *(CUP)* A source book of ideas for language teaching for all levels, including warm up activities, literary texts and songs.

Matthews, A et al - **At the Chalk Face** *(Nelson)* Edited articles from the British Council's newsletter in Portugal covering the theory and practice of language teaching.

Nuttall,C - **Teaching Reading Skills in a Foreign Language** *(Heinemann)* The book deals with teaching people to read in English as a foreign or second language.

Revell, J - **Teaching Techniques for Communicative English** *(Macmillan)* A tiny book that says as much as many tomes. A lot of ideas.

Swan, M - **Practical English Usage** *(OUP)* An alphabetical reference book of grammatical problems, so you can look up 'going to','unless'or'colons' and understand the entry.

Ur, P - **Discussions that Work** *(CUP)* The book offers guidelines on organisation and task centred activities for discussion. For elementary to advanced levels.

Ur, P - **Teaching Listening Comprehension** *(CUP)* This book aims to bridge the gap between theory and the development of listening comprehension skills in the classroom.

Wright, A et al - **Games for Language Teaching** *(CUP)* A resource book containing games for communicative language practice.

Also highly recommended:
The Collins COBUILD English Language Dictionary *(Collins)* Reading the introduction and the definitions; will help you select and explain words realistically and simply without using more difficult words than the ones you are trying to explain. Now also available on CD-ROM.

Wright, A - **One Thousand Pictures for Teachers to Copy** *(Collins ELT)* Useful guidance for artistically illiterate teachers on how to draw simple sketches on the blackboard.

Teaching magazines/journals
Practical English Teaching *(Mary Glasgow Publications)*. **Modern English Teacher** *(available from PO Box 129, Oxford OX2 8JU)* Both these periodicals contain practical teaching tips you can try out with your classes.
EFL Gazette *(available from 10 Wrights Lane, London W8 6TA)* Contains information on all aspects of EFL teaching and also materials to use in the classroom.

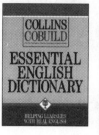
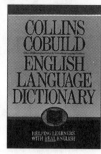
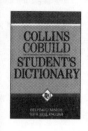

CAMBRIDGE
EXAMINATIONS, CERTIFICATES & DIPLOMAS

For Teachers of English as a Foreign Language

For Non-native Speakers			For Native Speakers *(or equivalent)*
Language development for teachers	**Teacher Training Courses**		
	Level	**Language development Language systems Methodology**	**Language systems Methodology**
Cambridge **E**xamination in **E**nglish for **L**anguage **T**eachers II	*In-service*	**D**iploma for **O**verseas **T**eachers of **E**nglish	**D**iploma in the **T**eaching of **E**nglish as a **F**oreign **L**anguage to **A**dults
	Early in-service	**C**ertificate for **O**verseas **T**eachers of **E**nglish	
Cambridge **E**xamination in **E**nglish for **L**anguage **T**eachers I	*Pre-service*		**C**ertificate in the **T**eaching of **E**nglish as a **F**oreign **L**anguage to **A**dults

The most widely used assessment schemes for EFL teachers

 University of Cambridge
Local Examinations Syndicate
International Examinations

 RSA
EXAMINATIONS BOARD

Trinity College London

'With strict guidelines for the institutions which run their courses, regular inspections and a proven track record, either (the RSA/Cambridge Certificate in TEFLA or the Trinity Certificate in TESOL) will equip a prospective teacher with a passport to work anywhere in the world - something that less established courses, even of a high standard, cannot provide.' **The Daily Telegraph**

Trinity College London
- for all the Positive Options!

.... Positive Career Options

Certificate in the Teaching of English to Speakers of Other Languages (CertTESOL)

• A first qualification for those with little or no previous experience • The essential foundations in classroom theory and practice • Emphasis is placed on classroom teaching and project work • Qualifies the trainee to teach both adults and children • Respected internationally, the first choice of thousands entering the profession worldwide • Available to both native and non-native English speakers at over sixty institutions in the UK and in centres overseas

Licentiate Diploma (LTCL TESOL)

• The advanced professional qualification for those with at least two years' teaching experience • Recognised by the British Council and by teaching institutions worldwide • The qualification for Directors of Studies and ELT Managers

.... Positive Options for Assessment

Graded Examinations in Spoken English for Speakers of Other Languages (ESOL)

• Examinations at twelve levels suitable for all ages and abilities from seven years to adult • Emphasis placed on communicative ability • Examinations held 'on demand' in familiar school surroundings • Fully-trained visiting Trinity College London examiners conduct live one-to-one interviews • Trinity College London examinations are available worldwide

'The most commonly accepted qualifications in Europe and elsewhere are certificates offered by Trinity College, London, and the Cambridge University examining board...' **The Observer.**

To: Geoffrey Smith, Trinity College London, 16 Park Crescent, London W1N 4AP, UK. *Telephone* (0)71 323 2328, *fax* (0)71 323 5201. | EFLG94 |

☐ **Please send me further details of Trinity College's Teacher Training Qualifications**

☐ **Please send me a syllabus and further details of Trinity College's Spoken English Examinations**

Name ....

Address ....

....

....

.... Telephone ....

KEY TO CERTIFICATE REFERENCE ADVERTISING

NORD ANGLIA INTERNATIONAL OVERSEAS RECRUITMENT

RECRUITING teachers with RSA/UCLES Cert. or Trinity College Cert. TESOL for Spain, Greece, Poland, Turkey, Hungary...

RECRUITING teacher trainers for short contracts in Eastern Europe.

RECRUITING teachers with business English experience for short contracts.

To join the register phone 061 491 4191.

Nord Anglia International, 10 Eden Place, Cheadle,Stockport, Cheshire, SK8 1AT

****Nord Anglia UK summer courses****
Apply March/April

Agency NW2305

TEACHING POSTS IN CENTRAL AND EASTERN EUROPE

Since 1990, more than 150 teachers have worked as volunteers with **East European Partnerships** in posts supported by the local Ministries of Education.

Current recruitment:

Posts in teacher training institutions in Poland, Czech Republic, Slovakia, the Baltic States and Russia.

Posts in high schools in Bulgaria, Hungary, Czech Republic and Slovakia (including science, history and geography)

Posts in technical universities in Hungary and Poland where ESP is required.

Volunteer Profile:

A degree in English or Modern languages; PGCE or TEFL qualification; minimum 2 years' classroom experience. English will be your mother tongue.

EEP Offers:

Equipment grants; NI contributions; endowment scheme; travel costs; health insurance; language training; skills adaption training.

East European Partnership, Carlton Hoouse, 27A Carlton Drive, London SW15 2BS
Tel: 081 780 2841 Fax: 081 780 9592

CfBT Education Services

CfBT Education Services celebrates 25 years in the EFL world this year. We have employed over 5,000 teachers in that time, and have managed contracts in countries as diverse as Germany and Mongolia. We are a small but flexible organisation , able to respond to teachers' and clients' requirements.

We recruit qualified and experienced teachers of EFL throughout the year for our projects in Brunei, Malaysia, Oman and Turkey. We have positions for teachers at tertiary, secondary and primary level, and there are occasional opportunities for subject teachers. On some contracts we can offer positions of responsibility, and professional development is encouraged on all projects.

We are well known for the personal and professional support we offer, and are proud of our reputation. Contact us to find out more about the opportunities that could enhance your career.

Fiona Johnson, **CfBT Education Services**, Quality House, Gyosei Campus, London Road, Reading RG1 5AQ.
Tel: 0734-756361   Fax: 0734-75636

FINDING A JOB

The reason behind any training is to find a job, so this section shows you how to go about finding your first teaching job, summer job, volunteering job, going for promotion, alternatives to actual teaching and even setting up your own business. It will also give you an insight in to the ways that EFL is taught and how technology is affecting it.

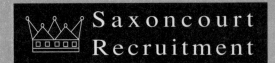

HOW TO FIND WORK

Newspapers, recruitment agencies and major employers

Newspapers

The following newspapers and newsletters regularly carry EFL, and ESP recruitment advertisements.(* - available from most newsagents). See also local English language newspapers in Section Four.

Worldwide

EFL Gazette (monthly) - available for £1.50 (1 issue) £22-UK, £25-Europe, £30-Rest of the World (yearly subscription) from 10 Wrights Lane, London W8 6TA UK, or from specialist bookshops in Britain.

Globetrotters, PO Box 741, Pwllheli, Gwynedd, LL53 6WA, UK.

The Guardian* (Tuesdays and Saturdays) - Education supplement (UK edition only) carries job advertisements.

Overseas Jobs Express (twice monthly) - available from PO Box 22, Brighton BNI 6HX.

Times Educational Supplement* (Fridays).

TESOL Newsletter - available from TESOL.

International Herald Tribune* (daily).

Ireland

Irish Independent* (daily); **Irish Times*** (daily).

Japan

The Language Teacher (monthly) - available from JALT

United Kingdom

ARELS bulletin will place free jobs wanted ads and circulate them to member schools in the UK- write to Arels, 2 Pontypool Place, Valentine Place, London SE1 8QS. The Department of Employment's **Overseas Placing Unit** (OPU) has a list of vacancies in the EC, and can be contacted via any Jobcentre in the UK.

Jobshops

At the following conferences teachers are recruited:

Japan

Japanese Association of Language Teachers (**JALT**) have a job Information Centre with about 100 employers who give interviews to qualifying applicants.

USA

TESOL job shop. Contact TESOL, as above.

Recruitment agencies

Sending a CV to a recruitment agency may be better than approaching individual employers. Established agencies will let you know when opportunities arise. An EFL specialist agency will tell you exactly what you need to know about a particular vacancy and should offer an interview supplying all the information you will require. Since agencies generally charge employers a percentage of salary, it is in their interest that you earn as much as possible. See p172-177 for addresses unless listed below:

ELT Banbury . Recruit mainly for Europe.

European Council of International Schools (ECIS). Recruit for Europe, Africa and the Far East. Mainly prefer teachers with specialist subjects to teach English in independent international schools.

English Worldwide (UK). Recruit for Europe, the Middle East, the Far East and South America.

English and Spanish Studies (for Spain only).

Basil Paterson (UK).

Central Bureau for Exchange arrange exchanges in Europe. Also recruit for Japan Exchange and Teaching (JET) scheme (see p26).

Hilderstone College (UK). Recruit for Shumei secondary schools in Japan.

Language Matters, 4 Blenheim Road, Moseley, Birmingham B13 9TY UK.

Nord Anglia International Ltd (UK).

Saxoncourt (UK) Ltd., 59 South Molton Street, London W1, recruit mainly for Japan, but also the Far East and Europe.

Teachers in Greece (for Greece only), Taxilou 79, Zographou, 15771 Athens, Greece.

Major employers

The following are major employers who have branches worldwide, and may be worth approaching for potential employment.

American Language Academy (USA).

ARA (UK- recruit for Middle East).

Berlitz International (USA). **Berlitz School** (UK).

Bell Educational Trust (UK - offer good conditions but prefer well-qualified teachers).

Benedict Schools (Switzerland).

British Aerospace (UK -recruit males for Saudi Arabia only).

British Council (UK - for Commonwealth nationals only. Sometimes recruit locally, but well-qualified teachers are offered lucrative London contracts. Expect to be moved every three years).

Educational Consulting Services (ECS) Ltd., PO. Box 25018, Arab Monetary Fund Building, Abu Dhabi, UAE. employ over 350 teachers in the Middle east and personally conducts regular interviews throughout the UK.

Centre for British Teachers (UK - run projects in Europe, the Middle and Far East, usually primary and secondary EFL).

ELS International Inc (USA). **ILC Recruitment** (UK).

inlingua (Switzerland and USA). Also **inlingua Pedagogical Department,** UK Branch, Essex House, 27 Temple Street, Birmingham B2 5DB UK.

International House, London (UK - have branches and affiliated schools around the world).

International Language Services (UK - for Sweden only).

Linguarama Ltd, (UK).

Applications can also be made to the schools listed in the country classifications of **Section Four**.

See **Keeping in Touch** (p168-169) and also **Voluntary Organisations** (p79).

WORKING IN THE UK & IRELAND

Job prospects, terms and conditions

The United Kingdom

Minimum salary: This varies considerably between areas - Oxford and Cambridge schools pay well while rates in London are relatively low. Try contacting three schools in the area you want to work to compare rates. You should get at least £8 per hour in the private sector; state colleges pay about twice that.

Tax and National Insurance: 25% plus 9% NI.

Visa requirements: EC nationals do not need a permit. Commonwealth citizens who have a grandparent with a British passport do not need a work permit, but need clearance first from their local British Embassy. Australians and New Zealanders under 26 can apply for a working holiday visa. Other Australians and New Zealanders as well as Americans and Canadians do not need a visa but must arrange a work permit before they enter the country. Your employer should help with this. Other nationals must apply for a visa at their local British Embassy.

Accommodation: £60-70 for a room in a shared flat in London and the south east, less elsewhere.

Other information: A certificate or a PGCE is usually considered the minimum requirement (see p27). There has always been a huge demand for teachers during the summer months when private language schools, colleges and, more recently, universities recruit for the annual influx of foreign students (see p67). Year round jobs are less frequent, with hundreds of qualified teachers returning from abroad competing for jobs, which has led to lower salaries. However, although it is hard for unqualified or newly qualified teachers to find well paid work in the UK, there is a demand for teachers with the RSA or Trinity Diploma (see p125). Non-British teachers with Qualified Teacher Status in their countries will find they can work in the primary or secondary system.

Most private school jobs involve teaching mixed nationality students of all levels, usually young adults. It is possible to teach English as a Second Language to immigrants.

There are also prospects for freelance and English for Specific Purposes teachers (ESP - see p148), some of whom can earn up to £20,000 per year. With the EC's Lingua programme and the growth of EFL in eastern Europe, there are also opportunities for teacher trainers. Geographically, London has the most language schools and also the most competition for jobs and the highest cost of living. Oxford, Cambridge and the south coast towns also have a large EFL market, but the rest of England and Wales are becoming more popular for foreign students, so jobs are also more prevalent. Scotland is now promoting itself as an independent EFL destination. A consortium of Scottish schools and the British Council are pushing EFL in Scotland especially in the Far East and Latin America.

State and private sector jobs in colleges and universities can be well paid, but competition for work remains fierce, with management positions being particularly scarce. If you want to progress in EFL as a career, you may increase your options if you work abroad.

There are also opportunities in the UK for spin off careers from EFL if you are an experienced teacher (see p75). For job sources in the UK see p65. For information about recognition schemes, designed to regulate the standards of schools and colleges, see p165.

Ireland

Minimum salary: Ir£8-10 per hour.

Tax and health insurance: 27% plus 7.75% social security. Be warned that if you stay for tinder 6 months you could be charged emergency tax after your first month - this could be up to 50%. Cheek with your employer.

Visa requirements: Your employer will arrange permits for non EC residents, but note that it is hard to get one unless you can convince them you are doing a job which can not be done by an EC citizen.

Accommodation: After the recent building boom in Ireland there is no shortage of accommodation. Expect to pay Ir£35-50 for a room in a shared house.

Other information: There has been a move to improve the image of language schools in Ireland after a proliferation of cowboy setups and a confusing array of teacher training certificates. For details on recognition schemes, see p165, and for recognised qualifications in Ireland, see p35. There are various staff associations and unions that teachers can approach, such as the National Association of Teachers of English as a Foreign Language in Ireland (NATEFLI).

Students in Ireland have traditionally been southern Europeans, mostly attending courses in the summer months. However, now that EFL is being more carefully regulated, Ireland is becoming popular for all nationalities throughout the year. Most language schools are in the Dublin area, but there has been a move to decentralise which has seen a growth in the number of schools in tourist areas such as Cork, Kerry, Limerick and Galway. Thanks also to an integrated marketing plan, which is now paying dividends, the future of EFL here looks promising. The Union of Students in Ireland (USI) arrange 9 month exchange programmes for teachers from the USA, for which no work permit is needed.

SUMMER SCHOOLS

Seasonal opportunities for experienced and unqualified teachers

As students have the time to travel and study English during their long summer holidays, schools put on special courses. There is a boom in July and August especially in the UK, Ireland and Canada, when the European schools are on holiday. In Australia and New Zealand the busy time is between December and March, when schools in Japan and the Far East are on holiday.

Established language schools run summer courses, as do colleges and universities, but EFL agents and teachers may hire out public buildings to run their own seasonal summer school. With so many courses being run, staff are in huge demand but salaries are not that good. Often courses are split into half a day of language learning and half a day of recreation - perhaps sight-seeing trips or sports activities - so courses need people to be lively administrators as much as language teachers. In Britain there are courses combining English with just about everything, from horse riding to sailing. In Australia and New Zealand it is also possible to combine teaching English with activity holidays, including sports like scuba diving and even bungee jumping. So if you have any experience in such activities you may be in demand.

Summer school contracts are usually for one to two months, and it is advisable to apply well in advance. As with any job in EFL, some sort of TEFL qualification will ensure you get a better paid job. Experienced teachers may also be able to become course directors or Director of Studies. In Britain, state sector colleges and, increasingly, universities also run summer courses. Pay tends to be quite high - up to £18 per hour in some colleges. Teachers on presessional courses who teach English for Academic Purposes to students going on to study at British universities should expect £250 a week, plus accommodation and all meals. Summer courses are traditionally where newly qualified teachers have their first classroom experience. Demand for teachers is so high that unqualified people have a good chance of being taken on. The courses are usually quite intensive and cater for multi-national students. If you have no previous teaching experience, or if you are interested in finding out about the particularities of teaching summer courses, read *Teaching English on Holiday Courses* by Nick Dawson, part of Longman's Handbook for Teachers series. Many schools prefer teachers with primary rather than TEFL experience, as some summer courses are for young learners.

Unfortunately summer schools in Britain have often had bad press, with stories of exploitative agents employing inexperienced teachers in inadequate premises. There has been a move to crack down on such operations, but one result of this has been to push students away from the established centres such as the south coast of England to the north of England, Ireland and Scotland. Students have found such areas less crowded, cheaper and friendlier. Prospective teachers can thus find potential employment throughout the British Isles. Conditions of pay still vary considerably, however, with Cambridge reportedly commanding the top rates of pay. London has too many teachers available to pay well, and has the highest cost of living. To find out if your potential employer is offering a decent salary, contact three schools in the area to work out an average. Around £7 should be a minimum hourly teaching rate with extra for social activities you are required to take part in.

Some schools offer full board and accommodation in residential summer schools, which is valuable for teachers returning from abroad for the summer, but they may offer very low salaries and you may be expected to look after the students outside class hours.

UK SUMMER SCHOOLS DIRECTORY
(R = recognised)

Abon Language School (R) 25, St John's Road, Clifton, Bristol BS8 2HD. Tel: (0272) 730354.
Anglo Continental (R), 33 Wimborne Road, Bournemouth. Tel: (0202) 557414, ext 213.
Anglolang (R), 20 Avenue Road, Scarborough, N. Yorkshire. Tel: (0723) 367141. Fax (0723) 378698.
AST School of English (R), Perth Aerodrome, Scone PH2 6NP, Scotland. Tel: (0738) 52311 Ext 241.
Bedford Study Centre (R) 95/96, Midland Road, Bedford MK40 1QE. Tel: (0234) 36-4161.
Bell Educational Trust (R), 1 Red Cross Lane, Cambridge CB2 2QX. Tel: (0223) 247242.
Berkeley School of English 43/45 Queens Road, Clifton, Bristol. Tel: (0272) 290604.
Bournemouth Teaching Service, 139 Charminger Road, Bournemouth. Tel: (0202) 521355.
Brighton and Hove School of English (R), 7-9 Wilbury Villas. Hove, East Sussex. BN3 6GB. Tel: (0273) 738182.
Buckswood Grange (R), Uckfield, East Sussex TN22 3PU. Tel: (0825) 761666.
Cambridge Academy of English (R), 65 High Street, Girton, Cambs CB3 OQD. Tel: (0223) 277230
The Cambridge School of English (R), 8 Herbrand Street, London WCIN IHZ. Tel: 071 734 4203.
Channel School of English (R), Bicclescombe Park, Ilfracombe, Devon, EX34 8JN. Tel: (0271) 862834
Churchill House (R), 40-42, Spencer Square, Ramsgate, Kent CT11 9LD. Tel: 0843 593630.

Clark's International Summer Schools (R), 28 Craiglockhart Drive South, Edinburgh EH14 IHZ. Tel: (031) 443 3298.

Concord College (R), Acton Burnell Hall, Shrewsbury, Shrops SY5 7PF. Tel: (06944) 631.

Concorde International (R), Arnett House, Hawks Lane, Canterbury, Kent CT1 2NU.Tel: 0227 451035.

Coventry Technical College The Butts, Coventry, CV7 3DG. Tel: (0203) 256793.

Devon English Centre (R), 1 Victoria Rd, Exmouth EX8 IDL. Tel: (0395) 265068.

Eastbourne School of English (R), 8 Trinity Trees, Eastbourne BN21 3LD Tel: (0323) 721759.

Edinburgh School of English (R), 271 Canon Gate, The Royal Mile, Edinburgh EH8 8BQ. Tel: (031) 5579200.

Edinburgh Tutorial College (R), 29 Chester St, Edinburgh EH3 7EN. Tel: (031) 225 9888.

EF International School of English (R), 1/2 Sussex Square, Brighton BN2 IFJ. Tel: (0273) 571780.

ELCO (R), Lowlands, Chorleywood Road, Rickmansworth, Herts. Tel: 0923 776731.

ELS (R), 3 Muirfield Crescent, Mill Harbour, London E14 9SZ. Tel: 071 512 0600.

English and Cultural Studies Centres (ECSC) (R) ,40 Village Rd, Enfield, Middx EN1 2EN. Tel: (081) 360 4118-

English in Chester (R), 9\11 Stanley Place, Chester, CH1 2LU. Tel: (0244) 318913/314457.

English Language Centre (R), 44 Pembroke Road, Bristol, BS8 3DT. Tel: (0272) 737216.

English Language Systems (R), The Old Rectory, Church Lane North, Old Whittington, Chesterfield, Derbyshire S41 9QY. Tel: (0246) 450503.

Essex House School of English (R), 4 Church Road, Clacton-on-Sea, C015 6AG, Essex. Tel: (0255) 423465.

Euro-Academy Ltd (R), 77a George St, Croydon, Surrey CRO 1LD. Tel: (081) 681 2905.

Eurocentre Brighton (R), Huntingdon House, 20 North Street, Brighton BNl 1EB. Tel: (0273) 24545.

Eurocentre Lee Green (R), 21 Meadowcourt Road, London SE3 9EU. Tel: (081) 318 5633.

Frances King School of English (R), 3 Queensberry Place, South Kensington SW7 2DL. Tel: (071) 584 6411.

Functional English (R), 5 Chubb Hill, Whitby, N Yorks Y021 1JU. Tel. (0947) 603933.

Greenwich School of English (R), 2/3 Turnpin Lane, London SE10 9JA. Tel: (081) 305 0370.

The Greylands School of English Ltd (R), 315 Portswood Road, Soton, S02 ILD. Tel: (0703) 550633.

Harrow School of English, 4 Gosling Close, Mill Green, Lyme Regis, Dorset, DT7 3PH. Tel: (02874) 3042.

Harven School of English (R), The Mascot, Coley Ave, Woking, Surrey GU22 7BT. Tel: (0483) 770969.

Hastings English Language Centre (R), St.Helens Park Rd. Hastings, Sussex TN34 2JW. Tel: (0424) 437048.

House of English (R), 24 Portland Place, Brighton BN2 lDG. Tel: (0273) 694618.

Hurtwood House School (R), Holmbury St Mary, Dorking, Surrey RH5 6NU. Tel: (0483) 277416,

International Community School (R), 10 York Terrace East, Regents Park, London NW1. Tel: (071) 935-1206.

International Homestays Programmes Ltd, 37 Park Road. Bromley, Kent BR1 3HJ. Tel: (071) 464 6925.

International House, Hastings (R), White Rock, Hastings, Sussex TN34 1JY. Tel: (0424) 720100.

International Language Institute (R), County House, Vicar Lane. Leeds LS1 7JH. Tel: (0532) 428893.

The International School (R), 1 Mount Radford Crescent, Exeter EX2 4EW. Tel: (0392) 54102.

ISCA School of English (R), PO Box 15, 4 Mt. Radford Crescent, Exeter, Devon, EX2 4JN. Tel: (0392) 55342.

ITS English School (R), 44, Cambridge Gardens, Hastings, East Sussex TN34 1EN. Tel: (0424) 438025.

Kent School of English (R), 3 Cranville Road, Broadstairs, Kent. Tel: (0843) 868207.

King's School of English (R), 25 Beckenham Road, Beckenham, Kent BR3 4PR. Tel: (081) 650 5891.

Lake School of English (R), 14B Park End Street, Oxford OX1 lHW. Tel: (0865) 724312.

Language Learning Centre, 7 Kings Road, Reading, Berkshire RGI 3AP. Tel: (0734) 582247.

London House (R), 51 Sea Road, Westgate-on-Sea, Kent CT8 8Ql. Tel: (0843) 31216.

LTC International College of English (R), Compton Park, Compton Place Rd, Eastboume, Sussex BN21 1EH. Tel: (0323) 727755.

Mayfield College of English (R), 24 Holland Road, Hove, Sussex BN3 1JJ. Tel: (0273) 779231.

Non Stop English Language School, 27 Grange, Rd, Eastbourne, E. Sussex BN21 4HG. Tel (0323) 27319

O.I.S.E.(R), Youth Language Centres, 1 King's Meadow, Ferry Hinksey Road, Oxford OX2 ODP. Tel: (0865) 792702.

The Oxford Academy (R), 18 Bardwell Road, Oxford OX2 6SP. Tel: (0865) 512174.

Oxford Study Centre Ltd (R), 17 Sunderland Ave, Oxford OX2 8DT Tel: (0865) 515243.

Penzance Language School, 21 Regents Square, Penzance PRI8 4BG. Tel: (0736) 67760/68520.

Pilgrims Language Courses (R), 8 Vernon Place, Canterbury, Kent. CT1 3HG. Tel: (0227) 762111.

Quest English International, 13 Victoria Road, Bath, Avon BA2 3QY. Tel: (0225) 448252.

Regent Summer Schools (R), 3rd Floor, 19-23 Oxford Street, London WIR IRF. Tel: (071) 734 1137.

RLC International, 27-28, George Street, Richmond TW9 1HY Tel: (081) 948 3333.

Richmond School of English, 6 & 8 Oxford Rd, Moseley, Birmingham B13 9EH. Tel: (021) 449 7748.

St Godric's College (R), 2 Arkwright Road, London NW3

Swandean School of English (R), 7 Oxford Rd, Worthing, W. Sussex BNll 1XG. Tel: (0903) 31330.

Universal Languages, 181 Earlseott Rd, London SW5 9RB. Tel: (071) 370 4755.

Woking and Chertsey Adult Education Institute, Danesfield Centre, Grange Road, Woking, Surrey. Tel: (0483) 721425.

Yorkshire International School, 12l St.Helens Gardens, Leeds LSI6 8BT. Tel: (0532) 611603.

WORKING IN NORTH AMERICA

Job prospects and conditions in the USA and Canada.

USA

Minimum salary: This inevitably varies from state to state, but expect around $20-40 per hour in the state sector and as little as $8-13 an hour in private language schools.

Tax and health insurance: 20-35% depending on the state. Social security tax is 7.5%. Most people have a private health insurance policy, which can cost $1,300 per year for a comprehensive policy. Some institutions have a group plan or offer subsidised rates.

Visa requirements: You must have a green card of permanent residence or a work permit. This can be a problem. There are two types of visa. The J1 visa is for 'Researchers, Teachers and Professors'. Obtaining it is a lengthy process; you must contact the head of a school, who will give you a form to return to the Foreign Student Department - who in turn will tell you which consulate to approach for the J1 visa. The H1B (working) visa can only be obtained if you are sponsored by a US company, and it is processed by the Immigration and Naturalisation service, as well as the Department of Labour.

Accommodation: From $500-600 per month in Manhattan to below $350 in rural areas. Allow around $30 per month for bills.

Other information: There is a huge number of immigrants in the United States who need to learn English. The market is known as English as a Second Language (ESL) for all language teaching within the country.

Although qualified US citizens should have no problem gaining employment, for non-Americans it is hard to get employment teaching EFL/ESL. As well as the differences in language, the RSA and Trinity certificate qualifications are not widely recognised, though many employers will treat the diploma as equivalent to an MA (see p00). It is unwise to try to work illegally, as there are stiff financial penalties for employers.

Education is decentralised, so conditions vary from state to state. There is no accrediting agency specifically for ESL programmes, although in some states, programmes must meet certain requirements. There are state sector teaching possibilities in public schools where ESL is taught from kindergarten to twelfth grade. Jobs tend to be well paid and secure, but you need to be certified as a teacher from a training establishment within the state you wish to work. External experience can count towards your certification, especially in California.

Unqualified teachers may be used in the adult education institutes, where conditions may be difficult. The Amnesty Programme was set up for immigrants in order to improve their standard of English, so that they could qualify for citizenship. Amnesty is offered if they attend an English language class - so the numbers attending such courses are enormous.

Canada

Minimum salary. Canadian $20/hour in the private sector (about $35/hour in state schools.

Tax and health insurance: The federal government and the local province income tax averages at 30%. Health care is free for residents in most provinces. There are insurance plans for those not covered by public schemes.

Visa requirements: Unless you emigrate, it is very hard for non-residents of Canada to obtain a work permit. Under immigration laws, you must demonstrate that you are more suitable than Canadian candidates for any prospective jobs. As there are so many highly qualified teachers in Canada, this rarely happens.

Accommodation: This is easy to find, although it can be expensive in Toronto and Vancouver.

Other information: If you do get a work permit, the standard of living is high in Canada. As a result of Canada's official bilingualism and its strongly multicultural character, teaching English as a Second Language (ESL) is a huge industry. Canada's open immigration policies are accompanied by publicly funded intensive ESL training for immigrants for up to six months, resulting in a huge demand for ESL teachers in the larger cities.

As with states in the USA, conditions vary from province to province. Generally ESL training takes place in post-secondary colleges and adult education departments. State schools also teach ESL, and tend to offer the highest salaries. Many universities also offer ESL and advanced English for Academic Purposes (EAP) courses. The federal and provincial governments offer in-house ESL training for francophone employees.

The Council of Second Language Programmes in Canada runs courses all year. For information on teaching on these programmes, contact **Council of Second Language Programmes in Canada, 151 Slater Street, Ottawa, Ontario, Canada KIP 5Nl.**

Many employers will treat the diploma as equivalent to an MA.

State schools also teach ESL, and tend to offer the highest salaries.

WORKING IN AUSTRALIA AND NEW ZEALAND

Job prospects, terms and conditions in Australasia.

Australia

Minimum salary: This varies from state to state. Only New South Wales has an industry award which determines rates of pay in the private EFL sector. Full time salaries in ELICOS (private schools) begin at A$26,175 per annum. Casual hourly rates begin at A$22.58.

Tax and health insurance: Averages at 30% if you have a tax file number. Without a file number, maximum marginal rates of around 50% are applied to every dollar of income. Some tax goes towards the government-run Medicare health plan, but for those on short contracts, contributions may be partly refunded on departure.

Visa requirements: New Zealand nationals do not need a visa or work permit. For other nationals, it is becoming harder to obtain work permits. If you are British and under 26, a working holiday visa is valid for one year, but officially you are not allowed to stay in one job for more than three months. If you are under 30, you can obtain a visa if you can persuade the authorities that you intend to return home and that the purpose of your visit is cultural or educational. Anyone registered as a full time student on a recognised course (eg. an MA) is entitled to work up to 20 hours a week if they hold a student visa. Otherwise you must emigrate or obtain a Temporary Residence visa which can only be obtained if you are sponsored by an Australian company, who must prove no Australian is available todo your job. Emigration may be easier to achieve, and is awarded on a points system. However, teaching EFL is not considered a 'wanted' profession for emigrants, so does not count on the points scale.

Accommodation: $90 for a room in a shared flat in Sydney, $55 elsewhere.

Other information: The different sectors in Australia are the private English Language Intensive Courses for Overseas Students (ELICOS) schools; the Government Funded Schools or Schemes such as TAFE (Technical and Further Education) and AMES (Adult Migration Education Service, for lower level learners); and universities, which are governed by the individual awards in each state for university employees. Generally, conditions do not differ greatly between these sectors, but teachers working on a holiday visa are unlikely to find work outside ELICOS centres.

Emigrants with a postgraduate qualification, such as a Masters Degree (see Section Five), could be eligible for the position of Director of Studies. However, such positions are quickly snapped up and are rarely open to those new to the scene.

The Independent Teachers' Association (ITA) is a union with a special section for EFL teachers. Their award has been accepted in New South Wales, which now has a set minimum wage, and they are working on other states to accept their conditions. Membership is $260 per year. Contact ITA (Tel: 02 267 5544). University employees can contact the Federated Australian University Staff Association (FA USA) Tel: 03 690 1855.

New Zealand

Minimum salary: NZ$20-27.50 per hour, NZ$25,100/year.

Tax and health insurance: 24%, rising to 33% on earnings over NZ$33,000. An accident compensation levy is paid by employees and employers. All visitors require private health insurance.

Visa requirements: Australian citizens do not require a work permit. Other nationalities can obtain a working holiday visa if they are under 27. Apply to your local New Zealand embassy. If you are over 27, you must have a letter of employment before applying for a work visa which will only be issued if New Zealanders are not available to do the work. This can be done within the country. Temporary work permits are also available for teachers with exceptional qualifications/ experience. Well qualified teachers might find emigration to be their best route.

Accommodation: NZ$80-100 for a shared flat in Auckland. NZ$60 for Christchurch. Teachers are expected to find their own accommodation, but this is not usually a problem

Other information: There is a demand for qualified teachers with more than three years' experience, and language schools sometimes recruit overseas for Director of Studies. Most vacancies arise in February-May and July-August. Auckland tends to be the best place to find work with around 20 private language schools. Christchurch on the South Island has several private schools.

New Zealand Qualification Authorities (NZQA) accredited schools prefer a Bachelors Degree and an RSA Cambridge TEFLA certificate, but this varies from school to school. Non-NZQA accredited schools have no minimum qualification. but such schools cannot accept students for courses of more than three months.

State schools may have vacancies to teach English as a Second Language (ESL) to immigrants. Polytechnics run ESL and/or EFL courses, and their teachers are well paid. Universities and technical institutes also run ESL or EAP programmes with good rates for teachers, although, like the polytechnics, work is likely to be part time only.

Food prices are very cheap, and general living costs are lower than in Europe, Australia or the USA.

AN INSIDER'S GUIDE: METHODOLOGY

Like all professions, EFL has its own history, phrases and terminology for its working methods. Here is a quick reference to the major developments, so you will have an idea of what people are talking about.

Grammar and translation

In the beginning there was grammar and translation. Language learners studied a text and learned the grammar with analysis of parts of speech and then translated it. The classroom language was overwhelmingly the mother tongue, not the language being learned and the aim was the imparting of content (knowledge of the language) rather than teaching a skill (ability to use the language). In the cyclical way of things, grammar is back with a bang, but translation has never quite recovered its hold on the classroom.

Louis Alexander, the distinguished coursebook author once said that a coursebook had three lives. First, its life in the methodologically advanced, affluent native speaker teacher-oriented metropolitan schools of the UK, the USA, and Western Europe, Latin America, and parts of the Far East. Then its life in schools in less affluent markets. And thirdly came its life in new markets coming on stream but non existent at the time a course was originally launched. In this way said Louis Alexander a coursebook might have a life of up to 15-20 years and different methods used by different generations of coursebooks might co-exist at in the world.

As with coursebooks, so with methodology. Grammar and translation is alive and well and living in a large number of classrooms, but is not a recommended approach for new teachers.

Audio-lingual/ direct method

In the Fifties and Sixties the audio-lingual method was adopted by language schools in the UK and US, influenced by the behaviourist psychology view. This method was characterised by a shift from teaching about language to teaching a language skill. Stress was placed on students speaking rather than listening to the teacher and on language practice rather than on translation. The use of the mother tongue became frowned upon in the classroom, as emphasis was firmly placed on breaking down the language into small structural units easily presented in simple English or through drawings and actions.

The direct method, as the application of the audio-lingual method was called, was highly structural. Students were taken up the verbal ladder from present continuous to present simple to present perfect. Highly ingenious, but very rigid, drills were developed to practise the new patterns learned in the classroom. Often the practice took place through language laboratories, with students sitting in booths listening to recordings, repeating and altering pattern sentences according to instructions.

This method has left its mark on teaching today with its insistence on structured progression; systematic lesson progression from presentation to practice to free expression; in the demand that teachers talk less and learners talk more; and in the use of English wherever possible. The rigid practice of structural patterns has fallen out of favour, as has to some extent the use of language laboratories.

The rigid practice of structural patterns has fallen out of favour, as has to some extent the use of language laboratories.

Situational teaching

The rigid structural progression and learning of language patterns was tempered somewhat by the incorporation of new patterns in situations - meeting a friend, losing and finding things and so on. Expressed through the work of Louis Alexander and Robert O'Neill, situational teaching bridged the gap between the structural approach and the functional approach that followed.

The functional/notional approach

At the end of the sixties, a major shift occurred in the way teachers understood language. Influenced by the research of Professor Noam Chomsky into language learning and the existence of a Language Learning Device (LAD) which is the ability of the brain to automatically make sense of the language it absorbs, David Wilkins at Reading University formulated the functional and notional approach to language description, which categorised language not into a structural framework, but into how it was used. This meant that instead of teaching tenses, teachers focused first on functions, such as how to greet, how to apologise. The they taught the appropriate structures in relation to the function being presented. The aim was to get learners using the language in a meaningful way as soon as possible. This format was enshrined in the

At the end of the sixties, a major shift occurred in the way teachers understood language.

Council of Europe Threshold Level Specification for English in 1974. Functional approaches to languages then caused a shift in emphasis from presentation of new structures in situations to the development of communication skills among learners. The functional approach is still central to the way we look at language analysis today.

The communicative approach

The communicative approach describes a way of applying a functional analysis of language to the classroom. Functionalism stresses the teaching of language as it is used in real life, so the stress is on the development of communicative skills - listening, speaking, reading and writing. Skills work in the classroom is not new, but the development of functional analysis meant that language could be taught in a different way. Take listening and reading, for example - a listening comprehension once had a text with a series of questions (mainly multiple choice). With a communicative approach stress was placed on problem solving - listening for gist, retrieving specific information, identifying locations and characters and even identifying the likely source and type of communication - an answerphone message, a radio broadcast or a lecture. In other words the aim became to make the learner conscious of the automatic processes that go on in them as native speakers.

Alongside this approach came the greater introduction of authentic materials - the use of materials not especially developed for learning English - in the classroom. Bus tickets and train timetables as well as newspaper ads became the raw material of reading and listening. At the same time, in developing speaking and writing skills, learners were asked to carry out roleplays and simulations, write specimen letters to newspapers, write film reviews and answer job advertisements.

Communicative teaching is enormously influential today. It has given learners a greater sense of relevance in the language they are learning and teachers have gained greater opportunities for creativity both in the classroom and in the development of their own materials.

But there has been a downside. With a clear eye on structural progression and informed teaching of lexis, communicative teachers have had great success. But the approach has inevitably favoured native or near-native speakers of English over the non-native speaker (most of English teachers) and, if unprofessional, could lead to an unstructured, 'phrase book' type of instruction in which little systematic knowledge of the grammatical framework or the pronunciation system was imparted.

Where are we now?

First, the pendulum has swung back, with the recognition of the importance of the grammatical framework, but teachers and writers have adopted a 'multi-syllabus' approach, in which a teaching programme includes not just a grammatical and lexical syllabus, but also a pronunciation, study skills and cross-cultural awareness.

Secondly, there's a growing focus on autonomous and independent learning to support the classroom teacher. This is reflected in the growth of self-access learning centres in schools as a supplement to their classwork. What makes learning centres different from libraries is that these materials are accompanied by graded worksheets and monitored by a qualified teacher so that students can read authentic and graded materials appropriate to their level.

The name of the teaching game now is 'eclecticism'. This doesn't mean, 'Do what you like', rather 'develop your own teaching style using the principles of good teaching and good classroom management that have been developed in EFL over the last 30-40 years'.

Alternatives

A couple of fringe developments have been and are now very influential in language teaching and learning.

Professor Stephen Krashen of the University of Southern California developed in the seventies and eighties, 'the natural approach' to learning language. Instead of strictly graded texts exactly at a presupposed level, Krashen proposed the idea of 'Comprehensible Input' - comprehension material that was just slightly above the level of the student. Although controversial on its introduction, many of Krashen's ideas have been quietly absorbed into language teaching materials and methods.

Research into how the brain learns and in particular the understanding of 'Whole brain learning' - recognising the particular characteristics of the right side of the brain have led to an important, but lesser known, subgroup of methods and materials, which we can categorise as humanistic disciplines. These are a mutually exclusive group of approaches usually developed by a charismatic psychologist or teacher. Foremost among these are 'Suggestopaedia' developed by Dr Georgi Lozanov in Bulgaria, 'The Silent Way' by Dr Caleb Gattegno in the US, 'Counselling Learning' by Father Charles Curran, 'Total Physical response' (TPR) developed by Professor James Asher.

Bus tickets and train timetables as well as newspaper ads became the raw material of reading and listening.

Recognising the particular characteristics of the right side of the brain have led to an important, but lesser known, subgroup of methods.

AN INSIDER'S GUIDE: TECHNOLOGY

All teachers are having to come to terms with the technological revolution brought about by the use of computers, telecommunications and videos in education. This is what you need to know to get you by.

The recent rapid advance of technology, together with dramatically falling prices means that a wider range of technological resources is becoming available to teachers. More resources means more opportunity to experiment, more ideas for what to do with your class, and the excitement and enthusiasm of learning something new that you can share with your students.

Discovering new ways of teaching, experimenting and finding out what works with your students' styles of learning, and your own styles of teaching are an essential part of the success of English language teaching. On training and refresher courses teachers are often very keen to find out more about using computers and video in the classroom. Recently there has been a lot more interest in multimedia - what it is and how you can use it in both classroom and self-access centre. As video, computers and multimedia do not often feature in general teacher training courses, yet could change your whole pattern of working, it is worth spending some time examining the options.

Video

Television is one of the most powerful and persuasive mediums of communication. Since we teach communication, video is an excellent source of effective lessons. There are two basic sorts of video you can use in the classroom, off-air (recorded by yourself or another teacher or the videos of TV programmes you can hire from your local video store), and published courses.

Off-air video is often the most useful, but you must ensure that you receive permission from the programme's producers before you re-broadcast it, or you could face legal action. For educational purposes, permission is often granted - contact the production company credited at the end of the programme. Students are highly motivated knowing the language is entirely authentic and up to date, and it is easier to find something that matches the interests of the whole class. 'The News' is a favourite, partly because everyone is interested in some item, and partly because there are so many ways of using it. You can, for example, ask students to watch the news one evening, use the video in class

the next day, then follow it up by using newspapers in the next day's classes. Some teachers have even prepared a standard set of exercises, structured in the format of a particular news programme, so that it works whatever the content of the news that day.

Obviously you can do more with off-air videos in higher level classes, but the range of exercises suitable for lower levels is surprising: advertisements are popular - short memorable presentations that serve as excellent mnemonic structures; limited language and often funny.

ELT publishers are producing an increasing number of video titles. Some are courses in themselves, others, especially the more recent titles, accompany coursebooks, adding another dimension to presentation phases and providing further practice and consolidation. There are published videos for all types of student; younger learners, general English, and business English for experienced business people, as well as students thinking of a business career. Many published videos feature a variety of story lines that continue from unit to unit throughout the course. Others feature short sketches or independent units that can be easily integrated into your scheme of work for this week - these are probably the best place to start experimenting with published videos.

As video has been around for quite a long time now there are several excellent resource books for teachers, full of lesson plans and ideas that cover all aspects, from making your own videos, to work with small and large classes to further ideas for exploiting coursebook videos.

Computers

As prices gradually continue to fall, private sector language schools are catching up with the state sector in the use of computing power, which in language learning is usually referred to as CALL (Computer Assisted Language Learning). CALL falls into three main areas; traditional CALL, the facilities available in office type applications, such as word-processors, and the increasingly influential CD ROM-based Multimedia packages.

Since we teach communication, video is an excellent source of effective lessons.

Students are highly motivated knowing the language is entirely authentic and up to date.

The traditional CALL packages put standard EFL type exercises, such as gap-fills, matching and multiple-choice onto computer screens. Many of these packages are Authoring Programs; the teacher/author enters the content (text, question content, etc.) into a standard program/exercise structure. It is very easy to understand and operate these programs as there are simple commands on each screen in use. The best traditional programs came out four or five years ago, with the notable exception of concordancing programs.

Pick a concordancing package that comes with plenty of texts.

A concordance is a list of all the instances of a particular word, part-word or phrase in a body of text, together with the line references. When you specify the word you are interested in, the concordancer highlights every instance of that word with as much context as you want on either side. This makes it especially suitable for experiential learning: your students can arrive at an understanding based on comparing different examples of the word's actual usage. In addition to vocabulary study, concordancers are a great help with grammar words; students can make and/or check hypotheses about how the language operates in a general or specific context. There are books full of ideas for using concordancing programs and manuals full of teaching suggestions. Although it is possible to input the text(s) of your choice, this can take a lot of time. If you have the choice, pick a concordancing package that comes with plenty of texts, covering a range of subjects, so there is always something to interest every student and ample instances of the teaching point you want to make.

Word-processing is probably the most useful program.

Computers with office-type applications, such as word-processing, spread-sheets and presentation programs, are becoming increasingly available in classrooms and self-access centres. Many adult learners use office-type applications at work. Learning to write formal or business letters on a computer and printing it out, rather than writing by hand, is far more motivating for these students. Even if your students are not familiar with word-processing or the particular package available to you, teaching them the basics is a subject for a lesson that the students are usually delighted to learn.

Word-processing is probably the most useful program, not least because there are endless ways of exploiting it in class. As well as the standard editing facilities, modern programs have built-in spelling-checkers, thesauruses, grammar and style checkers. They are also ideal for teachers to prepare, develop and store lessons, and so are probably the best place to start with CALL.

Multimedia

Multimedia is the continuing convergence of television, computers and the telephone. In ELT at the moment, multimedia is the integration of written text, sound, graphics, still photos, animation and full-motion video. A multimedia compatible computer can run any one or any combination of these at a time.

There is a wide range of exercise types; dictionary work, basic phrases, games, exercises - based on fairy stories for children and lessons based on dialogues animated by a video sequence or pictures of the speakers. These dialogues are a good illustration of multimedia; the learner can watch and listen to the whole scene or selected parts and phrases. Accompanying subtitles can be switched between different languages, turned off altogether or, like the sound, limited to one side of the dialogue. The learner can play either role, recording their voice, and then listening back.

Although there are a number of formats that can store different media together, CD ROM is emerging as the most popular. CD ROM is the same as a music CD, except that it reproduces words and pictures as well as sound.

As with video, some multimedia packages are courses in their own right, sometimes with accompanying workbooks. Others provide practice and consolidation through digital recordings of texts and listening exercises in coursebooks. Longman recently launched the first interactive CD ROM dictionary that allows learners to reference words by seeing and hearing, as well as reading, through a database taken from a complete range of dictionaries, including pronunciation, grammar and typical mistake dictionaries.

The current range of commercially available titles covers language learning for children, for general purposes and for business. Most publications so far cater for the lower levels; beginners to mid-intermediate. At these levels where learners tend to rely on translating, the translation facilities are particularly useful and can save a lot of time.

The format of CD ROM packages is self-explanatory and extremely simple to use. Multimedia in language learning provides a rich immersion environment that reduces the workload of the teacher in class and allows faster students to cover more. It encourages autonomous learning at home or in self-access use. Of all the technologies in language learning we can reasonably expect to hear and see a lot more of multimedia in the coming year.

SPIN-OFF CAREERS

You may find that the experience you have gained while teaching stands you in good stead for a career loosely related to EFL - in publishing or as an agent, for example.

Agents

Many EFL teachers who represent schools as a sideline find that it is so rewarding that they want to pursue it as a career. EFL teachers have direct access to the market, which schools in anglophone countries are trying to attract, so they are ideally placed to act as agents.

Start by writing to schools which advertise frequently, as they are probably the most keen to expand. Explain what you believe that you can offer them and ask for a commision of at least 10%. Some schools will work on an informal basis; paying your commission as and when you recruit students, but others may expect more commitment. In any case, carefully research the schools and their courses to try and ensure that they match the student's requirements.

Publishing

One of the more popular spin-off careers for EFL teachers is to move into ELT (English Language Teaching) publishing. If you want to get into publishing, do your homework carefully and learn how a publisher operates. Be very clear as to what you can offer them - and be aware of what you will get in return. Publishing is not the glamorous job many teachers hope it will be, and it is rarely well paid.

Becoming an editor

If you have taught EFL but have no previous editorial experience, the way in to being an editor is via a secretarial position, doing freelance work for a publisher as a reader who looks at new manuscripts, as a proofreader, or by trialling new books in your school. Previous editorial work - perhaps with a local newspaper overseas - will give you a head start over applicants who have only TEFL experience. There are also a limited number of courses which contain an editorial element - the Diploma in Printing and Publishing Studies at the London College of Printing, Elephant and Castle, London SE1 for example.

Once you are taken on by a publisher, you should be given in-house training. You will probably begin as an editorial assistant or as desk editor. You will be responsible for seeing an author's manuscript through to production of the final book. You will need to be aware of proofing symbols and will liaise with designers to ensure the copy fits on a page. A knowledge of desk top publishing packages also helps.

Sales representatives

The sales rep must know the publisher's list inside out, and must build u contacts with schools and bookshops in the area they represent. This may be in their native country but plenty of sales jobs involve travelling to or living in a country overseas and are often a good way into publishing for teachers with experience in a particular market.

You may also be required to give presentations at conferences or at schools, as well as organising stalls and displays for your publisher at trade fairs. You may need to arrange school visits for authors, commissioning editors or publishers, and entertain your visitors during their stay.

Some schools will work on an informal basis; paying your commission as and when you recruit students.

Lexicography

Lexicography is the act or skill involved in writing a dictionary. Becoming a lexicographer is a possible way into publishing, as well as a possible part time supplement to teaching EFL. The market for EFL related dictionaries has been fiercely competitive in recent years, and dictionary writing is booming.

Because there is a scarcity of people with dictionary experience, publishers are looking for people with some EFL experience. Obviously recruitment varies from publisher to publisher, but an Master of Arts (MA) in linguistics or a TEFL qualification would stand you in good stead. Some publishers will then shortlist candidates and give them a test to check their lexical aptitude. It is here that publishers can tell who will be suitable for the job. You will be expected to show you can make language pedagogically valuable.

The market for EFL related dictionaries has been fiercely competitive in recent years, and dictionary writing is booming.

It is likely that you will bc employed to work on a particular project. Most lexicographers can expect on-the-job training, though Longman offer a 2-3 week training course after a year on a particular project.

There are frequent vacancies for freelance lexicographers. This may be useful to part time teachers or those with young families. It may be possible to work from your home if you have computing facilities. A career in lexicography may lead on to project management, or into publishing. Another possibility is to move into marketing or promotions.

STARTING YOUR OWN LANGUAGE BUSINESS

Those of you with an entrepreneurial spirit may see the opportunities that EFL presents as a small business. Here are some ideas to start you thinking.

Many experienced EFL teachers - as well as a few business entrepreneurs - have seen how lucrative it can be to open their own language teaching business. Other people may decide that it is less of an investment to set up their own educational consultancy.

Starting a language school

The most important thing to realise if you are considering opening a language school is that you can expect at least a two year slog before your school is likely to break even. Many schools in the UK have not survived this period, partly because of the British Council's recognition scheme. The British Council will only consider recognising a private language school which has been operating for two years. Without recognition, many schools find that agents will not recruit for them - so they have no students to teach. Once you have reached the two year limit, make sure you meet the required standards to achieve recognition (see p165).

For the first few years, make sure you have the financial backing to survive, and make sure that if you take out a loan, you will eventually have the means to pay it back. Consult an accountant to see how much money you will need to get going. You will need some money to do some market research and marketing, and you must find how much you can realistically expect to charge your students. Then you must pay your rent, the teachers' salaries, your own salary, tax, bills and so on - in other words it will be a major investment.

If you are considering opening a school abroad, check out the legalities first. In Greece, for example, it is hard for a foreigner to open a school unless they at least have a Greek partner, although if you are an EU citizen, this ruling is technically illegal.

Before you make a final commitment, make sure you do some market research first. Find out what competition you have from other schools in the area, and try and offer something none of the other schools have - Business English or classes for younger learners, for example.

To get your clients, you will need to do a marketing campaign. Get a list of contacts (some new schools have contacts from their previous school and will attempt to poach them) and mailshot them. Try the personal approach - follow the mailshot up with a telephone call or a visit. Advertise as widely as possible, telling clients what you will do for them, rather than just saying what courses you run.

When you have won your clients, make sure your best clients are taught by your best teachers, yourself if needs be. You must also consider how you will recruit teachers. If you want to recruit from a native English speaking country, will it be worth offering to pay their airfare? Will you recruit highly qualified teachers, knowing they will expect higher salaries? Will you be strictly 'legal' and pay their tax and insurance contributions, or will you find loopholes to avoid this? All these factors may force you to put your prices up, or if avoided, force the quality of your school to drop.

Find out what your cash flow will be - as well as worrying about how much money you will get, you need to know when you will get it. It may take 120 days for some people to pay an invoice. If you have the finance, the patience, and the resilience, there is no reason why your school should not be a success, providing you have done the necessary research first.

Educational consultancies

If you do not want to be involved with finding and equipping school premises, but have the contacts to teach a large number of clients, it may be worth starting an educational consultancy. In this way you will only need an office, from which you can deal with your clients and your teachers.

Educational consultancies supply businesses or private individuals with teachers to teach at the client's premises. Although the initial investment will be less for a consultancy than for a school, the same principles of research, marketing and recruitment will apply. Once you have a reputation for supplying quality teachers to top clients, an agency can be a sound business.

If you are considering opening a school abroad, check out the legalities first.

Make sure your best clients are taught by your best teachers.

DEVELOPING A NEW CAREER

Working as an EFL teacher can lead to many opportunities. Here are some ways of using your experience.

If you are feeling jaded with teaching, there are opportunities for moving up in the EFL world, as well as using your experience to secure managerial positions in training and personnel departments of companies far removed from EFL.

Management

The traditional route for advancement in EFL is by going into school management. As teachers become more senior, they are given special responsibility for certain areas, then they may be made Assistant Director of Studies, Director of Studies and finally Principal. If a teacher stays abroad, they could become Director of Studies within four years. In anglophone countries competition will make such a move slower, but, in comparison to other industries, promotion to management in EFL tends to be rapid. Therefore, it can provide a useful springboard to management in other sectors. The communication skills gained within EFL are now recognised by recruiters in all sectors as a positive asset.

The communication skills gained within EFL are now recognised by recruiters in all sectors as a positive asset.

As the EFL industry becomes increasingly professional, management skills are becoming more sought after. The sort of problems a Principal or Director of Studies finds they are dealing with include enrolments in decline, staff asking for pay increases and so on. These are not usually areas covered on an academic course. In order to combat this, some TEFL or Linguistics orientated Master of Arts degrees (MAs) are now introducing a management component (see Section Five). Another alternative is for EFL teachers to take the Masters Degree in Business Administration (MBA).

IATEFL (The International Association of Teachers of English as a Foreign Language) has a Special Interest Group which produces newsletters and sets up conferences to share information about management. Members are usually in middle management, but for those interested in moving into management, the service shows what possibilities are available. For more information contact: Sue Leather, The IATEFL Management Special Interest Group (see p169).

There is a great demand for teacher trainers, especially in eastern Europe.

Lecturing

It is possible to use your TEFL experience to become a university or college lecturer in a related field. This can be a rewarding move - but competition for posts is fierce.

Jobs tend to be available to younger people with a Ph.D and EFL experience, or to older people with considerable practical experience, probably at a high level in a college.

Getting into lecturing can be a question of chance - look to see what sort of person they want. For example, a university may want a lecturer with experience in teaching children. If the candidate has this experience and shows academic potential and initiative, this may get them the job. Potential and initiative could be shown through writing articles on the subject for an educational journal - the job of lecturer requires research and writing skills.

It may be easier to get your first lecturing post in a non-anglophone country. Often a college that requires a Ph.D from a local candidate may accept a Masters from a native English speaking candidate.

Teacher training

There is a great demand for teacher trainers, especially in eastern Europe, because of the huge demand for English. and in the growing area of primary English. Make sure that teacher training is really what you are interested in before you make a commitment. Meet other teacher trainers, and be aware that it is a stressful occupation.

The advantages, however, include the potential to move into quasi-management, such as being in-service trainer or Head Teacher. The post also offers the potential to travel widely, to attend workshops and conferences, and the possibility of getting your articles published in educational journals.

Teacher trainers should have a good deal of teaching experience with all levels and nationalities. If you are prepared to advise other teachers, you need to have experienced anything they are likely to encounter. To prepare yourself, read *The Teacher Trainer, A practical journal for Modern Language teacher training*, (available from Pilgrims); the CUP series on Teacher Training and Development by Adrian Doff, Tessa Woodward and Michael Wallace; or the IATEFL Special Interest Group for Teacher Training newsletter (see p172 for addresses).

In the UK there are several courses in Teacher Training, see pages 149-156 for details.

VOLUNTEERING

Voluntary and aid organisations - working in the developing world

There are various organisations that recruit people to work as English teachers overseas, often in the developing world. Most developing countries are realising the importance of using experienced and qualified volunteers for their needs, and the days when people could take off for a year's adventure with most voluntary organisations has gone.

Today volunteers' average age is 30. Most organisations prefer to recruit teachers with at least two years' experience. Graduates have sometimes found two years' experience volunteering has revitalised their career, with head teachers keen to take them on in the state sector when they return. The British Council are sometimes interested in former volunteers, and OXFAM and the ODA (who fund VSO) often recruit people who have worked in the developing world. Volunteering is also a way into teacher training and materials development. If you are interested in volunteering, contact the following organisations (addresses p172-177).

Voluntary Service Overseas (VSO)
VSO usually offer two-year contracts, and volunteers are given a choice over which area of the world they would like to work in - although not a specific country. VSO have over 1500 volunteers operating in 50 developing countries. Before a volunteer is sent abroad, they will be given an orientation course. Furnished accommodation should be provided, along with medical and insurance cover and paid national insurance contributions. Airfares will also be paid - but usually only at the beginning and end of your contract. In between expect to pay for your own flights. Salaries are at local rates, so your living standard will not be high. As a volunteer, you do not have many rights or benefits, and only those committed to their work helping a particular country are advised to go.
VSO has English teachers in: Cambodia, China, Dominican Republic, Guinea-Bissau, Hong kong, Indonesia, Laos, Mongolia, Namibia, Pakistan, Sri Lanka, St Vincent and the Grenadines and Vietnam. Contact VSO for other destinations.

United Nations Volunteers (UNV)
VSO recruit and sponsor volunteers to work through the United Nations multi-national programme, the UNV. Work tends to be specialised, but allowances are larger and UNVs may be posted with their spouse and up to two children.

East European Partnership (EEP)
EEP is a branch of VSO, and was set up to contribute to the development of Eastern European countries. They are particularly interested in recruiting child carers and ELT/secondary level teachers for their projects in Albania, Bulgaria, the Czech and Slovakian Republics, Hungary, Poland and Romania. A TEFL qualification is preferred, especially for their teacher training projects. Teachers with specialist knowledge are also in demand to teach English for Specific Purposes (ESP). As with VSO, EEP volunteers are paid a local salary, but are provided with accommodation and free medical services. Posts are for one to two years.

Peace corps
Peace corps volunteers are particularly active in Eastern Europe. Returning volunteers are now offered state teaching jobs in the USA while they study for MEds.

WorldTeach
WorldTeach is a programme of Harvard University's social service organisation in America, and they have operations ill Africa, Asia, Central America and Eastern Europe. Most volunteers teach EFL on a one-year contract. Volunteers do not need any qualifications except a degree. Volunteers pay a fee of around $3000 to cover insurance, airfares and support services. They are then paid a local salary, and get free accommodation.

Useful organisations
If you want to talk to former volunteers, there are various recruiting agencies who will put you in contact with those in your area. **Returned Volunteer Action** (RVA) have an information pack, *Thinking about Volunteering?,* and also run 'Questioning Development Days' when you can meet former volunteers. Contact: **Returned Volunteer Action** (RVA), Amwell Street, London EC1R IUL.

Other voluntary organisations

Catholic Institute of International Relations, 22 Coleman Fields, London NI 1UL, UK.
Designers for Development Ltd., Campden Hill, Ilmington, Shipston-on-Stour, Warwickshire CV36 4JF UK. Fax: 0608 82643. (Min. 3 month contracts in Vietnam).
Skillshare Africa, 3 Belvoir Street. Leicester LE1 6SL UK. Tel: 0533 540517.

Graduates have sometimes found two years' experience volunteering has revitalised their career.

OXFAM and the ODA often recruit people who have worked in the developing world.

WORLD ENGLISH

This section is for EFL teachers looking for work outside their native country and for people seeking English training. There is general information about English language training in each country, teachers' pay, visa requirements, etc. Where possible, this is followed by a list of training establishments that have been put forward by independent sources. Training managers are advised to contact a number of schools in their area and refer to Section One before making a decision. Job seekers are advised to apply to a selection of schools in the area in which they wish to work and contact any local organisations for further information.

THE EUROPEAN UNION

Please note that the terms "European Union (EU)" and "European Community (EC)"are interchangeable for most purposes, although the European Commission is promoting the use of the term "European Union".

EC nationals no longer require a work permit in order to take up employment in another member state.

BELGIUM

Minimum salary: 550 francs per hour or 45-50,000 francs per month.

Tax and health insurance: Employers pay tax and health insurance if you have a contract. Freelance rates vary according to salary.

Visa requirements: Non-EC nationals can apply through their local Belgian Embassy. Proof of employment must be shown.

Accommodation: With Brussels being one of the major EC centres, expect to pay 15,000 francs per month, 10,000-12,000 francs outside the capital.

English language newspaper: *The Bulletin* (W).

Other information: There are many American, British and Belgian language schools. Degrees and TEFL qualifications preferred. The voluntary run Community Help Service in Brussels has a list of schools on 02 647 6780.

The standard of living is high in Belgium, though food is generally cheap. Despite the on-going tension between the Flemish and French languages, which has forced the country to have two distinct semi-autonomous districts, English is quietly becoming more prevalent. This is likely to continue with the importance of Brussels as an EC centre.

List of schools in Belgium

Access Bvba Taalbureau, Atealaan, 5,2200 Herentals.
Access Taal & Commumicatie, Abdy Van Tongerlo, Abdystraat 40, B-2260 Westerlo.
Belgo - British Courses, 21 Rue D'ecosse, 1060 Brussels.
Berlitz Language Centre, 28 Rue Saint Michel,1000 Brussels.
Berlitz Language Centre, Westinform 17-19, Monnikenwerve,8000 Brugge.
Berlitz Language Centre, 172 Leuvenselaan,3300 Tienen.
The British School Of Brussels, Leuvensesteenweg, 19,3080 Tervuren.
Brussels Language Centre, 55 Rue Des Drapiers, 1050 Brussels.
Crown Language Centre, 9 Rue Du Beguinage, 1000 Brussels.
The English Institute, 77 Rue Lesbroussart, 1050 Brussels.

inlingua School Of Languages, 62 Limburgstraat, 9000 Gent.
Institute of Modern Languages and Communications S.A., 20 Av. De La Toison D'or ,Bte. 21, 1060 Brussels.
Institut Pro Linguis S.C, Place De L'eglise,6717 Thiamont.
May International, 40 Rue Lesbroussart, 1050 Brussels.
Mitchell School Of English, 156 Rue Louis Hap, 1040 Brussels.
Peters School, 87 Rue Des 2 Eglises, 1040 Brussels.
Practicum, 24 Reep, 9000 Gent.
School Voor Europese Talen, 28 Charlottalei, 2018 Antwerpen.

DENMARK

Minimum salary: Salaries are set by law at 178.25 kroner per hour.

Tax: 52%

Visa requirements: Virtually impossible for non-EC nationals.

Accommodation: In and around Copenhagen, the cost of accommodation averages out at around 10,000 kroner per month. Elsewhere it can be considerably less, and standards are high.

Other information: Danish state teachers enjoy some of the highest salaries in the EC, primarily attributable to the fact that they are expected to be able to teach any subject to students of any age. As a result, the majority of Danish teachers have a very high standard of proficiency in English, with little need for native English speakers.

With local unemployment running at an average of 11%, the prospects of finding a teaching post in Denmark are currently very poor, particularly as the number of children of school age continues to decrease, and schools, universities and teacher training colleges alike, cut back on staffing.

Accustomed to free education, the private schooling sector continues to be small, and the problem of finding posts in the Danish public sector is only exacerbated by the need for non-native teachers to possess a sound knowledge of Danish.

Some opportunities may be found in institutes running part-time courses and evening classes, particularly in business English, and it is in this area where job-hunting efforts should be concentrated.

List of schools in Denmark

Access, Hamerensgade 8, 1267 Copenhagen K - branches in Odense & 4 other cities.
Activsprog, Rosenvægets Alle 32, 2100 Copenhagen - also Odense, Ärhus & Aalborg.
Ais Language Training Centre, Kongevejen 115, 2840 Holte - also Odense, Silkeborg, Esbjerg.
Aktiv Sprogservice I/S, Lindevej 9, 1877 Frederiksberg C.
Babel Sprogtræning, Vordingborggrade 18, 2100 Copenhagen - also Fredericia.
Berlitz International, Vimmelskaftet 42a, 1161 Copenhagen - also Äalborg.
Bls Sprogskole, Rolfsvej 14-16, 2000 Frederiksberg.
Cambridge Institute, Vimmelskaftet 48, 1161 Copenhagen - branches in 40 centres. Tel: 33133302.
European Education Centre Aps (Inlingua), Lyngbyvej 72, 2100 Copenhagen.
Elite Sprogcentret, Hoffmeyersvej 19, 2000 Frederiksberg.
Erhvervs Orienterede Sprogkurser, Betulavej 25, 3200 Helsinge.
Ibl Sproginstitut, Rosenvængets Alle 32, 2100 Copenhagen - also Arhus, Äalborg, Esbjerg, Kolding, Odense, Vejle.
Linguarama, Hvilevej 7, 2900 Hellerup.
Master-Ling, Sortedam Dossering 83, 2100 Copenhagen.
Praktisk Sprog Træning, Faksegade 13, 2100 Copenhagen.
Sprogklubben, Vendersgade 6, 1363 Copenhagen.

FRANCE

Minimum salary: Salaries for teachers vary immensely in France and will usually be considerably lower in the provinces than in Paris due to the lower cost of living. In universities the hourly rate may be as high as FF230, but paid three months later and with no long-term guarantee of work. Private language schools vary, but the lowest rate currently stands between FF50-100 per hour.
Tax and health insurance: English language teachers in France fall into two categories - a "salarié" (employee) or a "travailleur indèpendent" (self-employed). Status implies different rights and obligations. As a "salarié", social security contributions are deducted by your employer before you receive your pay slip and you are entitled to sick leave, holiday pay and certain other advantages. There may also be a "Convention Collective" which governs your sector. "Travailleurs indèpendants" are paid in "honoraires" (fees) which should be set significantly higher than salaries, due to the fact that social security contributions are paid separately. If you only teach a few hours a week you may not be covered by the French social security system.
Visa requirements: If you come from an EC country, you will need a "carte de Séjour de ressortissant de la CEE", which should be applied for within three months of arrival in France, or as soon as you find work. Non-EC residents will need different documentation and should contact and

should check with the relevant sources before setting off.
Accommodation: From around FF2,600 per month for a room in a shared flat in Paris, less in rural areas.
English language newspapers: *International Herald Tribune* (D); *Paris Passion* (US magazine).
Other information: Since 1971, the majority of French companies have been required by law to spend a fixed percentage of turnover on vocational training, with many allocating a large percentage to the development of their employees' English language skills, given the rapid developments within the European Community. Business English and English for Special Purposes (ESP) are two areas of opportunity, while the best paid jobs are often found at the Chambre de Commerces who do much of the training (including English teaching) for smaller firms. Although a degree is often enough, a TEFL qualification is preferred and most schools will expect a good knowledge of French.

Legislation at EC level is forcing developments within the French public teaching sector, opening access to a number of posts for non-nationals. For those wishing to keep in touch with these rapidly changing developments, it is advisable to obtain the *Bulletin Officiel du Ministère de l'Education Nationale*. An additional source of useful information on working and teaching in France is the "Centre d'Information et Documentation Jeunesse" (CIDJ). In Paris, the English Teaching Resource Centre aims to provide support to English teachers on a membership basis, and provides a sound base of materials and ideas.

List of schools in France

AABC, 20 Rue Gonot de Mauroy, 75009, Paris. Tel: 1 42661311.
Academic des Longues Appliquees, 60 Rue de Laxou, BP 3736-54098, Nancy.
Alexandra School, 32 Rue Amiral de Grasse, 66130 Grasse. Tel: 93368801.
Alpha Formation, 51 Rue Saint-Ferreol, 130001, Marseille. Tel: 91330072.
The American Centre, Belomeau, Avenue Jean-Paul Coste, Paris. Tel: 1 42384238.
Arc Langue, Chemin de la Haie, 64100 Bayonne. Tel: 59550566.
Audio-English, 44 allees de Tourny, 33000 Bordeaux. Tel: 56445405.
BEST, 24 Bd. Beranger, 37000 Tours. Tel: 47055533.
British Connection International, 279 Rue Crequi, 69007 Lyon. Tel: 72730255.
BTS Language Centre, 226 Route do Philipeville, 6001 Marcinelle. Tel: 71313076.
Collegium Palatinium, Dept EFL/CP, Chateau de Pourtales, 61 rue Melanie, 67000 Strasbourg. Tel: 88310107.
English Apart, 82 rue Jean Jaures, 29200 Brest.
The English Institute, 24 Rue Vieux Marche aux Vins, 67000 Strasbourg. Tel: 88325136.
English International, 8 Quaie Jules Courmont, 690021 Lyon.
The English Study Centre (TESC), 16 Rue Manuel, 13100

Aix-en-Province. Tel: 42380754.
Executive Language Services Group, 25 Boulevard
Sebastopol, 75001 Paris.Tel: 1 2366255.
Forum, 66 Rue Bretonnerie, 45000 Orleans. Tel:
38625245.
France Europe Consultants, 49 Rue Du Petit Bois, 35235
Thorigne. Tel: 99838934.
IFS, 23 Bis Boulevard de Louvain, 13008 Marseille.Tel:
91792503.
ILIC, 12 Rue Letellier, 75015 Paris. Tel: 1 45751962.
Info Langues Tassin, 169 Avenue Charles de Gaulle,
69160 Tassin. Tel: 78361111.
ISES, 70 bis Avenue Maignot, 37100 Tours (mainly ESP).
ITS Langues, 21 bis rue des Plantes, 75014 Paris. Tel: 1
40449848.
Language Studies System, 23 Rue Sommeiller, 74000
Annecy. Tel: 50528756.
Rapid English, BP410, 27404 Louviers. Fax: 32402256.
Riviera Plus, 22 Boulevard Dubouchage, 06000 Nice.Tel:
93626062.
Rothman Institute, 21 Avenue du Major General
Vanier.1000 Troyes. Tel: 25803041.
Sarl Executive Language Service, 25 Bld. Sebastopol
75001, Paris.
School Cool, 1c Chemion Etrer, 60270 Gouvieux. Tel:
44571504.
Wood Language Studies, 33 Cours De La Liberte, 69003
Lyon. Tel: 78601560.

GERMANY

Minimum salary: On contract, 2,400-3,000 DM, which is
1,600-2,000 DM net. Hourly rates vary from 20-45 DM per
45-minute lesson depending on the school and type of
class. Business English classes pay up to 60DM per hour.
Tax and health insurance: EC nationals can work tax-free
for the first two years. You are liable for back tax on your
first two years' salary if you stay beyond this period, at
33%. Freelances should take out a private health policy.
Visa requirements: Non-EC residents must get a job before
they enter the country to get a permit - which is usually
difficult.
Accommodation: 750-1,000 DM per month for a room in a
shared flat, through rents vary from city to city.
Accommodation is very difficult to find.
Other information: Germany's unification has slowed
economic growth up to 0%. Teachers new to Germany may
find the conditions very tough, pay in schools is low and
there are only a few full-time contracts available.

There is a core of contracted teachers working for the major
schools. Probably up to 90% of teachers work on a freelance
basis, working in *Volkshochscules* (Adult Education
Centres), private companies and smaller schools. It is a
hostile and competitive market, and many unqualified
teachers work for low wages.

Prerequisites for success as a freelance include possessing
initiative, having a high level of spoken Germany and being
prepared to work early mornings and late evenings. There

is considerable demand for business English and English
for Special purposes (ESP), with government grants
ensuring much lucrative in-company work, however, the
recent recession has resulted in significant cutbacks in
this area.

Transport is reasonably inexpensive while being fairly
efficient and Germany's federal capitals are pleasant,
relatively uncrowded places to live. A smart appearance
may be expected if you want to make a good impression.
You are advised to take about 6,000 DM with you for initial
expenses.

Demand for teachers in the former East Germany continues
to be high, although many Russian teachers have been
retrained to fill English teaching posts. Conditions in the
former East Germany are still difficult on the whole and
racism is rife.

The International Language Institute in Munich, is drawing
up proposals for two-month courses in specialised areas
such as banking, finance, and tourism, and consequently
native English speakers continue to be in demand.

Applications for work can be sent to The Central Placement
Office of the Federal Department of Employment, who
process overseas applications. Contact Zentralstelle fur
Arbeitsvermittlung Feuerbachstrasse 42, D-6000 Frankfurt
am Main 1.

List of schools in Germany

ASK Sprachenschule, 1 Kortlumstr 71, Bochum Tel:
23412910.
Benedict School, Gurzennichstr. 17,5 Koln 1 Tel:
41221212203.
Berlitz, Fredrich Wilhelm Strasse 30, 4100 Duisburg Tel:
(203) 27168.
Christopher Hills School of English, Sandeldamn 12, 6450
Hanatu.
Didacta, Hobonzollernring 27, 8580 Bayreuth.Tel: (49)
92127555.
English Language Centre, Altonaer Chausee, 89, 2000
Schenefeld. Tel: 830 2421.
English Language Institute, Sprachenchule 4, Ubersetzer
Am Zwinger 14, Bielfeld. Tel: 52169353- Also Alter
Kirchenweg 33A, 2000 Norderstedt. Tel: 405251660.
Europa-Universitat Viadrina, Sprachenzentrum. Postfach
776, Grosse Scharrnstr. 59, 0-1200 Frankfurt (Oder).
European Language School, Hansastrasse 44, 4600
Dortmund 1. Tel: 579496.
Euro-Sprachscule, Nuernberg Am Plarrer 6, D-8500
Nurnberg 80.
Eurozentrum. Koln, Sedanstrasse 31-33, D-5000, Koln 1
Tel: (221) 720831.
FBD Schulen, Katharinenstr 18, 7000 Stuttgart
1.Tel:71121580.
GLS, Sprachenzentrum, B. Jaeshke, Pestalozzistr 886, 1000
Berlin. Tel: 3135025.
Hallworth English Centre, Frauenstrasse, 118 Ulmdonau
Tel: (49) 73122668.

Helliwell Institute of English, Markt 15, 5040 Bruhl.Tel: 2232 12893.

inlingua Sprachschule, Konigstrasse 61, 4100 Duisberg, 1.Tel: 341334. Also Kaiserstrasse 37, 6000 Frankfurt I Tel: 231021. Fax: 234829. Also Knapper Strasse 38, 5880 Ludenscheid. Tel: 2351 20275. Also Schildern 8 D-4790 Paderborn 1.

inlingua Sprachschule Gmbh, Heinrichstr 4a, 6400 Fulda.

Intercom Language Services Muggenkampstr 38, 2000 Hamburg 20.

Linguotek Institut, Schluelterstrasse 18, D-2000, Hamburg 13. Tel: 40459520.

Modernes Lernstudio, Thielenplatz, Prinzenstr 1, 3000 Hannover. Tel: 51-1321861.

Neue Sprachschule, Rosastrasse 1, 7800 Freiburg 1.Tel: 761 24810/32026.

NSK Language and Training Services (language courses for industry), Comeniusstr. 2, D-2000 Nurnburg 40.Tel: 911441552.

Sprachschule Griffin, Reilstrasse 8,0-4020 Halle (Saale),Tel:503422.

Sprachstudio Lingua Nova, Thierschstrasse 36, 8000 Munich 22. Tel: 89221171.

The Principal, Stevens English Training, Rutten Scheider Strasse 68, 4300 Essen 1.

Vorbeck-Schule, 7614 Gengenbach. Tel: 049 7803/3361.

Dean of the Wirtschaftwissen-schaftliche Fakultat Ingolstadt, Auf der Schanz 49, D-8070 Ingolstadt (for lecturers in business English only)

GREECE

Minimum salary: Salaries for EFL teachers in Greece are low (around £4/$6 per hour) and many do private lessons to supplement their income. Private lessons are usually easy to arrange at 2,000-3,000 drachmas per hour, although some schools may discourage this or expect a cut of your pay. Most schools provide a generous bonus at the end of each term, but do not pay during the summer holidays. It is advisable that all teachers insist on a contract before commencing employment.

Tax and health insurance: Teachers are required to pay tax and social security (IKA). On a salary of around 150,000 drachmas per month (£400/$600) for example, these would amount to around 28,000 drachmas (£80/$120).

Visa requirements: As Greece is an EC country, British teachers have the right to work but will need a work/ residence permit. The employer is responsible for obtaining these but sometimes teachers may be paid "off the payroll" without papers. For non-EC nationals, a work permit will be arranged by your school, which will require a translated copy of your degree certificate (which is cheaper if done at a Greek consulate than in Greece itself). You may also require a doctor's certificate of good health. Permits take up to two months, though in practice you may find your contract is over before you actually get your permit. You may find it very hard to get a resident's permit unless you can claim *omogeneis* - being of Greek descent.

Accommodation: Prices can be high, especially in the Athens areas where a typical one-bedroom flat may cost £200/$300 per month. Landlords often require two or more months' rent as a deposit and this is not always returned. A phone is a great advantage, as the waiting list for installation is around 10 years, and the phone provides an invaluable source of communication, particularly if you intend to focus on private classes.

English language newspaper: *The Athens News* (D).

Other information: Greece has a huge EFL market and there are over 4,000 *frontisteria* (educational institutes). Most of these teach children aged 8-18, up to proficiency in the larger schools. Around 70,000 students take Cambridge exams each year. Most lessons are in the evening, when students have finished their state lessons. The introduction of English in state primary schools may reduce the number of children attending frontisteria, though this is unlikely in the short term.

Teachers need a degree, preferably in English, to be eligible for a work permit, but no TEFL qualifications are needed. Unqualified teachers will be paid less, and language schools are sporadically checked to ensure that everything is above board. Despite EC legislation, the government is attempting to protect local teachers' employment. This has made it virtually impossible for non-Greeks to own language schools.

Eating and drinking out are still cheap, but other costs are high. Foreign registered cars are prohibited if you work in Greece. Be warned that Athens has a chronic pollution problem, and that winters in Greece can be bleak, particularly in the north.

Note that schools in Greece recruit teachers for the whole academic year. Recruitment is normally made in May-June or in early September and there is little point in applying for posts mid-way through the year. The normal pattern is for teachers to approach schools in person as most teachers are taken on locally rather than from overseas. *The Athens News* carries job advertisements.

List of schools in Greece

Alpha Abatzolglou Economou, 10 Kosma Etolou St. 54643 Thessaloniki. Tel: 31 830535.

A Andrioponlon No3, 3 28 Octobrio, Tripolis.

Athens College, PO Box 65005,15410 Psychico, Athens.Tel: 1 6714621.

English Tuition Centre, 3 Pythias Street, Kypseli 1136, Athens.

Enossi Foreign Languages, Ermou 2, Syntagma, 10563 Athens. Tel: 3224 500 - a well-established school with 8 centres (6 in Athens, 1 in Larissa & 2 in Salonika)

Eurocentre, 7 Solomou Street 41222 Larissa.

Hambakis Schools of English, 1 Filellinon Street, Athens.Tel: 1 3017531/5.

Hellenic American Union, 22 Massalias Street, GR-106 80 Athens.

Homer Association, 52 Academias St, 10677 Athens.Tel: 1 3622887.

International Language Centre, 35 Votsi Street 262, 21 Patras.

Institute of English, French, German and Greek for Foreigners, Zavitsanou Sophia, 13 Joannou Gazi St. 31100 Lefkada. Tel: 64524514.

Institute of Foreign Languages, 41 Epidavrou St. 10441 Athens. Tel: 1 5142397.

ISIAA 93, Lamia 35100. Tel: 23 121028.

Makri's School of English, 2 Pardos G Olympion St. 60100 Katerini. Tel: 35122859.

G Michalopolous School of English, 24E Antistasis, Alexandria, 59300 Imathias, Thessaloniki. Tel: 333 322890.

New Centre, Arkarnanias 16, Athens 11526.

Peter Sfyrakis' School of Foreign Languages, 21 Nikiforou Foka St, 72200 Ierapetra, Crete. Tel: 84228700.

Protypo English Language School, 22 Deliyioryi Street, Volos 38221.

School of English, 8, Kosti Palama, Kavala 65302.

School of Foreign Languages, 12 P Isaldari St, Xylokastro. 20400 Korinth. Tel: 74324678.

The Director, SILITZIS School of Languages, 42 Koumoundourou 412 22 Larissa.

The A Trechas Language Centre, 20 Koundouriotou St. Keratsini. Tel: 1 432 0546. Also 34 Argostoliou St, Egaleo, Athens. Tel: 1 5617263.

Zoula Language Schools, Sanroco Square, Corfu. Tel: 66139330.

ITALY

Minimum salary: Salaries range from between 120,000 lire per month as a University "lettori", with contracts of a limited duration, while in private sector schools the pay varies greatly but an average figure of around 140,000 lire per month can be expected. Many teachers supplement their income with private lessons, translations and such like.

Tax and health insurance: 25-30% tax if you are on contract, plus 19% VAT if you are freelance. Private schools and universities should deduct tax and national insurance equivalents, and it is important to check that they do. Although your employer may pay health insurance, extra cover is desirable.

Visa requirements: For EC nationals, no visa is required, with work permits being issued by the police. This process is often slow and tiresome as a result. Non-EC nationals will find it difficult to get a work permit unless they are of Italian descent. It is essential to have employment before entering the country to get a work permit.

Accommodation: A typical flat now costs 1,000,000 lire per month in cities (less in rural areas), and as a result, flat sharing is increasingly common. Accommodation is difficult to find in the major cities and foreigners will often have to pay higher rents than the locals.

Other information: There are hundreds of private schools in Italy, as the state system is disorganised and the demand for English is huge. However, the recession has meant a decrease in student numbers and fiercer competition for jobs. Some schools will take on any native English teachers, but conditions are better if you are qualified.

The *Associazione Italiana Scuole di Lingua Inglese* (AISLI) at Via Campanella 16, 41100 Modena regulates the conditions in its member schools, so AISLI schools are generally recommended.

There are sometimes opportunities to work as university lecturers, but foreign lettori's salaries have dropped, pay is often delayed and classes are overcrowded.

Private lessons are actually illegal if you hold a contract, but self-employed teachers should be able to get plenty of in-company work as the business community increasingly needs English. A knowledge of Italian would be an asset.

Italy is expensive in the north. Government reports say that the small industrial cities in the north and centre offer the best standard of living but those with an appetite for Mediterranean living might prefer the south.

List of schools in Italy

ABC English School, Via San Rocco 7,23017 Morbegno (SO).

Accademia Britannica, Via Bruxelles 61, 04100 Latina. Tel: 773 491917.

Anglocentre, Via A de Gasperi, 23 70052, Bisceglie (BA).

Arlington Language Services, c.p.99 29100, Piacenza.

British Institute, Fontane 109, Rome. Tel: 6491979. Fax: 64815549. Also via Marghera 45, 20149 Milan. Tel: 2 48011149.

The British Institute of Florence, Palazzo Feroni, Via Tornalbuoni 2, Florence. Tel: 55 298866.

The British Language Centre Via Piazzi, Angolo Largo Pedrini, 23100 Sondrio. Tel: 342 216130.

The British Language Centre, Via Piazza, Roma 3 20038 Serengo.

Cambridge School, Via S Rochetto 3, Verona. Tel: 458003154. Fax: 458003154.

The Cambridge School, Pal. Casa, Bianca Via Origlia 38 84014 Nocera Inferiore, Salerno.

Centro di Lingue, Via Pozzo 30, Trento.Tel: 461981733. Fax: 461981687.

Centro Internazionale di Linguistica Streamline, Via Piave 34/b, 71100 Foggia. Tel: 039 88124204.

Centro Lingue Tradint, Via Jannozzi 8, S Donato Milanese (N1). Tel: 25231312.

The English Centre, Via Dei Mille 18, 07100 Sassari, Sardinia. Tel: 79 232154.

Language Centre, VL. Milano 20,21100 Varese. Tel: 0332 282732.

The English Institute, Corso Gelone 82, Siracuse, Sicily. Tel: 931 60875.

English House, Via Roma 177 85028 Rionero, Potenza.

The English Language Studio, Via Antonio Bondi, 27 40138 Bologna. Tel: 51347394. Fax: 51505952.

International Language School, Via Tibullo 10, Rome. Tel: 66547796. Fax: 66547796.

Lb Linguistico, Centro Insegnamento, Lingue Stanierc, Via Caserta 16, 95128 Catania, Sicily.

Language Centre, Via G Daita 29 90139 Palermo.

Lingua Due Villa, Pendola 15 57100 Livrono

Living Languages School, Via Magna Grecia 89100 Regio Calabria. Tel/Fax: 39 965330926.

Lord Byron College, Via Sparano 102, 70121 Bari. Tel: 80 232696.

Managerial English Consultants, Via Sforza Pallavicini 11, 009193 Rome. Tel: 6 654 2391.
Fax: 6 6871159.

Modern English School, Via Giordano Bruno 6, 45100 Rovigo. Tel: 425 200266.

Modern English Study Centre, via Borgonuova 14, 40125 Bologna. Tel: 51 227523.

Multimethod, I Go Richini 8,20122 Milan. Tel: 2583042. Fax: 289401235.

Oxford Inst Italiani, Via Senato 28 20121.

Oxford School, San Marco 1513, Venice. Fax: 415210785.

The Professionals, Via F Carcona 4,20149 Milan Tel: 2 48000035. Fax: 2 4814001.

Regency School, Via Arcivescovado 7,16121 Turin. Tel: 11517456. Fax: 11,541845.

Regent International Corsa Italia, 54 21047 Saronno.

The RTS Language Training, Via Tuscolana 4 00182 Roma.

Studio Linguistico Fonema, via Marconi 19, 50053 Sovigliana-Vinci, (Fl).Tel: 571 500551.

Wall Street Institute, Piazza Combattento 6. 4100 Ferrara. Tel: 532200231. Also Corso V.Emanuele 30, 20122 Milan. Tel: 2 76013959.

LUXEMBOURG

If you want to work in this tiny country, your opportunities are limited to two private schools, the English Language Centre and the International Language Centre. The state-controlled Centre de Langues also runs English courses (80 Boulevard George Patton,23-16 Luxembourg Tel:403914).

English language newspaper: *Luxembourg News Digest* (W).

Other information: English language teaching is nearly all done in the state system. There are no universities in the principality, so Luxembourg residents must take a BA in the UK or the USA to be able to teach - hence the high level of English teaching. The British Luxembourg Society is promoting an English language movement and has ties with the British Council. For information contact the British Council in Brussels - Tel:(02) 193600.

NETHERLANDS

Minimum salary: 1,900 guilders per month.

Tax and health insurance: Around 30%.

Visa requirements: Arranged by employer.

Accommodation: Availability of housing in the Netherlands is a particular problem and can be very expensive. Rented accommodation is often advertised in local newspapers from 350 guilders per month, but you can also contact the Netherlands Estate Agents Federation for suitable agents who deal with rented property.

Other information: As a full member of the European Community, all EC nationals have the right to live and work in the Netherlands without a work permit. UK nationals working in the Netherlands have the same rights as nationals of that country with regard to pay, working conditions, access to housing, vocational training, social security and trade union membership. Moreover, families and immediate dependents are entitled to join them and have similar rights. British nationals are free to enter the Netherlands for up to three months to look for work or set up in business. Visitors, even if looking for work, may be asked to prove that they have adequate means for the duration of their stay and that the cost of their return journey is secured.

Most Dutch people are fluent in English because of their excellent state system, and as a result opportunities to teach EFL are limited mainly to business English or English for Specific Purposes. In the state system teachers must be fluent in Dutch. Organisation in the private system is fairly chaotic.

List of schools in the Netherlands

Asa Studiecentrum, Kotterstraat 11,1826 Cd Alkmaar.

Asco,Nassauplein 8, 1815 Gm Alkmaar.

Alenpracticum Almelo, Nieuwstraat 171,7605 Ad Almelo.

Amerongen Talenpraktikum, De Kievit 1,3958 Dd Amerongen.

Berlitz Language Centre, Rokin 87-89,1012 Kl Amsterdam.

Bltc, Keizersgracht 389,1016 Ej Amsterdam.

Bressler's Business Language, Buiksloterdijk 284,1034 Zd Amsterdam.

Dinkgreve Handelsopleiding, Wilemsparkweg 31,1071 Gp Amsterdam.

Dutch College,P Calandlaan 42,1065 Kp Amsterdam.

Eerste Nederlandse Talenpraktikum,Kalverstr 112,1012 Pk Amsterdam.

Elseviers Talen,Jan Van Galenstraat 335,1061 Az Amsterdam.

Linguarama Nederland,Wtc Strawinskylaan 507,1077 Xx Amsterdam.

Europa Talenpraktikum, Vosselmanstraat 400,7311 Cl Apeldoorn.

School Of English, Eerste Wormenseweg 238,7331 Nt Apeldoorn.

Mieke Boot Instuitut, Waterbergseweg 13,6815 Al Arnhem.

Educational Holidays, Beukstraat 149,2565 Xz Den Haag.

Esp, Laan V Meerdervoort 834,2564 As Den Haag.

Fikkers Handelsinstituut, Anna Paulownastr 37a,2518 Bb Den Haag.

Linguarama Nederland, Venestraat 27,2525 Ca Den Haag.

Stichting Volwasseneducatie Deventer, Afd English Language Training, Postbus 639,7400 Ap Deventer.

Eerste Ned Talenpraktikum, Singel 355,3311 He Dordrecht.

Telencentrum Dordrecht, C De Wittstraat 50,3311 Kj Dordrecht.

Notenboom, Kerkakkerstraat 34,5616 Hc Eindhoven.
Instituut Schoevers, Markt 17,5611 Eb Eindhoven.
Trait D'union, Argonautenlaan 24a,5631 Ll Eindhoven.
A V C, Oringerbrink 43,7812 Jr Emmen.
Talenpraktikum Twente,Tav Dhr P De Wit,Ariensplein 2,7511 Jx Enschede.
Gebo, Boelekade 36-38,2806 Al Gouda.
Gouwe College, Turfsingel 67,2802 Bd Gouda.
Interphone Opleidingen, St Jorisstraat 17,5361 Hc Grave.
Linguaphone Instituut, Peperstraat 7,6127 As Grevenbicht, Huis Van Bewaring,de Koepel Afd Onderwijs,Harmenjansweg 4,2031 Wk Haarlem.
Erasmus College, Planetenlaan 5,2024 Eh Haarlem, Hendrik Ido Ambacht.
Meab Onderwijs-Instituut Bv, Herengracht 4,2312 Ld Leiden.
Leidse Onderwijsinstelling,Tav Mr Wirtz,Leidsedreef 2,2352 Ba Leiderdorp.
Avoc Teleninstituut, Heugemerweg 2d,6229 As Maastricht.
Bell College, Afd English LanguageTraining, Stationsstraat 17,6221 Bm Maastricht.
Instituut Meppel, Tav Dhr J G Rijpkema,Postbus 263,7940 Ag Meppel.
Zeeuwse Volksuniversiteit, Afd English Language Training, Postbus 724,4330 As Middleburg.
Onderwijsinstituut Netty Post, Haverstraat 2,1447 Ce Purmerend.
Class International, Bijlwerffstr 28b,3039 Vh Rotterdam.
Scholengem. G K Van Hogendorp, Postbus 290725,3001 Gb Rotterdam.
Interlingua Taalsupport Bv, Wijnhaven 99,3011 Wn Rotterdam.
Language Partners,Wtc,Beursplein 37,3011 A Rotterdam.
Instituut Schoevers, Postbus 10486,5000 Jl Tilburg.
B N M, Heinsbergenstr 27,502 Cd Uden, Flinckstraat 1/Keet,1506 Lk Zaandam, Niow ,Boslaan 6,3701 Cj Zeist.
Elseviers Talen, Westelijke Parallelweg 54,3331 Ew Zwijndrecht.
Boerhave Opleidingen, Hoogstraat 118,801 Bb Zwolle.
Interlingua Talenpraktikum, Burg van Royensingel 20 - 21,8011 ct Zwolle.

PORTUGAL

Minimum salary: 120,000 escudos per month, with the average rate of pay on an hourly basis estimated at approximately £12. A number of schools offer end of term bonus schemes.
Tax and health insurance: Not all schools offer health insurance and a minimum of class 3 NI is recommended. Teachers are liable to pay income tax and social security at the rate of 25-30%.
Visa requirements: Work permits and residents permits should be arranged by employers.
Accommodation: There is a severe housing shortage in Lisbon, while rents in Porto and the university town of Coimbra have also escalated dramatically. Expect to pay in the region of 40,000 escudos per month in a shared flat in these cities, less in smaller towns.
English language newspapers: *The Portugal Post* (W); *The Anglo-Portuguese News* (W); *The Algarve Gazette* (M).
Other information: Although Portugal is now no longer the EC's poorest country, its rapid economic growth and corresponding demand for English has slowed down. Student numbers have tailed off and competition for jobs is keen. There are probably more opportunities for teachers prepared to work in the smaller private language schools in the provinces, but pay is unlikely to be very high. The cost of living has also risen, and is comparable with northern Europe for many essentials (though eating and drinking out is still cheap). Housing is generally of low quality.

If you pay local health insurance, you are entitled to Caixa -basic medical treatment, but expect to wait several days for an appointment. A private health insurance policy is worth considering.

Ensure your timetables avoid a split shift, or your days will be very long. Travelling around Lisbon and Porto can take some time.

A degree is necessary to obtain a work permit, but in many schools qualifications are not essential. Such schools may expect you to work long hours. Others may offer you "green receipts", which in effect means you are self-employed and excluded from sick pay, holiday pay and bonuses. If this is the case, make sure you are paid enough to compensate. Private lessons are easy to find, especially for business English, and in-company work is lucrative.

The government are now promoting English at primary level, and there may be openings in the state sector. West Sussex Institute of Higher Education, TESOL section (Portugal) run an RSA course with a placement in The University of the Algarve. Contact them at Upper Bognor Road, Bognor Regis, PO21 1HR, UK.

The Portuguese climate is warm but expect a lot of rain in the winter. Northern Portugal is cheaper and generally friendlier than the south, but the weather is unreliable all year. In the Algarve, English is widely spoken and there is a large residential English population. Prices are higher here to reflect this.

MADEIRA

There are several private language schools on this island resort, especially in the capital, Funchhal. The island has no beaches, but is very scenic and stays warm and humid all year.

List of schools in Portugal

GEDI, Pq. Miraflores, Lt. 18-lj.A/B,1495 Alges.
INLINGUA, Campo Grande, 30 -1o A,1700 Lisboa.

The New Institute of Languages, Urb. Portela.Lt.197 - 5o B-C, 2685 Sacavem.

Cambridge School, Avenida de la Liberdade, 173-40,1200 Lisboa, Tel: 352 74 74, Fax: 353 47 29. Courses: CTEFLA, Business men, Companies, Juniors, UCLES exams. Employment: EC citizens, BA, CTEFLA/TESOL. Portugal's largest teaching chain - 7 locations.

Berlitz, Av. Conde Valbom, 6-4o,1000 Lisboa.

CENA-Cent. Est. Norte Americanos, R. Remedios, 62 - c/v,1200 Lisboa.

Centro de Instruçao Tecnica, Rua D.Estefania, 32-10 Dto,1000 Lisboa.

Centro Internacional Linguas, Av. Fontes P. de Melo, 25-1o Dto,1000 Lisboa.

Centro Linguas Estrangeiras de Cascais, Av. Marginal, BI.A - 30,2750 Cascais.

CETI, Av. Duque de Loule, 71 - 2,1000 Lisboa.

CIAL-Centro De Linguas, Av. Republica, 14-20, 1000 Lisboa, Tel: 351-1-3533733, Fax: 351-1-3523096. Qualified EFL teachers required on a full-time basis. Specialists in teaching general and business English to corporate employees.

Clube Conversaçao Inglesa 3M, R.Rodrigues Sampaio, 18-30,1100 Lisboa.

Inst.Linguas de Oeiras, R. Infante D. Pedro, 1 e 3-r/c, 2780 Oeiras.

Centro de Estudos IPFEL, R. Edith Cavell, 8,1900 Lisboa.

International House, Lisbon, Rua Marques Sa Da Bandeira 16, 1000 Lisboa, - Branches throughout Portugal.

Lisbon Language Learners, R.Conde Redondo, 33 - r/c E,1100 Lisboa.

Linguacoop, Av. Manuel da Maia, 46-10 D,1000 Lisboa.

INPR, Bernardo Lima, 5,1100 Lisboa.

Inst. Sinstrense de Linguas, R.Dr. Almeida Guerra, 26,2710 Sintra.

Know-How,Av. Alvares Cabral, 5-300,1200 Lisboa.

Lusodidacta, Av.Anto Augusto Aguiar, 24-70Do,1000 Lisboa.

PROLINGUAS, R.Saraiva Carvalho, 84 - Pt.2,1200 Lisboa.

Tell School, R. Soc.Farmaceutica, 30-1o,1100 LISBOA, World Trade Centre - Lisbon,Av. Brasil, 1-5o e 8o,1700 Lisboa.

Novo Instituto de Linguas, R. Cordeiro Ferreira, 19 C-1o D,1700 Lisboa.

Ecubal, Lombos,Barros Brancos,Porches, 8400 Lagoa Centro de Linguas de Alvide,R.Fonte Nino,Viv. Pe. Americo, 1o,Alvide, 2750 Cascais.

Big Ben School, R. Moinho Fanares, 4-1o,2725 Mem Martins.

Centro de Linguas de Queluz, Av.Dr. Miguel Bombarda,62 - 1oE,2745 Queluz.

ELTA, Av. Jose E. Garcia, 55-3o,2745 Queluz.

Instituto Franco-Britanico, R. 5 de Outubro, 10 -1o Dto, 2700 Amadora.

Language School, R.Alm.Candido Reis, 98,2870 Montijo. Celfibocage, Av. Luisa Todi, 288 -2o,2900 Setubal.

Centro de Linguas Intergarb,Tv. da Liberdade, 13-1o, 8200 Albufiera.

Centro de Linguas de Quarteira, R. Proj. 25 de Abril, 12,8125 Quartiera.

Class, R.Gen.Humberto Delgado,40-1o,7540 Santigo Do Cacem.

Curso de Linguas Estrangeiras, R.Dr. Miguel Bombarda,271 -1o,2600 Vila Franca De Xira.

English Institute Setubal, Av. 22 Dezembro, 88,2900 Setubal.

Encounter English, R.Letes, 42 - 2o,8000 Faro.

Instituto de Linguas de Faro, Av. 5 de Outubro,8000 Faro.

Interlingua, R. St. Isabel, 12,8500 Portimao.

Interlingua, R.Dr.Joaquim Telo, 32-1o E,8600 Lagos.

International Language School,Av. Rep.Guine Bissau, 26 - A,2900 Setubal.

English School of Loule,R.Jose F. Guerreiro, 66M, Galerias Do Mercado, 8100 Loul.

Mundilingua, R.Dr.Tefilo Braga, Ed.Rubi-1o, 8500 Portimao.

Weltsprachen-Institut, Qta. Carreira, 37 r/c - 2765 Sao Joao do Estoril, TEL: 4684032. Branch: R.Dr.Brito Camacho, 22-A-1o, 7800 Beja.

English at PLC, Praça Luis de Camoes 26, Apartado 73, 5001 Vila Real.

Escola de Linguas de Agueda, R. Jose G.Pimenta, 3750 Agueda.

Royal School of Languages, Av. Dr.Lourenco Peixinho, 92-2o,3800 Aveiro. Tel: (034) 2956. Fax: (034) 382870. Also schools in Agueda, Ovar, Guarda, Porto. All modern schools renowned for their outstanding staff and their expertise in teaching foreign languages, Portuguese for foreigners and summer language courses abroad.

Escola de Linguas de Ovar, R.Ferreira de Castro, 124 - 1o A/B,3880 Ovar.

INESP,R.Dr.Alberto Souto, 20-2o,3800 Aveiro.

Instituto Britanico, R.Cons.Janu rio, 119/21,4700 Braga.

Inst.Britanico de Ponte Lima, R.Dr. Ferreira Carmo, 4990 Ponte De Lima.

Instituto Inlas do Porto, R. S da Bandeira, 522-1o, 4000 Porto.

Inst. de Linguas de Paredes,Av. Republica, Casteloes Cepeda, 4580 Paredes.

ISLA, Bo S.Jo de Brito. 5300 Bragan A, Manitoba,C. Com. Premar, lj.72,4490 Povoa De Varzim.

Lancaster College, Pta 25 Abril, 35-1o E, 4400 V. Nova De Gaia.

Whyte Institute, Lg. das Almas, 10-2o E/F, 4900 Viana Do Castelo.

Casa de Inglaterra,R.Alexandre Herculano, 134,3000 Coimbra.

Centro Linguas de Santarem, Lg. Pe. Francisco N. Silva, 2000 Santar M.

The English Language Centre,R. Calouste Gulbenkian,22-r/c C, 3080 Figueira Da Foz.

The English School of Coruche, R.Guerreiros, 11, 2100 Coruche.,

Gab. Tecnico de Linguas, R. Hermenegildo Capelo, 2 - 2o,2400 Leiria.

IF Ingles Funcional, R. Com. almeida Henriques, 32, 2400 Leiria.

IF Ingles Funcional , Av. Vidreiro, 95 - 2o, 2430 Marinha Grande.

IF - Ingles Funcional, R. Afonso Albuquerque, 73-A, 2460 Alcoba A.

Instituto Britanico, R.Municipio, Lt. B - 1o C, 2400 Leiria.

Instituto de Linguas, R. Valverde 1, 2350 Torres Novas.

Inst. Linguas Cast.o Branco, Av. 1o Maio, 39-S - lj E, 6000 Castelo Branco.

Instituto de Linguas do Fundao, Urb. Rebordao, Lt.17 - r/c,6230 Fundao.

Lancaster College, Rua C. Civico, Ed. A.Seguradora, 2o, 6200 Ccvilha.

Muntilinguas, R.Miguel Bombarda, 34-1o, 2000 Santar M.

Linguacultura, R. Dr.Joaquim Jacinto,110,2300 Tomar.

Linguacultura, Lg. St.o Antonio, 6-1o Esq., 2200 Abrantes.

Inter Way, Po. Jose Fontana, 11 -1oDto, 1000 Lisboa.

Inst.Nacional de Administradao, Centro de Linguas, Palacio Marquus de Oeiras, 2780 Oeiras.

Tjaereborg Studio, Av. Liberdade, 166-4o F,1200 Lisboa.

SPAIN

Minimum salary: The rates of pay for EFL teachers ranges from 130,000 pesetas to 180,000. A teacher can also charge up to 2,500 pesetas an hour for a private class on a one-to-one basis. However, due to the large number of EFL teachers entering Spain it is essentially that you are prepared to put considerable effort into finding work.

A minimum salary should be in the region of 105,000 pesetas per month for 25 teaching hours per week. Employers may pay a fixed salary for 10-14 hours and give the rest cash in hand on an hourly basis. Before agreeing to these terms, check and sick pay.

Tax and health insurance: 2% taxation rate on gross salary, deducted at source. EC nationals are entitled to medical treatment, but it is advisable to get private health insurance, particularly since many Spaniards do. Employers pay half of national health insurance contributions.

Visa requirements: All EC nationals are allowed to work in Spain without work permits. Non-EC nationals must obtain a resident's permit from their own country. A work permit can be obtained within Spain, through your employer, but they are not easy to obtain.

Accommodation: The average price of accommodation in a shared 2-3 bedroom flat in the centre of a major town is about 50,000 pesetas, slightly more in Madrid and Barcelona.

Other information: Spain's education system is undergoing *La Reforma*, the introduction of more modern teaching methods into the state system. English will also be taught at primary level. This may make it harder for teachers to find work in the private sector in the long term, especially if the high rates of unemployment continue. Although the boom in EFL is slowing down in Spain, and competition for school work is fierce, there is still scope for freelance private and agency work.

Schools usually recruit in September and January, when many teachers have left because of the often surprisingly cold winters (especially in Madrid). Qualifications and experience are an invaluable asset.

English and Spanish Studies, 26-40 Kensington High Street, London W8 4PF recruit for teachers to work in Spain. Tel: 071 938 2222. Try also the English Educational Services, Alcala 20-22, 28014 Madrid. Tel: 531 4783.

List of schools in Spain

Academia Saint Patricks, Calle Caracuel No.1, 17402 Girona.

AHIZKE/CIM, Loramendi 7, Apartado 191, Mondragon Guipuzcoa.

Alce Idiomas, Nogales 2, 33006 Oviedo. Tel: 85 254543.

Berlitz (branches around Spain), Gran Via 80-4, 28103 Madrid. Tel: 1 542 3586.

Big Ben College, Plaza Quintiliano 13, Calahorra 26500 La Rioja.

Britannia School, Leopoldo Lugones 3, 1 B 33420 Lugones, Asturias.

Britannia School, Leopoldo, Lugones 33420. Tel: 85 26 2800. Also Raset 22, Barcelona 08021. Tel: 3 200 0100. Fax: 414 4699.

British Language Centre, Bravo Murillo, Po.de la Habana 62, bajo A, 28036 Madrid. Tel: 1 5649177.

Callan Method School of English, Calle Alfredo Vicenti 6, bajo 15004, La Coruna.

Centro Atlantico, Villanueva, 2dpdo., 28001 Madrid. Tel: 1 435 3661. Fax: 1 578 1435.

Centro De Idiomas Liverpool, Libreros 11, 10, 28801 Alcala de Henares, Madrid. Tel: 1 881 3184.

Centro Linguistico del Maresme, Virgen De Montserrat.Tel: 35 55 5403 (Jenifer Grau).

El Centro Britanico, Republica De El Salvador 26-10m, (Edificio Simago), 15701 Santiago De Compostela, La Coruna. Tel: 8159 7490.

English Activity Centre, Pedro Frances 22a, 07800 Ibiza. Tel: 7131 5828.

The English Centre, San Francisco 10, 33400 Aviles, Asturias. Tel: 8554 5933.

The English College, c/ Andalucia 2/4, Gijon 33208, Asturias.

English Studies, SA Avendiade.. Arteijo, 8-1 15004 La Coruna.

Fiac School of English, Mayor 19, 08221 Terrassa, Barcelona.

FLAC, Escola D'Idiomes Moderns Les Valls, 10 2/0 08201 Sabadell, Barcelona.

Glossa English Language Centre, Rambla De Cataluna. 9, 78 20 2A 08008 Barcelona.

Idiomas Oxford, Calvo Sotelo 8-1, 26003 Logrono.Tel: 4124 41332.

Idiomas Progreso, Plaza Progreso 12, 07013 Palma De Mallorca. Tel: 7123 8036.

inlingua Idiomas C/o., Greforio Fernandez 6, 47006 Valladolid.

inlingua Idiomas, Maestro Falla no.5,2,12 Puerto del Rosario 35600 Fuerteventura, Canary Islands.

inlingua idiomas, Tomas Morales 28, 35003 Las Palmas de Gran Canaria. Tel: 2836 0671.

Interr ang, PI Padre Jean de Mariana, 3-2 45002 Toledo.

Key School Princes, 3-1 36001 Pontevedra.

Lawton School, Cura Sama 7, 33202 Gijon, Asturias. Tel: 8534 9609.

Manchester School, San Bernado 81,33201 Gijon, Alicante Tel: 8535 8619.Fax: 8535 6932.

Nelson English School, Jorge Manrique 1, Santa Cruz, Tenerife.

The New School, Calle Sant Joan 2, 2a Reus Tarragona.Tel: 77 330775.

Number Nine English Language Centre, Sant Onofre 1, 07760 Ciutadella De Menorca, Baleares. Tel: 7138 4058.

Principal English Centre, Aptdo. 85, Puerto De Santa Maria, Cadiz.

Skills, Trinidad 94, 12002 Castellon. Tel: 6424 2668.

Stanton School of English, Colon 26, 03001 Alicante. Tel: 65207581.

Trafalgar idiomas, Avda Castilla 12,33203 Gijon, Asturias Tel: 85 332361.

Warwick House Centro Linguistico Cultural, Lopez Gomez, 18-2 Valladolid 47002.

Windsor School of English, Virgen De Loreto 19-1, 41011 Sevilla.

Yaga School, Maria De Molina, 40-lo 28006 Madrid.

York House, English Language Centre, Muntaner 479, 08021 Barcelona. Tel: 32 113200.

Acento - The Language Company, Ruiz De Alarcon 7, 21 41007 Sevilla.

Afoban, Alfonso Xii,30 41002 Sevilla.

Aljarafe Language Academy, Crta. Castilleja-Tomares,83 Tomares, Sevilla.

Berlitz, Edif. Forum,1 Mod. 3 Av. Luis Morales,S/N 41018 Sevilla.

Britannia School Of English, Juan Diaz De Solés, 9, Bl. 2 41010 Sevilla.

CLIC (Centro de Lenguas é Intercambio Cultural), Santa Ana, 1141002, Sevilla. Tel: 34-5-437 4500/438 6007. Fax: 437 18 06. CLIC is medium-sized school, specialising in Spanish as a foreign language and all types of EFL courses. Our Spanish could be a "springboard" in helping you find future work as an EFL teacher in Andalusia.

English Way, Platero,30 San Juan De Aznalfarache, Sevilla.

Epicenter, Niebla ,13 41011 Sevilla.

Eurocentre, Puerta De Jerez 3,1 41001 Sevilla.

Modern School, Gerona,11 41003 Sevilla.

The Oxford School, Maron Feria, 4 41800 Sanlúcar La Mayor, Sevilla.

Passport to English, Segura,14 - 16 41001 Sevilla,

Ripolles, Adriano,3 41001 Sevilla.

Rolleston, Melliza,1 Dos Hermanas,Sevilla.

Tower Centre, Asuncion,43 41011 Sevilla.

Wall Street Institute, Av. República Argentina 24,P12 D 41011 Sevilla.

Windsor School of English, Virgen De Loreto,19 41011 Sevilla.

Academia Andaluza de Idiomas, Crta. El Punto, 9 Conil, Cadiz.

Cenro Cooperativo De Idiomas,Clavel,2 11300 La Linea,Cadiz

"Communication", Academia De Idiomas, Sociedad Cooperativa Andaluza, C/ Camilo José Cela, 12, 1a, 11160 Barbate, Cadiz.

The English Academy, Cruz ,15 11370 Los Barrios,Cadiz.

The English Centre, Aptdo. Correos 85, 11500 Puerto De Santa Maria, Cadiz. Tel: 34 56 850560, Fax: 873804. We specialise in small children and need highly professional infant/primary teachers with Tefl qualifications and experience, offering dedicated, quality education.

International House, Canovas Del Castillo,33 11001 Cadiz.

Language Study Centre, Corredera Baja, 15 Bajo Chiclana De La Frontera,Cadiz.

Preston English Centre, Edif. El Carmen Chapineria,3 Jerez De La Frontera,Cadiz.

St Patrick's Caracuel, 1 Jerez De La Frontera,Cadiz.

Trinity School S.L., C/ Golondrina (Plaza Jardines) No.17 Bajo, 11500 Puerto De Santa Maria, Cadiz. Tel: 34-(9) 56-871926. Fax: 541918. Summer Spanish courses, all year Spanish courses (groups). Also courses in France, United Kingdom, America. Translations and more.

Centro De Ingles,Tejon Y Marin,S/N 14003 Cordoba,

English Language Centre, Jesús Maria,9 - 1d,14003 Cordoba.

Eurolingua, San Felipe, 3 14003 Cordoba.

Idiomaster, Los Maristas, 2 Lucena,Cordoba.

International House, Rodriguez Sanchez,15 14003 Cordoba.

Linguasec, Malaga,1 14003 Cordoba.

Piccadilly English Institute, Los Chopos, 8 14006 Cordoba.

Centro De Estudios De La Lengua Inglesa, Edif. Edimburgo,Plaza Nia,21003 Huelva.

International House, Rico,19 21001 Huelva, Onoba Idiomas,Rasco 19-2,21001 Huelva.

Audio Jeam, Pza. Ayuntamiento 2, 46002 Valencia.

Centre of English Studies, Jai Alai 5, 46010 Valencia.

Cnt. Estudios Norteamericanos, Aparisi y Guijarro 5, 46005 Valencia.

International House, Pascual y Genis 16, 46002 Valencia. Tel: 352.06.42.

London House, Baron de S. Petrillo 23bajo, 46020 Benimaclet.

Oxford Centre, Alvaro de Bazan 16, 46010 Valencia.

The Institute of English, Santiago Garcia 8, 46100 Burjasot (Valencia)

American Institute, El Bachiller 13, 46010 Valencia.

Apple Idiomas, Aben al Abbar 6, 46021 Valencia. Tel: 362.25.45.

Aupi, Jesus 43, 46007 Valencia.

Centro de Estudios de Ingles, Garrigues 2, 46001 Valencia. Tel: 352.21.02.

Centro de Ingles Luz, Passage Luz 8bajo, 46010 Valencia. Tel: 361.40.74.

inlingua, Ribera 13, 46002 Valencia.

THE REST OF EUROPE

ALBANIA

Despite years of isolation, the general level of English is quite good, especially in Tirana, perhaps because English offers Albanians a means of leaving the country. They are going through an uneasy transitionary period at the moment, which has resulted in a short supply of food and books. Tertiary demand for English is huge, though college entry requirements are strict. Should you wish to work in this interesting, but unstable, country, contact the British Council resource centre in Tirana or Fakulteti Histori-Filogogja, Universiteti Tiranes, Tirana.

AUSTRIA

Minimum salary: 150-200 schillings per hour, 15,000 schillings per month on contract.

Tax and health insurance: Income tax is charged at the rate of approximately 40% of your salary.

Visa requirements: December 1993 heralded a change in visa requirements following Austria's membership of the EEA (European Economic Area). EC nationals are to be afforded the same opportunities as Austrians when applying for a job and work permits are no longer required. Within three months, foreigners are required to apply for an identity card for EEA citizens at the Austrian Immigration Office. For detailed information, contact your local Austrian embassy or consulate.

Accommodation: About 6,000 schillings per month for a one-bedroom flat in Vienna or Salzburg - slightly cheaper elsewhere. Apartments are difficult to find, but agencies can help.

English language newspaper: *New Gazette* (M).

Other information: Teachers in Austria are civil servants and therefore teaching posts used to be restricted to Austrian citizens. By law it is now possible for citizens of EEA members to be employed as teachers in Austrian state schools or universities. Knowledge of German is a basic entry requirement for such posts. Other opportunities exist for temporary employment as assistant teachers or under exchange schemes. For further details contact: Bundesministerium fur Unterricht und Kunst, Minoritenplatz 5, A-1010 Wien (Tel: 0222 531 200), the Central Bureau for Education Visits and Exchanges (CBEVE), Seymour Mews House, Seymour Mews, London W1H 9PE (Tel: 071 486 5102), or inlingua teacher service for Austria, Birmingham (Tel: 021 643 3472).

There are a number of private language schools which tend to be well organised and are often prepared to take on unqualified teachers - as long as they have a degree. There is also a demand for in-company business English, but a knowledge of German is a prerequisite for teaching in this area. Food is expensive in Austria, although restaurants and drinks are relatively cheap.

List of schools in Austria

Graz International Bilingual School (GIBS), Klusemannstrasse 25, A-8053, Graz. Tel: 0316/27 38 48-40. Fax: 38 47 29. GIBS is a German-English bilingual school. The student body is predominantly Austrian; GIBS seeks to give quality education, emphasising individual attention along with special attention to self-directed learning in workshops, cross-curricular teaching.

Innsbruck International High School, Schönberg 26, A-6141, Innsbruck.

Lizner International School Auhof, Aubrunnerweg 4, A-4040, Linz.

Salzburg International Preparatory School, Moosstrasse 106, A- 5020 , Salzburg.

American International School, Salmannsdorferstrasse 47, A-1190, Wien.

Vienna International School, Strasse Der Menschenrechte 1, A- 1220, Wien.

Danube International School, Gudrunstrasse 184, A-1100, Wien.

The International Montessori Preschool Vienna, Mahlerstrasse 9/13, A-1010 , Wien.

Kindergarten Alt Wien, Am Heumarkt 23, A-1030, Wien.

Amerika-Institut, Operngasse 4, 1010 Wien.

Austro-American Society, Stallburggasse 2, 1010 Wien.

Austro-British Society, Wickenburggasse 19, 1080 Wien.

Berlitz Sprachschulen Gesmbh, Graben 13, 1010 Wien.

Business Language Center, Trattnerhof 2, 1010 Wien.

Didactica Akademie F. Wirtschaft Und Sprachen, Schottenfeldgasse 13-15, 1070 Wien.

English For Kids, 232 Vienna, A-Baumgartner-Str. 44a/7042, 1230 Wien. Tel: 0222/6674579. Summer courses for kids from 5 to 18. English round the clock - have fun and learn!

English Language Centre Hietzing, In Der Hagenau 7, 1130 Wien.

inlingua Sprachschule, Neuer Markt 1, 1010 Wien.

Institut Cef, Garnisongasse 10, 1090 Wien.

International House Vienna, Schwedenplatz 2/55, 1010 Wien.

Jelinek & Jelinek Privatlehrinstitut, Rudolfsplatz 3, 1010 Wien.
Mini-Schools & English Language Day Camp, Postfach 160, 1220 Wien.
Sight & Sound Studio Gesmbh, Schubertring 12, 1031 Wien.
Spidi-Spracheninstitut Der Industrie, Lotringerstrasse 12, 1031 Wien.
Sprachstudio J.-J. Rousseau, Untere Viaduktgasse 43, 1030 Wien.
Sprachinstitut Vienna, Universitätsstr. 6, 1090 Wien.
Super Language Learning Sprachinstitut, Florianigasse 55, 1080 Wien.
Verband Wiener Volksbildung, Wiener Volkshochschulen, Hollergasse 22, 1150 Wien
Berufsforderungsinstitut, Kinderspitalgasse 5, 1090 Wien.

BULGARIA

Minimum salary: Currently Bulgarian EFL teachers charge an average of 100 Leva per private lesson (45 minutes), which is about £2.25. It should be noted that prices in Bulgaria are subject to constant growth as a consequence of the increasing inflation rate.

Tax and health insurance: The majority of teachers will be required to pay income tax. The rate of tax varies and is progressively increased. Its highest annual rate of 52% is applied to an annual income of 270,000 Bulgarian Leva which is equivalent to about £6,000. Health insurance is still not developed in Bulgaria apart from the general social security system. It is advisable to take out a private health insurance policy.

Visa requirements: All non-Bulgarian citizens need to obtain an entry visa, which may be obtained from the Bulgarian Consular Service in any country. Within 48 hours of arrival, all foreigners are required make an address registration with the respective Visa and Passport Office of Police. If your employer is Bulgarian you will be issued with a "labour visa", which permits residence for up to a year. In its present application, the authorities are rather lenient towards employees originating from the EC and US, however, as the system evolves, it may become more stringent.

Accommodation: Prices vary, depending on location, size and type of building, etc. Renting prices are currently US$ 5-15 per sq. metre. However, accommodation is often provided free with your contract of employment.

Other information: Air fares are usually paid for and some contracts may include free flights for your family. Conditions continue to be hard and inflation is still very high. Expect food shortages and fuel rationing, especially in winter. Other basic necessities are often unobtainable. However, Bulgarians are highly motivated in their desire to learn English. As a teacher, expect to have a high profile in the community. Bulgaria has a surprising developed ELT structure.

The Central Bureau for Educational Visits and Exchanges arrange for EFL teachers to work for the Bulgarian Ministry of Education in local ELMS. There are EFL opportunities in language centres such as the Institute for Foreign Students in Sofia which runs intensive courses for professionals. The British Council have recruited lecturers for Bulgarian universities, but generally need teacher trainers. The East European Partnership (EEP) also recruit volunteers to teach in Bulgaria.

List of schools in Bulgaria

Alliance, Centre for Teaching of Foreign Languages, 3 Slaveikov Square, 1000 Sofia.
Centre for Language Qualification, National Palace of Culture, Administrative Bldg., 2nd Floor, Room 131, Sofia.
Institute of Tourism, Park Ezero, 8000 Bourgas.
Meridian 22, 6 Dimiter Blagoev Street, Sofia.
Pharos Ltd., 2 "S.Vrachansky" Street, Vasrajdane Square, Sofia.

CROATIA

Minimum salary: Average rates for EFL teachers are difficult to establish, varying according to the size of school and its general reputation. Native English speakers are paid up to 50% more than locals - about 550 DM net per month.

Tax and health insurance: Paid by the employer, so teachers receive a net salary. They generally amount to 130% of gross income.

Visa requirements: Both visas and work permits are required, however, a work permit can be arranged on arrival in Croatia.

Accommodation: Average rent is 300 DM per month for a one-bedroom flat. Flats are not easy to find and landlords ask for rent be paid in foreign currency.

Other information: There is a significant increase in interest for native English speaking teachers throughout Croatia, but the outlook will depend very much on the political and economic situation. The British Council in Zagreb advises teachers who want to work in Croatia to contact them first to establish working conditions. Inflation rates are soaring and work permits can be difficult to obtain. Schools generally require their teachers to have a university degree and a teaching diploma.

List of schools in Croatia

Centar za strane jezike, Trg republike 2, 58000 Split.
Class, Jankomirska 1, 41000 Zagreb.
The English Workshop, Medulinska 61, 52000 Pula.
Lancon, Jurisiceva 1, 4000 Zagreb.
Linguae, Zeljka Marca 4, 51000 Rijeka.
Octopus, Savska 13, 41000 Zagreb.
Radnicko sveuciliste, Bozidar Maslaric, 5400 Osijek.
Verba, M. Gorkog 5, 51000 Rijeka.

CYPRUS

Minimum salary: Salaries vary significantly, with no minimum guidelines. Private institutes may in some cases pay only hourly or weekly and not at all during holiday periods.

Tax and health insurance: It is advisable for all non-Cypriot nationalities to take out personal insurance against illness and accident. Information on income tax rates can be obtained from the Ministry of Finance, Department of Inland Revenue, Nicosia.

Visa requirements: All non-Cypriots require work permits before taking employment in Cyprus. These are not normally granted by the government of Cyprus unless the vacant position cannot be filled by a Cypriot. It is the responsibility of the prospective employer to obtain a work permit for the applicant before engaging their services. Travel to Cyprus is inadvisable before a work permit has been issued.

Accommodation: Rented accommodation in the large towns is plentiful and is comparatively inexpensive. The rent of a furnished, three-bedroom house for example, in a respectable area should cost C£350-500. Unfurnished flats of a similar size and situation cost C£150-180, and shared accommodation is also widely available and inexpensive.

English language newspapers: Advertisements in the local English language newspapers may be helpful in finding employment and include *The Cyprus Mail* (P.O. Box 1144, Nicosia) and the *Cyprus Weekly* (Archbishop Makarios III Avenue, Mitsis Building 3, Office 216, Nicosia).

Other information: As a former British colony, English is widely spoken and the state system is fairly efficient. There are a number of private language schools which may recruit native English speakers. English is taught in the last years of the state primary schools and in the secondary schools but many students take additional private lessons and sit for a number of English examinations. The Ministry of Education normally requires teachers to have a degree in the subject being taught and it is therefore advisable for prospective teachers to clear their qualifications with the Ministry of Education in Nicosia.

List of schools in Cyprus

Ashley Janice, Arch Makarios III Avenue, Kanika Street,
CDA Coaching Centre, 5 Akritas Street, Larnaca.
Europa Language Centre, 3 Kypranoros Street, Nicosia.
Forum Language Centre, 47a Prodromou Street, Strovolos, Nicosia.
Linguaphone Institute, 21 P Katelari Street, Nicosia.
Masouras Private Institute, D Lipertus Street, Zenia Zoe Court, Flat 103, Paphos.
Proodos Institute, 2 Asopios Street, Nicosia.
Richmond Institute, 9 Chr Kannaouros Street, Dasoupolis, Nicosia.
Themis Tutorial, 6a Einar Gzerstad Street, Larnaca.
Thomas Michaelides, 52 Golgon Street, Limassol. Limassol.

THE CZECH REPUBLIC

Minimum salary: Foreign teachers are paid on the same basis as Czech teachers, which is about 3,000 Czech crowns per month after tax. Private lessons pay 100 crowns per hour.

Tax and health insurance: Medical insurance is usually paid by employers. Tax is charged at the rate of 15-20%, although you may be able to claim some of this back if your you are on a short-term contract.

Visa requirements: Not necessary for EU nationals, but other nationalities should apply to their Czech Embassy. Work and residence permits will usually be arranged by your employer. Teachers under contract will qualify for a residence permit which is necessary for any kind of employment. It is best to apply for this long-term residence permit prior to entry at any Czech Embassy. Application may also be made upon arrival as a tourist. When applying for the permit you will be asked to present your contract, as well as other documents including confirmation of housing arrangements, and that you hold no police record in the Czech Republic.

Accommodation: This may be subsidised or arranged by your employer - often with a local family or student hostel. Central Prague is short of housing and outlying areas tend to be drab concrete estates. Expect to pay 1,500 to 4,000 crowns a month in Prague. You must be prepared to travel fairly long distances to work.

Other information: The Czech Republic is the wealthier half of former Czechoslovakia, and enjoys a fairly stable political environment. There is a thriving EFL market, particularly in Prague and Brno. Teaching may well involve travelling to give in-company lessons. Expect to work 14-22 hours per week, mainly early mornings or early evening. Private lessons are easy to come by and there are numerous private language schools - some more reputable than others. The Bell School in Prague and ILC in Brno are two major international organisations now established in the Czech Republic. There are also many opportunities to work in the state sector in secondary schools. Although these offer competitive salaries and free accommodation, teachers are expected to pay their own travel expenses.

The Academic Information Agency (Tel: + 42 2 26 7010) helps foreign teachers find jobs at local schools. Foreign teachers are not expected to speak Czech and will tend to teach conversation classes, although you may also be required to teach grammar.

Outside the main cities there are still shortages of many essential food items, particularly fruit and vegetables. Books are expensive and in short supply. Transport and eating out is cheap, though in Prague restaurants tend to be busy.

Addresses

Ministry of Education, Karmelitska 9, 11000 Prague 1 - recruit for general state schools.
Pedagogicky Ustav Prahy, Na Porici 4, 11000 Prague 1 - recruit for state schools in the Prague area.
Pro-English, Mala Strana, 5 Hellichova (4th Floor), Prague.

FINLAND

Minimum salary: 100 markka an hour, 6,000 per month. Some employers pay airfares.
Tax and health insurance: Tax is 20-28%, while employers pay health insurance.
Visa requirements: A letter of employment must be submitted to any Finnish Embassy. An academic qualification is needed. Permits will initially be renewable after three months. It is possible to enter on a tourist visa, find employment, and then leave the country to apply for a work and residence permit.
Accommodation: Rent is usually paid at 60-75 markka per square metre. Expect to pay 1,200 markka per month, which includes heating. Some employers may pay your rent.
Other information: Most language schools and commercial colleges (Kauppaloulu) are concentrated in Helsinki and the south of Finland, usually offering evening courses to supplement state school English. Business English in particular is in great demand as Finland moves towards European integration. Many employers offer English language learning as a perk for their employees. As a result, many private English language schools arrange in-company work. Private in-company work lessons are also possible.

Teaching qualifications are not necessary, but there have been reports of schools neglecting teachers' legal rights when this is the case. Eating and drinking out are very expensive. Expect long, dark winters.

Addresses:

The Federation of Finnish-British Societies, Puistokatu 1bA, 00140 Helsinki, Tel: 639625, recruits qualified teachers year round.
Lansi-Suomen opisto, 32700 Huittinen. Tel: 8 3267866.
Richard Lewis Communications plc, 107 High Street, Winchester, Hants SO23 9AH, UK - recruits Business English teachers.

HUNGARY

Minimum salary: 15-25,000 forints per month for c. 20 hours/week in the private sector (15,000 in the state sector). Private lessons pay 300-800 forints an hour and are easy to find.
Tax and health insurance: 62%.
Accommodation: In Budapest there is a housing shortage and you should expect to pay 15-30,000 frorints per month

- potentially more than your basic salary. State sector and many private sector schools should subsidise your rent or provide free accommodation. Student hostels are a short-term solution.
Visa requirements: To prevent another glut of unemployed teachers, regulations have been tightened. You must have a job offer before entry. You will then be issued with one-month permit (costing $20), which can be extended at your local police station.
Other information: EFL is big business in Hungary and native speakers are needed in private schools, state schools and universities. English has replaced Russian as a requirement for university entrance. There are over 300 private language schools, many of which belong to The Chamber of Language Schools - a recognition body. For a fee of $20 they put teachers on a database which is circulated to members; contact: Eva Vajda, Nyelviskolak Kamaraja, Rath Gyorgy u.24, 1122 Budapest. Tel: 155 4664.

Teaching standards are generally high in Hungary. The larger private schools will expect good qualifications, but state primary and secondary schools take on unqualified assistants, which is a good way to get some experience, but not a great income. The state sector has no formal recruitment policy, so jobs are difficult to track down - try IATEFL Hungary. In secondary schools, you may need to speak Hungarian.

The East European Parnership (EEP), the Fulbright Program and the US Peace Corps recruit for voluntary work in Hungary (see p00). The Central Bureau in London recruit qualified teachers for summer camps.

Addresses:

The Budapest Pedagogical Institute, Horveth Mihaly Ter 8, Budapest 8 - recruits for schools in Budapest.
The English Teachers' Assoc. of the National Pedagogical Institute, Bolyai u.14, 1023 Budapest -
IATEFL Hungary, Kecskemet, Akademia Korut 20.L.31, 6000 Budapest.
IH Budapest, POB 95, Budapest 1364.
recruits for schools outside Budapest.
RLC International, 27-28 George Street, Richmond, Surrey T9 1HY, UK - recruits for Hungary.

ICELAND

Minimum salary: 80,000-90,000 krona per month.
Tax and health insurance: 38%.
Visa requirements: Your employer must arrange a work permit before you enter.
Accommodation: 20,000-30,000 krona per month for a one-bedroom flat, often part of a contract, otherwise hard to find.
Other information: Because of its limited population and high general level of English, EFL work is limited, especially in the current recession. Expect a harsh climate but if you enjoy outdoor living, thermal springs and volcanic landscape, this could be the place for you.

Malta

Minimum salary: 3,300-3,500 Maltese pounds per year.
Tax: 30%.
Visa restrictions: Work permits will be arranged by your employer.
Accommodation: 60 Maltese pounds per month for a bedsit.
English language newspaper: *The Times (D)*.
Other information: English is the official language on this tiny Mediterranean island. In theory, only Maltese nationals can teach here, but the surprisingly large EFL market, especially in the summer when foreign students take advantage of its relatively cheap courses and nice climate, often means a shortage of qualified teachers. Business English is also big. The Federation of English Language Teaching Organisations in Malta (FELTOM) monitors standards of schools on Malta. Tel: Sliema 356 310427.

List of schools in Malta

AM Language Studio, 14 Tigne St., Sliema. Tel: 318673.
inlingua, 9 Fawwara Lane, Off Tower Lane, Sliema. Tel: 313158.
Institute of English Language Studies, Manoel Court, Parisio St., Sliema. Tel: 335367.
NSTS English Language Centre, 220 St Paul St., Valletta.
Revival English Language Institute, Trinity Hall, Taliana Lane, Gzira. Tel: 331853.

Norway

Minimum salary: 95 krona an hour, up to 400 krona for business English.
Tax and health insurance: 35-40%.
Visa requirements: Very hard to obtain unless you live with a Norwegian or have a specialised skill, such as in EAP.
Accommodation: 2,500 krona a month for a one-bedroom flat in Oslo, 2,000 krona elsewhere.
Other information: Children learn English from age 9, but English language tuition tends to be informal evening classes. With possible entry into the EC, there has been a growth in business English. There is fierce competition for jobs, and unemployment is high.

Poland

Minimum salary: Average salary when working for a state school is about 1,500,000 zloty (about US $80) a month for about 18 contact hours a week. Some schools may offer "extra hours" and may pay more for this. The basic salary may be slightly more in "social schools", which are funded by the Ministry of Education and parents (60%), and local regional authorities (40%). Private language schools pay more - 120,000-150,000 zloty per hour.

Tax and health insurance: No taxation for two years. Health insurance, if paid by the school, amounts to 48% of total salary, however, schools are very reluctant to cover this, and it is generally advisable to obtain your own insurance cover from your native country.
Visa requirements: Visas have been abolished and there is no need for them if a teacher comes for a short period of time (say a month). Any period longer than this will require the school to apply, on a teacher's behalf, for a work permit to Wojewodzke Urzad Pracy, 44 Czerniakowska Street, 00-717 Warszawa. It usually takes a about a month to come through. A teacher may also get a "working visa" before their departure at their local Polish consulate with employers' sponsorship.
Accommodation: About 2,000,000-3,000,000 zloty for a one-bedroom flat - less with a family or when a school arranges it. If you work in the state sector through a scheme or voluntary organisation, like the VSO or Teachers for Poland, you will be offered accommodation with board or its equivalent. Finding accommodation in the large cities is not easy and is often expensive, and it should be remembered that gas and electricity are expensive. In order to live at a reasonable standard in a large city in Poland, expect to spend an average of 8-10 million zloty per month.
Other information: If you want to find a state post in a school on your own, contact: The Ministry of National Education, Department of International Cooperation, Mrs Katarzyna Malec, Al. I Armii Wojska Polskiego 25, Warszawa, Poland (Tel:+ 297241 ext. 655).

Conditions are improving steadily in Poland. With the collapse of communism and the move to a market economy, there has been a huge demand for English and an increase in the number of private language schools. The Polish Association for Standards in English (PASE), monitors schools in Poland. Native English speaking teachers are in demand, and qualifications are not always essential. Now that Britain has lifted visa restrictions to Poles visiting the UK, British English has the edge on US English. There is a need for business English, and in-company work can be extremely lucrative. The British Council and the Peace Corps have invested heavily in Poland. There are opportunities for teachers in the state sector, although pay is likely to be low.

The Central Bureau and EEP also recruit for Poland.

List of schools and addresses

American English School, Oddzial Warszawa-Cztery, Kondratowicza 25a m 33, 03-285 Warszawa.
Angloschool, ul Elblaska 65/84, Warszawa.
Bakalarz, Prywatne Studium Jezykowe, ul Rakowiecka 45/25, 02-528 Warszawa. Tel: 489 889
British Council English Language Centre, Warsaw Technical University, ul. Filtowa 2, 00-611 Warszawa. Tel: 25 82 87.
Elan, Mokotowska 9 m 6, Warszawa. Tel: 25 19 91.
English Unlimited, Osrodek Nauczania Jez Obcych, Margerytki 52, 04-908 Warszawa. Tel: 40 55 19.

International House - Bydgoszcz, Pl Piastowski 5, 85-012 Bydgoszcz. Tel: 22 35 15.
Langhelp, Al Jerozolimskie 23/34, Warszawa. Tel: 21 44 34.
Omnibus, Pl Wolnosci 5, 61-738 Poznan. Tel: 52 79 08.
World, ul Basztowa 17, 31-143 Krakow. Tel: 22 91 61.
Yes, ul Chelmonskiego 6 m 18, Lodz. Tel: 43 95 26.

ROMANIA

Conditions remain difficult - inflation is high without pay increases to match. Although there is a lack of resources to develop English training, there is a great deal of interest in the language and Romanian schools have always taught two foreign languages from the age of seven. Nearly all opportunities are in the state sector with local salaries. The British Council has a local operation, the Soros Foundation has set up a school Timisoara and the EEP sends volunteers (see p79).

Addresses:

ABB Power Ventures Ltd, CS-MR/PS, PO Box 8131, CH-8050 Zurich, Switzerland - recruits for in-company teachers in Romania.
Technical University, Timisoara - funded by the Soros Foundation.

SERBIA AND MONTENEGRO

Minimum salary: Average rates of pay for EFL teachers range from DEM 150-200 monthly in private language schools.
Visa requirements: Contact your local Yugoslav Embassy for details.

Accommodation: For a flat of approximately 40 sq. metres, it will cost roughly DEM 150 per month.
Other information: Many private language schools in Yugoslavia will welcome EFL teachers, as there continue to be a high demand for such teachers.

SKOPJE (MACEDONIA)

Still struggling for international recognition, its economy is unhealthy. Average monthly salaries of $100. Despite the volatility of the region and the low rates of pay, the British Council reports growing interest in its resource centre in Skopje.

SLOVAKIA

With a weaker economy than the Czech republic, conditions are much more difficult. The capital Bratislava's proximity to Vienna has led to a demand for German and private English schools are scarce. English is more popular in the eastern town of Kosice. The EEP and the Peace Corps recruit teachers on a voluntary basis (see p79).

SLOVENIA

Minimum salary: £7/hour freelance, £500/month nett (21 teaching hours/week.
Tax and health insurance: Income tax of 12-20%, social security charges of 22.6%. Foreigners have the same right to health services as Slovenes.
Visa requirements: A work permit is required. Contact your local embassy/consulate.
Accommodation: One room - about £180/month; two bedroom apartment - about £300/month, plus bills.
Other information: As this was the first state of the former Yugoslavia to gain independence, it is the most stable. Most foreign teachers work freelance and schools will usually expect teachers to have a degree in English.

List of schools in Slovenia

ACCENT on Language, Ljubljanska 36, 61230 Domzale. Tel: 061 712 658.
Babylon, Komenskega 11, 61000 Ljubljana.Tel: 061317980
CTJ, Vilharjeva 21, 61000 Ljubljana. Tel: 061 317 865.
CZT, Gospodarska zbornica Slovenije, 69252 Radenci. Tel: 069 65 059.

SWEDEN

Minimum salary: Every language school employer pays union rates, even if none of the employees is a union member. At present this works out at just over 100 krona/45 minute lesson. This can be supplemented with private lessons.
Tax and health insurance: Payable by your employer, roughly 30% of your income. Local taxes can be high.

Visa requirements: A work permit must be obtained before you enter Sweden. To get one takes about six weeks and it will be initially valid for nine months. Permits are not possible to obtain for private language schools. International Language Services, based at the Salisbury School of English, arrange visas for the teachers they recruit for Folk University in Stockholm. The Folk University places teachers in its network of adult institutions, known as the British Centres, throughout the country.

Accommodation: 2,000 Krona per month for a shared flat, probably a third of your income. Finding accommodation can be a real problem, especially in Stockholm. Make sure your employer helps you find somewhere. The standard of housing is invariably high.

Other information: Swedish children learn English from age 10. General English courses were subsidised by council grants, but cut-backs have made lessons more expensive. As a result, schools have had a drop in numbers. Nevertheless, the prospect of joining the EC has maintained demand, especially for business English. Many companies now have language departments. Adult education is also very popular in Sweden. Eating out and drinking is very expensive. Sweden is good for the outdoor life, but the winters are long.

SWITZERLAND

Minimum salary: 30-38 Swiss francs per hour, up to 125 SF in some schools. Teaching higher level classes is better paid.

Tax and health insurance: Basic of 18-20%. This varies from canton to canton. Contact the local canton, which should have an office that deals with foreign workers. Some cantons levy a church tax, although this can be claimed back. A 35% 'withholding tax' is levied on interest from bank accounts, so it is advisable to invest money elsewhere.

Visa requirements: This is a problem. Although your employer should arrange a work permit, processing it is particularly rigorous. You must have employment before you enter the country. However, those in the country on a student visa are allowed to work a few hours a week.

Accommodation: 1,800-2,000SF per month in Geneva for a two-bedroom flat, less elsewhere.

Other information: Because of the work permit situation, most native English speakers tend to be married to Swiss nationals or teach part time in addition to other employment. Teaching conditions vary between the 26 autonomous education departments, but state-run schools and colleges require Swiss qualifications. Because the Swiss must learn the other languages of the country before English at school, many go to private schools for English tuition. So teaching opportunities tend to be in private shools teaching general EFL. The RSA and Trinity certificates are becoming more widely recognised.

Although riddled with bureaucracy and one of the most expensive countries in Europe, employers are usually generous about maternity leave and sick pay. English

Teachers Association of Switzerlgnd (ETAS) publish a booklet entitled *Legally Lost? Brief Information for English Teachers Working in Switzerland,* available from Silvia Dingwall, Stermenstr.7, 5415 Nussbaumen, Switzerland.

List of schools in Switzerland

Alpha Sprachstudio, Freidstrasse 72, 8032 Zurich.
Bell School, Zurich Todistrasse 1, 8002 Zurich. Tel: 1 2810781.
Ecole Club Migros Geneve, 3 rue du Prince, 1204 Geneva. Tel: 22 286555.
Ecole Club Migros Lausanne, Place de la Palud 22. Case Postale 313, 1000 Lausanne 17. Tel: 21 202631.
Ecole Club Migros Neuchatel, 3 rue du Musee, 2001 Neuchatel. Tel: 38 258348.
ELCRA-BELL, Chemin des Sports 8 1203 Geneva. Tel: 22 3441225.
Migros Klubschule Aarau, Herzogstrasse 26, 5000 Aarau.Tel: 64 246431.
Migros Klubschule Baden, Hochhaus Hotel Linde, Hellingerstr. 22, 5400 Baden. Tel: 56 226206.
Migros Klubchule Basel, Jurastrasse 4, 4053 Basel.Tel: 61 350066.
Migros Klubschule Bern, Marktgasse 46, 3011 Bern.Tel: 31 222021.
Migros Klubschule Luzern, Schweizerhofquai 1, 6004 Luzern. Tel: 41 515656.
Scuola Club Migros Lugano, Via Pretorio 15,6900 Lugano. Tel: 91 227621.
TASIS, The American School in Switzerland, CH 6926 Monagnola-Lugano. Tel: 91 546471.

TURKEY

Minimum salary: A CTEFLA teacher can expect a salary of about £400-500 month (in lira) in a private language school, and slightly more in a private secondary school in Istanbul. Rates are slightly lower in Ankara (a cheaper city) and you may be poorly paid in Izmir. Provincial rates vary, but are generally less than Istanbul and Ankara. All Turkish salaries are quoted net of tax, normally in Turkish Lira. University ELT posts can be very well paid indeed by Turkish standards, but there is a correspondingly long queue of applicants.

Tax and health insurance: Salaries are quoted net of tax. There is a legal requirement for schools to register their teachers under the state social security scheme (if the teacher requests it). It is not necessary to have a work permit to be registered. However, the service provided is generally considered to be very inadequate. It is worth investing in private health insurance policies and visits to private health centres can be very reasonably priced. Dentists are very expensive. There are health schemes available for Turkish insurance companies, and some organisations are beginning to offer them as part of the overall package. Be sure to discuss this point at interview.

Visa requirements: Visas and work permits are necessary. A work visa must be obtained from a Turkish Consulate in your country before departure. There is a charge for this service. The necessary documents for this should be provided by the Turkish employer. Residence permits are arranged on arrival. Owing to the length of time it can take for schools in the provinces to get teachers' qualifications processed (a necessary condition for the issuing of a work visa), many schools ask their prospective teachers to come in on a tourist visa and arrange work visas after arrival. The school pays a fine regularly until the documents are processed, as the teacher is technically working illegally. The legal responsibility for acquiring working permission rests with the teacher (even though all schools do the work for their teachers), so a foreign teacher has no legal defence against breach of contract by the school.

Accommodation: Most schools provide accommodation for their teachers, often in shared flats. Accommodation in Istanbul costs 50% more than other areas. Most flats in Turkey are unfurnished - your employer should help you find furnished accommodation.

English language newspaper: *Turkish Daily News* (D)

Other information: Turkey has a huge and growing EFL market as it tries to shift closer to the European Community and develops its tourist infrastructure. Despite the boom, unqualified teachers are not in great demand - except for short-term, holiday "bonus" work. Generally a degree, plus an RSA or Trinity certificate in TEFL will be the minimum requirement in order to obtain a work permit.

The 18-25 age group is growing fast, and with it a demand for English. The English medium secondary schools and colleges generally offer better terms and conditions than private language schools.

With national unemployment of around 15%, your pay may be 2-3 times the rate of a local university professor, even if by western standards this is a moderate wage. Inflation fluctuates dramatically, so check that wages are adjusted.

Istanbul tends to be the most popular destination, and is relatively expensive - and polluted. Istanbul, Izmir and Ankara, are fairly western orientated, however, further east, in addition to the Kurdish unrest, life is still fairly traditional and is also predominantly Muslim, so women may find conditions difficult. Dealing with sex, politics and religions should be avoided in the classroom.

List of schools in Turkey

Akademi School of English, PK 234, 21001 Bahar Sokar No 2, Diyarbakir. Tel: (90) 83242297. Fax: 83217908.
Ankara University, Rektorlugu, Beslevler, Ankara. Tel: 41234361.
Best English, Mesrutiyet Caddesi no 2/8, Ankara. Tel: 4172536.
Cadgil, Yabanci Dil Ogritum Kurumu, Altiparmak Rihtim, Pastanesi Ustu, Bursa. Tel: 24122522. Also: Setbasi Akdemir Sokak, Bursa. Tel 90 741 225220.
Dilko English Centres, PO Box 152, Kadilkoy, 81300 Istanbul. Tel: 1 3380170.
Elissa English, Ihsaniye Mah 41, Sokak 48, Bandirma, Balikesir.

The English Centre, Rumeli Cad. 92/4, Zeki Bey Apt., Osmanbey, Istanbul. Tel: 1 470983.
English Fast, via Mr. K. Humphries, 9 Denmark Street, London WC2H 6LS, UK.
Evrim, Ozel Evrim Yabanci, Dil Kurasi, Cengiz Topel Caddesi 8/2, Camlibel, Mersin. Tel: 74121893.
International School, Eser Apt.A Blok Kasap, Sokak 1617, Esentepe, Istanbul.
Istanbul Turco-British Association, Suleyman Nazif Sokak 68, Nisantasi, 80220 Istanbul. Tel: 1 132 8200.
Istanbul University, Rektorlugu Beyarzit, Istanbul. Tel: 1 522 1489.
Kapani Ishani, Cumhuriyet Buvari, Gumruk, Izmir.
Kumlu Dersanerleri, Bursa Merkez, Basak Caddesi, Bursa. Tel: 241 20465.
Kent English, Mithatpasa Cad. 46/3, Kizilay, Ankara.
New Kent English, 1477 No. SK 32, Alsancak, Izmir. Tel: 51632737.

COUNTRIES OF THE FORMER USSR

THE BALTIC STATES

As Estonia, Latvia and Lithuania re-establish independence, tax systems remain minimal or non-existent. Accommodation remains a real problem, so if it is part of your contract it will be a huge bonus. Otherwise you may find yourself in a student hostel. English is in demand, and there are a number of private language schools being set up, often by cooperatives of state teachers who work in them in the evenings. Universities are also crying out for teachers. In Latvia and Lithuania, the English syllabus is part of the school curriculum which is being rewritten, but expect local salaries if you work in the state system. Business English and private lessons pay better, possibly even in hard currency. Non-qualified teachers can also find work giving conversation lessons. Conditions are changing quickly in the Baltics, but books remain in short supply. Nevertheless, motivation is high and the level of English is surprisingly good. The Peace Corps are active in the Baltics.

ESTONIA

Minimum salary: 1,500 kroone per month (around $100).
Visa requirements: None. Work permits are easy to obtain.
Other information: Because of Estonia's close ties with Finland, it is better off economically and English is widespread. Private language schools are crying out for teachers. The Soros Foundation has a centre in Tallin, where the British Council plans to open a resource centre.

LATVIA

Minimum salary: 8,000 roubles per month (about $45). Experienced teachers could earn up to 50,000 roubles with in-company work.
Visa requirements: Work permits are easy to obtain and

visas can be purchased.

Other information: Teaching material is scarce, although the government is trying to get publishers to print using local materials. The government are keen to promote English signs, which were in Russian and Latvian, and are now in English and Latvian, but Russian remains the second language. The British Council has resource centres in Lazaetes, Lela and Riga, but economically the country is in a mess.

LITHUANIA

Minimum salary: Expect the equivalent of $50 a month.
Visa requirements: As Estonia.
Other information: The country's currency problems mean materials and foreign expertise are hard to come by. The Soros Foundation has a centre in Vilnius, where the British Council has a resource centre.

GEORGIA

Minimum salary: 5,000 roubles per month (the equivalent of $15).
Tax and health insurance: Tax is at source and quite low. Private health insurance is recommended.
Visa requirements: Entry visas are issued on arrival. Work permits can be obtained by your employer.
Accommodation: Usually part of a contract, or expensive for foreigners.
Other information: Conditions are difficult in Georgia, and there is civil war in the north west. Inflation is very high, but English is in demand and some private lessons may pay in hard currency. Take your own materials as these are very scarce. There are also fuel shortages, hence little heating and public transport. The British Council in Tbilisi will give advice to those who are tempted by this adventurous but cultured and friendly country where teachers are warmly appreciated. Contact David Rowson at the British Council centre. Tel: Tbilisi 78832 230232. Fax: 78832 983250.

RUSSIA

Minimum salary: 3,000 roubles per month (about $6).
Tax: There are plans to tax foreigners at 40% of hard currency earnings, but if paid a local salary, this will not affect you.
Visa requirements: Single entry visas only can be obtained from your local consulate (£10-15). Work permits are not necessary.
Accommodation: Usually provided, but often in student hostels. A flat in Moscow will cost at least $150 a month.
Other information: The rouble has plummeted in value, as the Russian economy faces hyper-inflation. Russia, like the other former states of the USSR, is desperate for English teachers but lacks the resources to meet demand. The local salary quoted above would require teachers in Moscow and St. Petersburg to give private lessons to supplement this basic income. Most native-English speakers are only taken on as language assistants. Teaching methods are still traditional and a knowledge of

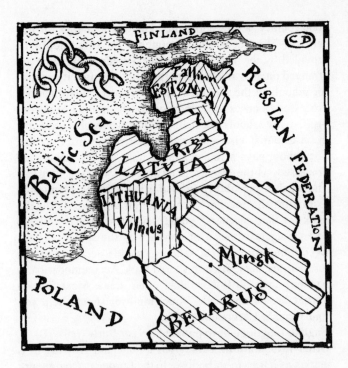

Russian helps. The Linguistic Association of Teachers of English at the University of Moscow (LATEUM) and the Moscow Association of Applied Linguistics (Maal) aim to provide cooperation between English teachers inside Russia and abroad.

List of institutions in Russia

Moscow MV Lomonosov University, Sparrow Hills, Moscow 117234.
Director of Centre for Intensive Foreign Language Instruction, Sparrow Hills, Building 2, Moscow119899.
St Petersburg University, Universitetskaya, Naberezhnaya 7/9, B-164, St Petersburg 199164.
Russian Academy of Sciences, Universitetskaya Naberezhnaya 5, St Petersburg 199034.
St Petersburg University of Humanities and Social Sciences, Ulitsa Fuckhika 16, St Petersburg 192238.

UKRAINE

Minimum salary: The equivalent of $1 an hour. The official minimum salary is the equivalent of $8 a month.
Tax: Paid by your employer if you are on contract, otherwise a complex system of six different taxes.
Visa requirements: If you are invited by an employer, you do not need a work permit. Visas are issued on arrival.
Accommodation: The equivalent of $50 a month for a modest flat.
Other information: There are many private language schools in the Ukraine and teachers should find work easily. Business English is lucrative and foreign teachers can have a good standard of living. The British Council are setting up a centre in Kiev. The Slavonic Center runs business and children's classes and plans to run a summer camp. Contact Eugeny Samartsev, The Slavonic Center, 16 Rozi Luxemburg, 252021 Kiev. Fax: 2779797.

LATIN AMERICA

Despite the diversity of this huge area, the best opportunities for native speaker teachers are with the established organisations, such as the Culturas, the LAURELS schools or the Binational centres. International House and ELS also have Latin American operations. The Latin American British Cultural Institutes (LABCI) have centres in Brazil, Uruguay, Mexico and Paraguay. These Cultural Institutes (Culturas) have close ties with the British Council. Some have British Council postings.

Culturas are non-profit making and generally have better conditions than private language schools. Culturas will usually offer teachers a rent allowance for at least the first six months, and help find accommodation. Private health schemes are also offered. They mainly recruit locally and prefer teachers with the RSA certificate. In Mexico and Brazil the Culturas may run RSA Diploma courses. Other centres may be prepared to take on and train unqualified teachers.

The Latin American Union of Registered English Language Schools (LAURELS) was founded in Brazil in 1987 and is an association of private self regulating language schools. The schools are thus reputable and offer good conditions.

Throughout Latin America, telephones are cheap locally but expensive externally. Numbers frequently change. Remember, however, that making disparaging remarks about Latin American countries is considered highly offensive amongst the local population. Remember also that the Latin American academic year runs from February to December.

ARGENTINA

Minimum salary: The equivalent of $1,000-1,500 per month. The union-demanded minimum wage for local labour is $536 per month.
Tax and health insurance: Local medical care is expensive. Private medical insurance is recommended.
Visa requirements: The government welcomes qualified immigrants, especially Brits (despite the Falklands conflict) You can apply for a residents permit after two years.
Accommodation: Averages at a third of your salary and hard to find.
English language newspapers: *Buenos Aires Herald (D).*
Other information: The Argentinian economy is forecast to grow 5% next year, and inflation is low by Latin American standards. There is a demand for Cambridge exams, which private schools have offered since the British Council closed during the Falklands Crisis. The Council now runs teacher training courses. The standard of English in Argentina is generally high, so few teachers are recruited from outside the country. You will be in more demand if you are qualified and speak Spanish.

BOLIVIA

Opportunities occasionally arise in Bolivia, one of Latin America's poorer countries. Positions are usually in English medium secondary schools or with voluntary organisations (see p79).

BRAZIL

Minimum salary: Varies from about $300 per month to $1000 per month or more depending on experience, qualifications and type of school. The hourly rate depending on the incremental level is between Pds 5-6.60. Teachers are paid 13 months in the year. Many teachers supplement their income with private classes which can be quite lucrative. Inflation is currently running at about 30% a month, so check pay is adjusted and issued regularly.
Tax and health insurance: Health insurance can be taken out locally with different rates for different levels of cover. There are a number of other benefits offered by well-established institutes, including contributions to private medical insurance schemes. Members of the middle class take out private medical insurance and the recommended schemes are: Golden Cross, Bradesco Saude, Sulamerica, Itau and Unimed. Tax is levied at around 25% of the salary, which includes a contribution to the national medical scheme.
Visa requirements: At least six months should be set aside for getting a working visa. Work can be obtained illegally by visitors on tourist visas, but is obviously not to be recommended. Good schools are unlikely to take the risk of employing such a teacher. It also leaves the teacher vulnerable to exploitation and the possibility of an eight day deportation order. Teachers should contact: Dr Paulo Cavalcant Pessoa, Chefe do Setor de Estrangeiro, Departamento de Policia Federal, Av Martin Luther King - 321, Cais do Apolo, Recife - PE, 50080-090. Tel: + 55 081 424 1444.
Accommodation: Some schools provide free accommodation. To rent a two-bedroom flat in Boa Viagem for example, a middle-class district of Recife, will currently cost in the region of Pds 130-200 per month.
English language newspaper: *Brazil Herald* (D).
Other information: Contributing to the huge demand for fee-paying English courses in Brazil is the poor teaching in the state sector, caused by crowded classrooms, under-funding, poorly paid teachers and a maximum of two hours a week on the timetable adding up to insufficient input in the secondary sector. The secondary level timetable is devised in such a way that a child studies in either the morning or the afternoon, but not both. This leaves plenty of time that both child and parent want to fill in a constructive manner.

The recession has made competition for jobs even more intense and a foreign language qualification is a definite advantage on your CV. One of the most noticeable features of the commercial sector is the large number of well-trained non-native speakers. They are certainly needed as the requirements for obtaining visas for foreign teachers are lengthy and bureaucratic. As the UK has a large pool of itinerant EFL teachers, it is frustrating for British schools not to be able to employ more of them. Qualified teachers are guaranteed as much work as they want, but are no doubt put off by the negative effect of inflation on living standards. In fact Brazil is a safe and professionally rewarding country in which to work. Teachers will not save a great deal, but they can enjoy a reasonable standard of living in a country which is seldom dull. Brazil is highly susceptible to American cultural influences and English is perceived to as the key to membership of an international culture club.

Much is made of the activities of criminals by expatriates, the local media and foreign press. Care should obviously be taken not to flash money or display expensive cameras, watches or bags.

Some useful background reading can be found in the *South American Handbook* and Fodor's *Guide to Brazil*. Internal flights within Brazil are extremely expensive and if you intend to travel a lot on your own account it is worth investigating air passes, which are only issued outside Brazil, by airline companies.

List of schools in Brazil

Cultura Inglesa - Goiana, Rua 86 No. 07 - Setor 74083-330 Goiana - Go. Tel: 55 62 241-4516, Fax: 241-2582. Member Brazilian Association of Culturas Inglesas, PET, FCE, CAE, CPE, CEELT centre, Communicative Learner-centred Approach, Teamwork Highly Valued.
Sbci, Av Dos Andradas, 536 Juiz De Fora Mg.
Sbci, R Antonio De Alburquerque 746, Belo Horizonte Hg.
Sbci, Rua Do Progresso 239, Recife Pe.
Sbci, Rua Raul Pompeia 231, Rio De Janeiro Rj.
Sbci, Ponta Verde, R Eng Marion De Gusmao 603, Maceio Al.
Ccli, R Dr Silvio Henrique Braune 15, Nova Friburgo Rj.
Cultura Inglesa, R Ponta Grossa 1565, Dourados Ms.
Sbci, Rua Marechal Deodoro 1326, Franca Sp.
Sbci, R Visc De Inhauma 980, Ribeirao Preto Sp.
Sbci, Rua Julia Da Costa 1500, Curitiba Pr.
Sbci, R Humberto De Campos, Campo Grande Ms.
Sbci, Pca Rosalco Ribeiro 10, Maceio Al.
Sbci, R Joao Pinheiro 808, Uberlandia Mg.
Centro De Cultura Inglesa, Rua 12 De Outubro 227, Cuiaba Mt.
Sbci, Av Rio Grande Do Sul 1411, Joao Possoa Pb.
Sbci, Av Guilherme Ferreira 650, Uberaba Mg,
Sbci, Rua Maranhao 416, Sao Paulo Sp.
Sbci, Rua Acu 495, Petropolis, Natal Rn.
Cultura Inglesa, Av. Barao De Maruim 761, Aracaju, Sergipe 49015-040. Tel: 55 97 224-7360/4637. Fax:

221-1195. Member ABCI/ centre for Cambridge and Oxford EFL exams/ self-access centre with multi-media computers/ student body of 900.
Sbci, R Plinio Moscoso 945, Jardim Apopema, Salvador Ba.
Sbci, R Ana Bilmar 171, Aldeota, Fortaleza Ce.
Sbci, R Jeronimo Coelho 233, Joinville Sc.
Sbci, Av Simoa Gomes 400, Garanhuns Pe,
Inst Academico De Cultura Inglesa, R Conde De Porto Alegre 59, Duque De Caxias Rj.
Cultura Inglesa, Av Ouze 1281, Ituiutaba Mg.
Sbci, Seps 709/908 Conjunto B, Brasilia Df.
Sbci, R. Sao Sebastiao 1530, Sao Carlos Ä Sp.
Sbci, R Mal Floriano Peixoto 433, Blumenau Sc.
Sbci, Av Rio Branco 17, Haringa Pr.
Cultura Inglesa, Av Bernardo Vieira De Melo 2101, Jaboatao Pe.
Sbci, Casa Forte, Av 17 De Agosto 223, Recife Pe.
Cultura Inglesa, R. Natal 553 V. Municipal, Arianopolis, Manaus ÄAm.
Cambridge Sociedade Brasileira do Cultura Inglesa, Rua Piaui 1234, Londrina 86020 320 Pr. Tel: 043 324-1092.Fax: 324-8391. University of Cambridge authorised Centre for PET, FCE, CAE, CPE and Oxford/ARELS Oral Examinations.
Sbci, R Paula Xavier 501, Ponta Grossa Pr.
Sbci, Praca Mauricio Cardoso 49, Porto Alegre Rs.
Cultura Inglesa, R. Eduardo De Moraes 147, Bairro Novo Olinda Pe.
Cultura Inglesa, Av Tiradentes 670, 36300 Sao Joao Del Rei MG. Tel: (032) 371-4377, Fax: (032) 371-4377.
Sbci, Av. Gov. Jose Malcher 1094, Belem Pa.
Centro De Cultura Inglesa, Av Guapore 2.236, Cacoal - RO, CEP 78.975-000. Tel: 55 (69) 441-2833. Fax: 441-5346. Always pioneering. Not only an English learning centre, but also a teaching training centre since 1981 in a town founded 22 years ago.
Cultura Inglesa, Visinde De Alburquerque 205, Madalena, Recife Pe.
Britannia Special English Studies - Juniors, R. Barao da Torre 599 - Rio de Janeiro, CEP 22411, Rj. Tel:55 21 239-8044. Fax: 55 21 286-0861. Special English classes for children and adolescents, small groups, modern classroom resources, video classes, trips to England. Preparation for PET Cambridge exam.
Cultura Inglesa, Rua Goias 1507, Londrina Pr, School House, Rua 4, No. 80 Esq. Rua 3, Goiania Go.
Universitas, R Gongalves Dias 858, Belo Horizonte Mg.
Seven Language & Culture, R. Bela Cintra 898, Consolacao, Sao Paulo Ä Sp.
Britannia Schools, Rua Garcia D'Avila 58, Ipanema, Rio De Janeiro RJ, 22421. Tel: (55 21) 511-0940. Fax: (55 21) 511-0893. Six high quality schools - Rio, Sao Paulo, Porto Alegre - general English, executives, public exam preparation. Further education schemes for teachers.
Ibi, Sep Sul Entrequadra 710/910, Brasilia Df,
Casa Branca, R Machado De Assis 372 Boqueirao, Santos Sp.
CelÄLep, Av. Cidade Jardim 625, Sao Paulo Ä Sp.
English Forever, R. Rio Grande Do Sul, 356, Pituba, Salvador Ä Ba.

Britannic English Course, R Joao Ivo Da Silva 125, Recife Pe.

Liberty English Centre, R Amintas De Barros 1059, Curitiba Pr.

Britannia Special English Studies, R Dr. Timoteo, 752 Moinhos De Vent, Porto Alegre Ä Rs.

Instituto Britanico, R. Dep Carvalho Deda 640, Salgado Filho, Aracaju Ä Se.

CHILE

Minimum salary: 150,000-200,000 pesos per month. Inflation is about 30%. Private lessons will pay 1,000-3,000 pesos per hour. One-to-one lessons in multi-national companies are in demand and are potentially lucrative.

Tax and health insurance: Payable by employer.

Visa requirements: These are easy to obtain at any time for British or Irish nationals, but are harder for US nationals. Your employer can arrange work permits. Temporary work and residents permits are issued for one year, when they can be extended to become permanent permits.

Accommodation: 60,000-70,000 pesos per month for a studio flat in the cities.

Other information: It is not recommended to go to Chile without employment unless you have contacts in the country. English is more in demand for the new "democratic" Chile, and private schools have mushroomed.

The British Culturas and North American Cultural Institutes are major employers throughout Chile, although outside Santiago and Vina del Mar there are few, if any, opportunities for private school work. In the two main cities expect a mixture of in-class and in-company teaching. Santiago is well stocked with English language bookshops, and the Instituto Chileno Britanico has a good library of teaching material.

The Chileans consider themselves "the English of South America", and value privacy. They are not very flamboyant. Chile is one of the most wealthy and stable of the South American countries.

COLOMBIA

Minimum salary: In all major cities prospects for EFL teachers are good, as there are plenty of jobs available. However, it should be pointed out that the quality and conditions of these jobs is variable. The average monthly salary for a full-time teacher at the British Council is in the region of 750,000 pesos (approximately £650) - probably one of the highest figures among the institutions in Bogota. The British Council and many other institutes pay 14 salaries per year.

Tax and health insurance: With a normal work visa and earnings above 250,000 pesos, teachers will pay tax according to their salaries and this could be anything from 8% upwards. If the employer is not in a private health scheme, it is strongly recommended for the teacher to join one, since the public health service is poor - annual cost of approximately 300,000 Colombian pesos.

Visa requirements: All non-Columbian teachers are required to hold a permit. the British Council arranges a Service Visa for its employees. Any reputable institute will obtain a work permit and visa for its teachers. If an institute is reluctant or unable to obtain such papers, it is probably not a very reliable concern.

Accommodation: In Bogota and most other cities, expect to pay about 250,000 pesos for a one-bedroom flat in a reasonably exclusive area of the city.

Other information: Red tape is a problem and delays in issuing of visas and work permits must be expected. Colombia's bad reputation is exaggerated. However, problems do exist and the British Embassy does put certain travel restriction on British Council employees form time to time and certain areas of the country are best avoided. It is also advisable to register with your appropriate Embassy on arrival

There is a growing professional class that need English in Colombia, and despite low wages, teachers can have a good standard of living. There are English Medium International Schools, Centro Americanos and British Council centres in Bogota and Cali. The Council are coordinating the Colombian Framework of English and English Language Teaching Officer training scheme with the ODA, which will help establish more ELT resource centres. However, most opportunities are in private language schools. Many of these have difficulty in getting work permits unless teachers are qualified and experienced, and can be poorly paid. American English may be preferred.

A fascinating country, but some areas are definitely no-go. Check with your Embassy before you go to remote locations. It is not advisable to take children as kidnappings are possible. The main cities have bad traffic problems and water and electricity cuts are common. Electrical goods and cars are expensive.

List of schools in Colombia

Academia Ingles Para Niños, Calle 106 No 16Ä26, Bogota.

Advanced Learning Service, Transversal 20 No 120Ä15, Bogota.

Aprender Ltda, Calle 17 No 4Ä68 Ql. 501, Bogota.

Aspect, Calle 79a No 8Ä26, Bogota.

BBC De Londres, Calle 59 No 6Ä21, Bogota.

Babel, Avenida 15 No 124Ä49 Cf. 205, Bogota.

Bi Cultural Institute, Avenida 7 No 123Ä97 Of. 202, Bogota.

Britanico Americano De Idomas, Avenida 13 No 103Ä62, Bogota.

Carol Keeney, Carrera 4 No 69Ä06, Bogota.

Centro Audiovisual De Ingles Chelga, Calle 137 No 25Ä26, Bogota.

Centro Colombo Andino, Calle 19 No 3Ä16 Of. 203, Bogota.

Centro De Ingles Lincoln, Calle 49 No 9Ä37, Bogota.

Centro De Idiomas Winston Salem, Calle 45 No 13Ä75, Bogota.

Centro De Lengua Inglesa, Calle 61 No 13Ä44 Of. 402, Bogota.

Coningles, Calle 63 No 13Ä24 Of. 502, Bogota.

English For Infants (John Dewey), Diagonal 110 No 40Ä85, Bogota.

English Language & Culture Institute (Elci), Calle 90 No 10Ä51, Bogota.

Escuela De Idiomas Berlitz, Calle 83 No 19Ä24, Bogota.

Genelor International, Avenida 78 No 20Ä49 Piso 20, Bogota.

I.C.L., Calle 119 No 9aÄ25, Bogota.

Ingles Cantando Y Jugando, Calle 106 No 16Ä26, Bogota.

Instituto Anglo Americano De Idiomas, Carrera 16a No 85Ä34 Of. 204, Bogota.

Instituto Electronico De Idiomas, Carrera 6 No 12Ä64 Piso, Bogota.

Instituto Meyer, Calle 17 No 10Ä16 Piso 80, Bogota.

Interlingua Ltda., Carrera 18 No 90Ä38, Bogota.

International Language Institute Ltda, Carrera 11 No.65-28 Piso 3, Bogota,Tel: 571 235-8132/52. Fax: 310-2892. Or: Carrera 13 No.5-79, Castillo Grande, Cartagena. Ten years offering regular, conversation, business and intensive English, Spanish and French for adults and children: personalised and communicative methodology.

International System, Transversal 6 No 51 A 33, Bogota.

K.O.E De Columbia, Calle 101 A No 31Ä02, Bogota.

Life Ltda., Transversal 19 No 100Ä52, Bogota.

The British Council, Calle 87 No 12Ä79, Bogota.

Oxford Centre, A.A. 102420, Santate de Bogota.

Ways' English School, Calle 101 No 13 A 17, Bogota.

Boston School of English Ltda, Carrera 43 No 44Ä02, Barranquilla.

California Institute Of English, Carera 51 No 80Ä130, Barranquilla.

Centro De Lenguas Modernas, Carrera 38 No 69 C 65, Barranquilla.

Esquela De Ingles, Calle 53 No 38Ä25, Barranquilla.

IdiomasÄMuneraÄCros Ltda, Carrera 58 No 72Ä105, A.A. 52032, Barranquilla.

Instituto De Lenguas Modernas, Carrera 41 No 52Ä05, Baranquilla.

Instituto Experimental De Atlantico, "jos Celestino Mutis", Calle 70 No 38Ä08, Barranquilla.

Instituto De Ingles Thelma Tyzon, Carrera 59 No 74Ä73, Barranquilla.

Avc, Carrera 45 El Palo 52Ä59, Cali.

Centro De Idiomas Winston Salem, Avenida La Ceste No 10Ä27, Santa Teresita, Cali.

Instituto Bridge Centro De Idiomas, Carrera 65 No 49 A 09, Cali.

Centro De Idiomas Y Turismo De Cartagena, Popa Calle 30 No 20Ä 177, Cartagena.

Ceico, Calle Siete Infantes, San Diego, Cartagena.

International Language Institute Ltda, Carrera 13 No 5Ä79 Castillogrande, Cartagena.

Instituto De Ingles, Calle 42 B No 48Ä45, Ibagu.

Business Language Centre Ltda, Carrera 49 No 15Ä85, Medellin,

Centro De Idiomas Winston Salem, Transversal 74 No C2Ä33 Laureies, Medellin.

Easy English, Carrera 45 A No 34 Sur 29 Torre No 4, Portal Del Cerro , A. A. 80511, Envigado, Medellin.

El Centro Ingles, El Poblado Carrera 10 A.No 36Ä39, Medellin.

Centro Anglo Frances, Carrera 11 No 6Ä12, Neiva.

International Language Institute Ltda., Carrera 5a No 21Ä35, Neiva.

Boston School Of English Ltda., Cra. 43 No 44Ä02, Barranquilla.

Costa Rica

Minimum salary: The equivalent of $300 per month. Tax: 10%.

Visa requirements: Rarely a problem.

Accommodation: $100-200 a month for a shared flat.

Other information: One of the safest and most expensive Latin American countries. There are many private language schools, but often with huge classes of mixed ability and poor facilities. Qualified teachers who speak Spanish could work in the private bilingual schools. Qualified teachers enjoy a reasonable standard of living in a beautiful, friendly and diverse country.

The Instituto Britanico, Apdo.8184 San Jose 1000 can provide infomation. Tel: 25 0256.

Cuba

Minimum salary: The state system has a set wage. The private sector pays a small salary in dollars which is convertible on the black market.

Tax and health insurance: Free.

Visa requirements: There is a restricted immigration policy, so it is hard to get a work permit. Apply to the local Cuban embassy, or contact the British Council in Havana.

Accommodation: Difficult to find.

Other information: Cuba is likely to face economic difficulties now that Russia no longer helps its economy. However, the growing tourism market may cause growth in demand for English.

Ecuador

Minimum salary: There are a many private language schools in Quito which vary in quality from very poor to reasonable. It is not difficult for native English speakers to obtain work, but rates of pay are poor and most take on additional private students. The British Council has two teaching centres in Ecuador, which pay well, but they recruit through their central offices in London and not locally. Salary is the equivalent of $1/hour for a 25-hour contact week.

Tax and health insurance: Since most EFL teachers are employed "informally", they are not likely to have to pay local tax or to contribute to the local social security scheme (which is in any case hopelessly inadequate). You are advised to take out health insurance in your home country. If tax is applicable it will be in the region of 10%.

Visa requirements: In theory all foreigners are required to have a residence visa and a work permit in order to be employed. They should be sponsored by their employer before they enter. However, in practice, most private language schools employ native speakers either illegally or for a short term only (a Tourist Visa last three months and can be renewed once for three more months without too much difficulty).

Accommodation: Apartments are available for US$125-250 per month depending on size and location.

Other information: Inflation is very high, but Ecuador is more stable and generally cheaper than many of its neighbours. There are around 20 private schools in Quito, many of which take on unqualified teachers. There are also opportunities in the coastal business centre, Guayaquil, but this is more expensive than the capital.

List of language schools in Ecuador

Benedict, 9 De Octubre 1515, Y Orellana, Quito.
Lingua Franca, Edifcio Jerico, 12 De Octubre 2449 y Orellana, Casilla 17-2-68, Quito. Tel: 546075. Fax: 593-2-568664. Small, dynamic operation - General English, ESP and one-to-one for professionals. Minimum requirement RSA Cert. & one year's experience.
Quito Language And Culture Centre, Republica De El Salvador, 639 Y Portugal, Quito.

GUATEMALA

Tourists require a visa unless they fly direct. Work permits can be obtained by your employer after arrival. Political conditions have improved considerably, but it is still an unstable country.

MEXICO

Minimum salary: The average rate of pay is between $400-600 per month for a minimum number of classes. Private teaching is possible to supplement basic pay.

Tax and health insurance: Taxation is approximately 35%, but it varies, as does the cost of health insurance, which is not cheap.

Visa requirements: It is illegal for a foreigner to work in any capacity without a work permit, and this is difficult and expensive to obtain. Very few institutions are prepared to offer a contract for a foreigner and scarcely any will do so without a personal interview. This applies to both private and public sector entities. Take originals of qualifications or an authorised copy. Where a work permit is needed, your employer in Mexico will handle everything through the Mexican government, who will advise your local embassy when work permit clearance is received. For further information contact: Simon Brewster, Director of Operations of the Instituto Anglo Mexicano de Cultura, Rio Nazas 116, Col. Cuauhtemoc, Mexico, D.F.

Accommodation: Shared accommodation will cost about US$150 per month. Furnished accommodation is rare, so check with your employer who should be able to help with this.

Other information: Mexico City has a severe pollution problem and is not recommended for children. Now that Mexico has joined the free trade agreement with Canada and the USA, demand for English should increase.

List of schools in Mexico

Univ. Autonoma De Aguascalientes, Rio Tamesis 438, 20100 Aguascalientes, Ags.
Univ. Aut De Baja California Sur, Carr. Al Sur. Km. 5.5, 23080 La Paz, Bcs.
Univ. Aut Del Carmen, Fac. De Ciencias Educativas, 24170 Cd. Del Carmen , Camp Alabama 2401, Quintas Del Sol, 31250 Chiuahua, Chih.
Universidad Aut. De Chiapas, Apdo. Postal No. 933, 29000 Tuxtla Gutierrez, Chis Cipresses No. 12, Fracc. Los Laureles, 30780 Tapachula , Chis.
Univ Aut De Coahuila, Depto. De Idiomas, Hidalgo Y Gonzalez Lobo, Col. Republica De Oriente, 25280 Saltillo, Coah.
Universidad De Colima, Escuela De Lenguas Extranjeras, Josefa Ortiz De Dominguez S/N, 28950 Villa De Alvarez, Col.
Univ. Aut. De Guerrero, Av. Lazaro Cardenas 86, 39000 Chilpancingo, Gro.
Universidad De Guanajuato, Centro De Idiomas, Lascurian De Retana 5, 36000 Guanajuato , Gto.
Universidad Autonoma De Hidalgo, Centro De Lenguas, Carr. Pachuca/Tulancingo S/N, 42000 Pachuca, Hgo.
Universidad De Guadalajara, Esc Superior De Lenguas Modernas, Apdo. Postal 2Ä416, 44280 Guadalajara, Jal.
Univ Autonoma Del Edo De Mexico, Centro De Ensenanza De Lenguas, Rafael M. Hidalgo No. 401 Pte., 50130 Toluca, Edo De Mexico.
Universidad Michoacana De Sn. N.H., Apartado Postal 225ÄC, 58260 Morelia, Mich.
U Autonoma Del Edo De Morelos, Centro De Lenguas, Rayon 7 BÄ Centro, 62000 Cuernavaca, Mor.
Univ. Aut. De Neuvo Leon, Fac. Filosofia Y Letras, Apdo. Postal 3024, 64000 Monterrey, Nl,
Mil Cumbres No. 4853, Col. Villa Mitras, 64170 Monterrey, Nl
Univ Aut Benito Juarez De Oaxaca, Centro De Idiomas, Armenta Y Lopez 700, Centro, 68000 Oaxaca De Juarez, Oax.
Universida Autonoma De Puebla, Dpto Lenguas, 4 Sur 104, 72000 Puebla, Pue.
U Autonoma De Queretaro, Escuela De Idiomas, Cerro De Las Campanas, 76010 Queretaro, Qro.
Univ. Aut. De San Luis Potosi, Centro De Idiomas, Zaragoza No. 410, 78200 San Luis Potosi, S.L.P.
Universidad De Sonora, Idiomas, Rosales Y Blvd. Luis Encinas, 83000 Hermosillo, Son, Av Universidad, Centro De Ensenanza Idiomas, Zona Cultura , 86000 Villahermosa, Tab.
U Autonoma De Tlaxcala, Depto De Filosofia Y Letras, Carretera A San Gabriel S/N, 90000 Tlaxcala , Tlax.
Univ. Veracruzana Udih, Fac. De Idiomas, Fco Moreno

Esq Ezequiel Alatriste, 91020 Xalapa, Ver.
Univ Aut De Yucatan, Fac. De Educacion, Calle 61 No 525 (Entre 66 Y 68), 97000 Merida , Yuc.
Universidad Autonoma De Zacatecas, Centro De Idiomas, Alameda 422, 98000 Zacatecas, Zac.

NICARAGUA

Teaching posts at universities offer good conditions. The Nicaragua Solidarity Campaign may recruit and help with airfare, as do the Peace Corps (see p79). Thieving is common. A knowledge of the political situation will help you integrate with the local people who are very hospitable.

Visa requirements: UK citizens do not require a visa to enter the country. To stay for a maximum of three months, you must show return tickets and have at least $300. Other nationalities require a tourist visa, available by sending passports to their respective Nicaraguan embassies. Work permits must be obtained before entering Nicaragua. Schools must submit a work permit request to the respective Nicaraguan embassy.

PERU

Minimum salary: Rates are good if you are recruited for English medium secondary schools. Inflation is rife, but expect the equivalent of $4 an hour for a 30-hour week.
Tax: 25%, payable by your employer, usually deducted at source.
Visa requirements: You must obtain an employment contract from a school in Peru and get the Peruvian Consulate to countersign and "legalise"it. The Consulate will send this to Peru and work permits are issued there. Obtaining permits can take over a year, and can be difficult to obtain unless you can prove a Peruvian cannot do your job. Take originals of qualifications or an authorised copy if you wish to work legally. Most people work illegally under a tourist visa.
Accommodation: One-third of your salary for a shared flat. Furnished acconunodation is rare - see if your employer can provide it.
English language newspapers: *Lima Times* (W).
Other information: It is not advisable to go on spec without at least a contact in Peru. There are grave economical difficulties and some parts are still no-go areas because of terrorists.

URUGUAY

The standard of EFL teaching in Uruguay is very high, and few schools recruit externally, but if you are there, you may find work from the list below.

List of schools in Uruguay

British Schools, Maximo Tajes esq Havre, Carrasco, Montevideo.

Dickens Institute, 21 De Setiembro 3090, Cp 11300 Montevideo.
English Studio Centre, Obligado 1221, Montevideo.
Instituto Cultural Anglo-Uruguayo, Casilla de Correo 5087 Sec.1, San Jose 1426, Montevideo.
London Institute, Caramuru 5609, Av. Brasil 2846, Montevideo.
St Patrick's College, Av J.M. Ferrari 1307, Montevideo.

VENEZUELA

Minimum salary: The average rate of pay teachers at the British Council, who hold the RSA Diploma and with two years post diploma experience, is in the region of £700 per month.
Visa requirements: There are a variety of visas, including a tourist visa, "transeunte", business "transeunte", work and transit "transeunte". "Transeunte" may be translated as "temporary", however, it may last a considerable time and allows the holder to undertake paid employment but also renders the holder liable for income tax. The business "transeunte" is issued to foreign nationals who go to Venezuela to carry out commercial activities or paid technical, scientific, artistic or cultural activities. This visa lasts for 120 days and it is non-renewable. It allows the holder multiple entries into Venezuela, however it may only be awarded twice a year. Work permits must be obtained before entering the country, and your employer will get authorisation from the government.
English language newspaper: *The Daily Journal* (D), written primarily for the American reader.
Other information: Although the oil boom has died somewhat, there is a great demand for English, although American English is more common. Remember that this is one of the most expensive and cosmopolitan countries in South America, and salaries should reflect this. Caracas is generally dry, warm and sunny thoughout the year, but temperatures and humidity elsewhere vary with altitude. The unit of currency is the "Bolivar" and the national language is Spanish.

List of schools in Venezuela

Berlitz Escuela de Idiomas, Av. Madrid, Urb. Las Mercedes, Caracas 1060.
The British Council, Torre La Noria, Piso 6, Paseo Enrique Eraso, Urb. Las Mercedes, Aptdo. 65131, Caracas 1065.
Centro Venezolano-Americano, Av. Principal Jose Marti, Urb. Las Mercedes, Caracas 1060.
English Lab, Quinta Penalba, Av. Venezuela, Urb. El Rosal, Caracas 1060.
Instituto de Ingles Britanico, Av. Avila No. 52, Urb. San Bernadino, Caracas 1011.
Instituto Loscher-Ebbinghaus SRL, Quinta Magal, Av. Venezuela, Urb. El Rosal, Caracas 1060.
Instituto Venezolano-Britanico, Quinta Guaricha, Av. Los Manguitos, Urb. Sabana Grande, Caracas 1050.

THE FAR EAST

BRUNEI

Minimum salary: 2,350-2,400 Brunei dollars per month. You must have a degree and at least two years' teaching experience. Top salary is up to B$70,000. Most posts are recruited by the Centre for British Teachers who recruit for the Ministry of Education (see p64).
Tax and health insurance: Normally no personal income tax. Health insurance is usually part of the package.
Visa requirements: The Brunei High Commission will supply a visa with proof of job offer - either before or after your arrival. Your passport is stamped on arrival for a period decided at the discretion of the immigration officer. The work permit application form is filled in by your employer and submitted to the Commissioner of Labour in Brunei. If the job offer comes from the private sector, the company must obtain a labour licence before they can apply for a work permit.
Accommodation: Usually provided or subsidised as part of the job package, otherwise prohibitively expensive - 1,500 Brunei dollars a month. At least a three-month deposit is demanded.
English language newspapers: *Borneo Bulletin (D)*.
Other information: The standard of living is similar to northern Europe in this wealthy country. Have a medical and dental check-up before you go. Public transport is limited and most schools insist that teachers have a clean driving licence and buy a car out there. Some kind of car loan scheme is usually offered. Brunei is a Muslim country, so teachers are advised to dress "modestly". Take enough shoes with you - it is difficult to buy any over English size five.

CAMBODIA

Minimum salary: The equivalent of £18,000 unless accommodation is provided.
Tax and health insurance: Probably no tax. Take out private health insurance.
Visa requirements: These will be arranged by your employer.
Accommodation: The equivalent of £1,500 per month for a two-room villa in Phnom Penh. The shortage of accommodation for aid workers has forced prices up dramatically.
Other information: Because the UN are virtually running the country, English is very popular, especially business English. CFBT and VSO recruit teachers and teacher trainers (see p64 and 79). However, the Khmer Rouge are still active and many parts of Cambodia remain dangerous.

HONG KONG

Minimum salary: HK$100 per hour, though qualified teachers should get double this.
Tax and health insurance: 15%.
Visa requirements: UK nationals can get a work permit in Hong Kong. Other nationalities must be sponsored before they can get a permit.
Accommodation: Expect to pay a minimum of HK$1,500 for a shared, very small flat. Many teachers stay in hostels. Accommodation is larger in outlying islands, such as Lamma and Cheung Chau, but these are becoming more expensive.
English language newspapers: *Hong Kong Standard, International Herald Tribune, South China Morning Post(D)*
Other information: There are enough people needing private lessons to be a full-time freelance teacher. English is becoming more important as Chinese control approaches. Qualifications are not essential, and native English speakers are needed to give conversation lessons in box-rooms around Chung King Mansions (40 Nathan Road). Some schools also offer 'coffee shop' style conversation classes to up to 20 students. Generally a degree is preferred, and a diploma will give you the cream of the jobs, such as working for the state island schools. Contact the Hong Kong Government Office, 6 Grafton St., London W1X 3LB UK for secondary school opportunities. The British Council in Hong Kong is the largest in the east and is a good source of information. Many teachers find supplementary work with publishers or doing voice-overs for films.

List of schools in Hong Kong

First Class Language Centre, 22a Bank Tower, 351-353 King's Road, North Point. Tel: (5) 887 7555.
Josiah's Institute of English, 2nd and 3rd floors, 88 Lockhard Road, Wanchai.
Hong Kong English Club, Grd flr., 176b Nathan Road, Tsimshatsui, Kowloon. Tel: (3) 722 1300.

CHINA

Minimum salary: Varies considerably but expect around 700-1,000 yuan per month for a lesser qualified "foreign teacher", while "foreign experts", who are required to have an MA can expect about 1,400-2,500 yuan a month. Negotiate before you go to China.

Tax and health insurance: No tax and free health care is provided.

Visa requirements: You must get a letter of invitation from your prospective employer to take to your local Chinese Embassy to receive a visa. You have to undergo a medical examination, including an HIV test, before you are allowed into China. Get it done before you go or may have to have additional, more risky, tests within China. You can apply for a residence permit after three months.

Accommodation: Usually provided by employer, and varies in quality from poor to inadequate. Expect sporadic heating and hot water. South of the Yangtse river there may be no heating as it is "warmer", although the winters are bleak.

English language newspaper: *China Daily* (D).

Other information: Chinese institutions employ two types of foreign teachers. The first is a "Foreign Expert", who should have an MA in a relevant discipline and some experience of teaching at the tertiary level. Chinese institutions will pay the salary, airfares, accommodation costs and some baggage costs for such teachers. The second type of teacher is a "Foreign Teacher", whose salary is considerably lower (often less than half) than that of the "Foreign Expert", and air fares are not paid. Qualifications required vary, ranging from just native English speaker to several years' experience. For both types of post, applications should be made to the State Bureau of Foreign Experts, Friendship Hotel, Beijing 100873, or to the Education Section of the Embassy of the Peoples Republic of China, 5-13 Birch Grove, Acton, London W3 9SW or directly to an institution in China.

Applications can also be made in February to the British Council, Overseas Educational Appointments Department, 15 Medlock Street, Manchester M15 4AA. VSO also recruits English teachers, mainly for teacher training colleges in China.

There are no private language schools in China, although some hotels and large companies have their own language training facilities, for which they normally recruit locally.

Living conditions tend to be harder living away from Beijing, where western food is available. The Chinese are highly motivated and interested in foreigners, but expect traditional learning methods and few (if any) facilities such as cassettes, books and photocopiers. Nevertheless, China looks likely to open up, especially with the influx of western technology, which has brought satellite television into the country. For further information obtain the following book, which includes a comprehensive list of Chinese colleges and universities: *Living in China - A Guide to Teaching and Studying in China including Taiwan,* published by China Books and Periodicals Inc.

INDONESIA

Minimum salary: $12,000-20,000 pa depending on qualifications and experience.

Tax and health insurance: Most language schools have some kind of health insurance policy for teachers, but it is advisable to arrange cover privately before arriving in Indonesia. Generally though medical services are poor and many EFL teachers fly out to Singapore.

Visa requirements: Officially work permits and visas are required to teach in Indonesia. There are two main types of visa: DINAS, a six month visa issued to many EFL teachers; KIMS, under which you pay a much lower rate of tax. Many prospective EFL teachers arrive in Indonesia on tourist visas, and once they have found a job, go to Singapore to obtain a Business Visa, which can subsequently be changed to KIMS or DINAS. It is worth bearing in mind that passports do have to be surrendered at regular intervals, sometimes for as long as six weeks at a time, while visas are being renewed.

Accommodation: Usually provided by employers, mostly in bungalows or houses. If not, it is becoming increasingly expensive, especially in Jakarta, where rent for a small house near the centre is $3,000-5,000 pa., but for a larger-style house the average price is nearer $10,000. Landlords usually expect expatriates to pay two years' rent in advance, and it is advisable to seek legal advice to ensure your lease is in order if you do pay in advance. Employers may be prepared to offer you an initial loan.

English language newspaper: *The Indonesian Times, Indonesian Observer,* and the *Jakarta Post* (D).

Other information: English is booming in Indonesia, and most opportunities for teachers are in Jakarta, Surabaya and Bandung. North American and Australian EFL teachers dominate the area. Qualified teachers can command far higher rates than unqualified staff, and business English is the key area of demand growth.

Language schools, which are "Yayasans" or foundations, are able to compete commercially with one another and appear to be doing well. Along with Indonesia's growing economy has come an increased demand for, and awareness of the importance of, English language learning.

Public transport tends to be poor, over-crowded and dangerous, and most foreign nationals find they prefer to spend the extra on taxi fares, which are still relatively cheap. Women should dress discreetly. Jakarta is very dirty and non-violent crime is common. New shopping malls have opened in Jakarta in recent years and provide a comprehensive range of services, including facilities for making international telephone calls and for sending faxes. Most western products can be obtained in supermarkets in Jakarta, although these products command a premium.

List of schools in Indonesia

ALT (American Language Training), Jalan R.S. Fatmawati No. 42 A, Keb. Baru, Jakarta Selatan. Tel: 769 1001. Five schools.

EEC (English Education Centre), Jalan Let Jen S.Parman 66, Slipi, Jakarta Barat. Tel: 567 1144.

EEP (Executive English Programs), Jalan Wijaya VIII No.4, Kebayoran Baru, Jakarta Selatan. Tel: 722 0812. Branch in Bandung.

ELS International, Jalan Tanjung karang 7 C-D, Jakarta Pusat. Tel: 323211.

ELTI (English Language Training International), Complex Wijaya Grand Centre, Blok F83, 84 A & B, Jalan Wijaya II, Keb. Baru, Jakarta Selatan. Tel: 720 2957. Branches in Yogyakarta, Semarang and Solo.

IALF (Indonesia-Australia Language Foundation), Wisma Budi, Suite 503, Jalan HR Rasuna Said Kav. C-6, Kuningan, Jakarta Selatan 12940. Tel: 521 3350. Branch in Bali.

ILP (International Language Programs), Jalan Panglima Polin IX/2, Kebayoran Baru, Jakarta Sealtan. Tel: 722 2408. Branch in Surabaya.

SIT (School for International Training), Jalan Hayam Wuruk 120 C-D, Jakarta Pusat. Tel: 629 3340.

TBI (The British Institute), Setiabudi Building 2, Jalan HR Rasuna Said, Kuningan, Jakarta Selatan. Tel: 512 044. Branch in Bandung.

JAPAN

Minimum salary: Since it is difficult to get a visa, many schools offer teachers just enough to get them a visa. Monthly pay therefore begins at around 260,000 yen per month for between 25-30 contact hours per week. Better schools pay more. Expect less outside Tokyo.

Tax and health insurance: Income tax is around 10% and local tax is about 5%. The Japanese health insurance system is complicated, with some places running a local health scheme which may cover up to 70% of our medical costs, based on your previous year's salary - so initially it is for a minimal fee. Some prefectures will not allow foreigners to join the local scheme, however, and private medical insurance is strongly advised. Larger schools will often offer a private insurance scheme, which you may be able to join.

Visa requirements: Japanese law requires teachers to have a valid work visa, and it is impossible to apply for a work visa unless you are sponsored by an employer. The application process is lengthy, and usually involves a wait of up to three months before the visa is granted. Consequently teachers intending to work in Japan are strongly advised to arrange employment before they arrive. It is illegal to work on a tourist visa, even if a work visa is being processed in the meantime. Students are entitled to work on a part-time basis if they have an official student visa. In order to get a visa, you need various documents including a guarantee of monthly salary in excess of 260,000 yen. Although it is illegal to work on a tourist visa, it is possible to use such a visa to solicit and secure a firm offer of employment. However, if you find work on a tourist visa, you will need to leave the country and re-enter with sponsorship from your employer, getting the change of status endorsed by an overseas Japanese embassy. You cannot change your status without leaving Japan.

Accommodation: Accommodation is a big enough problem in Japan and many Japanese landlords are reluctant to rent to foreigners, so it is worth getting a Japanese intermediary to help you. Most landlords require six months rent in advance, four months of which is non-returnable "key-money". Most good schools will help teachers find suitable accommodation with rents varying from 60,000-85,000 yen per month for a small one-bedroom unfurnished flat, 80,000 yen in Tokyo.

English language newspaper: Monday's edition of *The Japan Times* carries the best selection of teaching jobs. Also the *Asahi Evening News*, the *Daily Yomiuri*, and the *Mainichi Daily News* (D).

Other information: Despite the recession, Japan remains a massive EFL market, with a large proportion of children's work (you may teach children as young as two!). Travelling to and from work can be long and arduous; the climate is oppressive in the summer. The Japanese have a strong work ethic, which is reflected in teachers' contracts (25-30 hours per week is the norm, with often only 10 days holiday a year, not including public holidays). Most work takes place in the afternoons and evenings.

State education concentrates on reading and writing, so private language schools which concentrate on "conversation" are popular. There remains no regulation of language schools, which means that standards vary. However, the economic downturn in Japan has meant that many of the worst schools have closed, and the better schools have significantly improved their teaching standards. The Japan Association of College English (JACET) is aiming to improve state education, especially at primary level.

Foreigners are known as "gaijin" and it is estimated to take at least six months to adjust culturally and economically. Japan is generally safe, but teachers, especially women, should not allow themselves to be lulled into a false sense of security, as sexual and racial harassment is becoming increasingly frequent.

The best time to look for work is March - just before the start of the Japanese academic year in April. September is another possibility. The government is clamping down on illegal workers, but the National Union of Workers and Kanto Union Teachers' Federation will help legal teachers know their rights.

See ELS (USA), Hilderstone College and information on the JET scheme (p26) for details of their recruitment schemes to Japan.

List of schools in Japan

Aeon Institute of Foreign Languages, Nihonseimei Building 7f 1-1 3 Shimoishii Okayama-shi 700.

Attorney Foreign Language Institute, Osaka Ekimae Daiichi Building, 1-3-1 Umeda Kita-ku, Osaka.

American Academy, 4-1-3 Kudan Kita Chiyoda-Ku Tokyo 102.

AEON 7F Nihonseimei Okayama Daini Building 1-1-3 Shimoishii Okayama.

American School of Business, 1-17-4 Higashi Ikebukuro Toshima-Ku Tokyo 170.

Azabu Academy No 401 Shuwa-Roppongi Building 3-14-12 Roppongi Minato-ku Tokyo 106.

Berkley House Gogaku Centre 4-2 Go-bancho Chiyoda-ku Tokyo 102.

Berlitz Schools of Languages (Japan) Inc., Kowa BLDG. 1,5f, 11-41, Alasaka 1-chrome, Minato-ku, Tokyo 107.

Bernard Group, 2-8-11 Takezono, Tsukuba City, Ibaraki-Ken, 305 (recruit for British-owned schools).

Cambridge English School, Dogenzaka 225 Building, 2-23-14 Dogenzaka Shibuya-ku Tokyo 150.

Cambridge School of English, Kikumura 91 Building1-41-20 Higashi, Ikebukuro Toshima-ku, Tokyo 170.

Cosmopolitan Language Institute Yashima B Building 4F 1-8-9 Yesu Chuo-ku Tokyo 104.

CIC English Schools, Kawamoto Building, Imadegawaagaru Nishigawa Karasuma-dori, Kamigyo-ku Kyoto.

DEH, 7-5 Nakamachi, Naka-ku, Hiroshima 730.

David English House 2-3F Nakano Building 1-5-17 Kamiyacho Naka-ku Horoshima 730.

EEC Foreign Languages Institute, Shikata Building, 2F, 4-43 Nakazald-Nishi, 2-chrome, Kita-ku, Osaka 530.

ELEC Eigo Kenkyujo (The English Language Education Council) 3-8 Kanda Jimbo-cho Chiyoda-ku Tokyo 101.

Executive Gogaku Centre (Executive Language Centre) 1 Kasumigaseki Building 12F 3-2-5 Kasumigaseki Chiyoda-ku Tokyo 100.

FCC (Fukuoka Communication Centre), Dai Roku Okabe Building 5F Hakata Eki Higashi 2-4-17 Hakata-ku Fukuoka 812.

F L Centre (Foreign Language Centre), 1 Iwasaki Building 3F 2-19-20 Shibuya-ku Tokyo 150.

Gateway Gakuin Rokko Atelier House 3-1-15 Yamada-cho Nada-ku Kobe.

ICA Kokusai Kaiwa Gakuin (International Conversation Academy)l Mikasa No 2 Building 1-16-10 Nishi Ikebukuro Toshima-ku, Tokyo 171.

IF Foreign Language Institute, 7F Shin Nakashima Building, 1-9-20 Nishi Nakashima Yodogawa-ku, Osaka.

Kains English School in Gakko, 1-5-2 Ohtemon Chuo-ku Fukuoka 810.

Kyoto English Centre, Sumitomo Seimei Building, Shijo-Karasuma Nishi-iru Shimogyo-ku Kyoto

Kobe Language Centre, 3-18 Wakinoharnacho, 1-chome, Chuo-ku, Kobe 651.Tel: (78) 2614316.

Language Education Centre 7-32-chome Ohtemachi Nakaku Hiroshima-shi 730.

Matty's School of English, 3-15-9 Shonan-takatori, Yokosuka 234. Tel: (468) 658717.

Mobara English Institute, 618-1 Takashi, Mobara-shi Chiba-ken 297. Tel: (475) 224785.

Plus Alpha (Agency) 2-25-20 Denenchofu, Ota-Ku, Tokyo 145.

Queens School of English, 3f Yuzuki Bldg 4-7-14 Minamiyawata, Ichikawa 272.

Pegasus Language Services, Sankei Building 1-7-2 Otemachi Chiyoda-ku Tokyo 100.

REC School of Foreign Language, Nijojo-mae Ebisugawasagaru Higashihorikawa-dori Nakagyo-ku, Kyoto.

Royal English Language Centre, 4-31-3-2 Chyo Hakata-ku Fukuoka 812.

Seido Language Institute, 12-6 Funado-cho Ashiya-shi Kyoto.

Sun Eikaiwa School, 6F Cherisu Hachoubori Building 6-7 Hachoubori Naka-ku Hiroshima-shi 730.

Shane Corporation, 4f Kimura Building 4-14-12 Nishi Funa Funabashi Shi Chiba Ken.273.

Shane Corporation, Yutaka Daini Building 4F Higashi Kasai 6-2-8 Edogawa-Ku Tokyo.

Shane Schools:

Fujisawa, 251 Fujisawa Homon Building, 6F 484-25 Fujisawa, Fujisawa City, Kanagawa.

Kasai-134, DAJ2 Yukata Building 4F, G-2-8 Highashi Kasai, Edogawa-ku, Tokyo.

Nishi Funabashi-237, Kimura Building, 4F, 4-14-12 Nishifuna, Funabashi City, Chiba.

Omiya-331, Maehara bldg. 2F, 2-455-2 Sakuragicho, Omiya City, Saitama.

Stanton School of English, 12 Gobancho Chiyoda-ku Tokyo 102.

Chunichi Bunka Centre, 4-5F Chunichi Building 4-4-1 Sakae Naka-ku Nagoya 460.

Smith Ohokayama Eikaiwa School, 2-4-9 Ohokayama Meguro-ku, Tokyo 152.

Ten'noji Academy of Business and Languages, 2-9-36 Matsuzaki- cho Abeno-ku Osaka.

Tokyo YMCA College of English, 7 Kanda Mitoshiro-Cho Chiyoda-ku Tokyo T-101.

Tokyo Language Centre, Tatsunama Bldg 1-2-19 Yaesu, Chuo-Ku Tokyo 103.

Tokyo English Centre (TEC) 7-9 Uguisudai-cho Shibuyaku Tokyo 150.

Toefl Academy, 1-12-4 Kundankita, Chiyoda-ku Tokyo 102. Tel: (3) 2303500.

World Language School Inc Tokiwa Soga Ginko Building, 4F 1-22-8 Jinnan Shibuya-ku Tokyo 171.

Yoko Ishikawa, 480 GO, Takaatano, Anjo, 730.

MALAYSIA

Minimum salary: Malaysian $3,000-3,500 per month.

Tax and health insurance: 17-20%. Some employers will arrange health insurance. If not, take a private policy. Local doctors are inexpensive.

Visa requirements: Visa and work permit regulations are very strict. Teachers must have a work permit to work either privately or in the public system. Permits are only issued for jobs for which no suitably qualified Malaysian is available. As a result there are almost no expatriate teachers in the public sector and few in the private system, irrespective of the subject offered. Those teachers who do obtain employment often do so through entering the country on a tourist visa, securing a post, and then leaving the country to get their work permit.

Accommodation: Malaysian $550 for an unfurnished, shared flat in Kuala Lumpur or Petling Jaya where accommodation is scarce. Elsewhere, the price is considerably reduced and is about Malaysian $350.

English language newspaper: *Malay Mail, The Borneo Post, New Straits Times*, and *The Star* (D).

Other information: The Prime Minister is promoting English and demand is high in the business community, the state and private sectors. Economic growth has meant high inflation, but clothes, food and restaurants are relatively inexpensive. Public transport is generally good, although trains are slow. EFL books are readily available. Women should dress modestly outside the big cities, especially on the more conservative east coast, and it should be noted that Malaysia is predominantly Muslim.

The Malaysian Ministry of Education, Pusat Bandar Damansara, Blok J, 50604, Kuala Lumpur, sometimes recruits experienced teachers for lucrative university posts. The Centre for British Teachers and ELS also recruit.

List of schools in Malaysia

The English Language Centre, 1st Floor, Lot 2067, Block 10, K.C.L.D., Jalan Keretapi, PO Box 253, 93150 Kuching, Sarawak.

The Kinabulu Commercial College, 3rd & 4th Floors, Wisma Sabah, Kota Kinabulu, Sabah.

NEPAL

Current opportunities for TEFL in Nepal are not good, due to stringent visa restrictions. However, with the unquestioned demand for wider access to the English language, the medium-to-long term outlook is fairly promising.

Visa requirements: Unless you are employed by an official organisation such as the British Council, a Diplomatic Mission or a UN Agency, it is impossible to secure anything more than a tourist visa for Nepal. The tourist visa is usually valid for one month on entry and can be extended for two additional months but further extensions beyond a total initial stay of three months are never approved. A tourist visa does not entitle you to work legally during your stay. At present, none of the bi-lateral or multi-lateral donors are involved in EFL/ESL programmes though there are signs that this position may change within the next two years. This means that it is unlikely that you could obtain employment and hence a non-tourist visa through an official organisation.

Other information: There are a myriad of private language schools in Kathmandu which are run as businesses by enterprising Nepalese. Some of these (illegally) recruit tourists as teaching staff and are generally unable to assist in the process of changing the visa status of their employees from "tourist" to "non-tourist". These schools are usually poorly resourced, and do not pay a living wage to those who work for them.

The British Council has a small Direct Teaching Operation in Nepal which at present is staffed almost entirely by part-time teachers, as the volume of work does not yet justify more than one contract post. They do hope to expand however, and the possibility of the creation of an additional post is likely during the next two years. The minimum qualification for a teacher at the British Council is the RSA/ UCLES CTEFLA (or equivalent) with at least two years relevant experience, but an RSA/UCLES DTEFLA (or equivalent) is preferred. Contact address: The British Council, Kantipath, P.O. Box 640, Kathmandu, Nepal (Tel: + 2213 05/2237 96/2226 98).

The American Language Centre runs courses for Nepalese intending to study in the USA under US Government Scholarship schemes and also teaches business-oriented language courses for employees of local companies. Contact address: Mr Chris Gamm, The Director, P.O. Box 58, Kathmandu, Nepal.

SINGAPORE

Minimum salary: 2,000-2,200 Singapore dollars per month.

Tax and health insurance: 12%. There is also a compulsory savings tax, which you can reclaim with interest when you leave the country.

Visa requirements: You must secure a job before you arrive. Your employer will arrange a work permit. Non-graduates need to take an AIDS test to enter.

Accommodation: 400 Singapore dollars per month for a room in a shared flat.

English language newspapers: *Business Times. Straits Tinies, The News Paper* (D).

Other information: Singapore is a modern, repressive country. The Singapore High Commission in London have a recruitment office linked to the National University of Singapore. Contact: 071 235 4562. Teachers in government schools and colleges should have a relevant qualification and preferably five years' experience, but are rewarded with a salary of 5,000 Singapore dollars tax free. International House and the British Council can supply details of other language schools.

SOUTH KOREA

Minimum salary: 1,400,000 won per month, more for qualified and experienced teachers.

Tax and health insurance: Free with a contract for two years, but very high after this period - most teachers leave at this time. Private medical insurance is recommended.

Visa requirements: Obtainable from your local Korean embassy, who will want to see sponsorship from an employer before you can get a work permit. Many teachers work illegally with a tourist visa.

Accommodation: 250,000 won per month for a one room flat in Seoul, 150,000 won elsewhere. Rates may be lower if you put down a large deposit.

English language newspapers: *Korean Herald, Korean Times* (D).

Other information: English is essential for university entrance and because state system English is poor, students are very motivated in private schools. It is easy to find work, particularly in Seoul and Pusan. The Koreans go out of their way to make foreigners feel at home. English for Academic Purposes (EAP) and business English are popular and lucrative. Some places prefer American English - many students are keen to live there. Public transport, including an underground, is good in the huge capital, Seoul.

TAIWAN

Minimum salary: New Taiwanese $8,500-$9,000 per month, or $370 an hour.

Tax and health insurance: 20% tax. Proof of tax payment will help you get a visa extension. Take out a private health insurance policy.

Visa requirements: These have been tightened and you must now have sponsorship and a degree to obtain a work permit. If you enter on a tourist visa and find work, you must leave the country to apply for a work permit. You also need a health certificate, including an AIDS test.

Accommodation: New Taiwanese $7,500 per month for a room in a shared flat, cheaper outside central Taipei. Most landlords will want three months' rent in advance.

English language newspapers: *China Post, China News, China Daily News (D).*

Other information: Since the government clamped down on illegal teachers, some schools have found that they have been unable to get permits for the teachers they hire. Check your school can guarantee a permit. With low unemployment and a healthy economy, there is plenty of in-company and private work, and falling rates may rise again now some of the cowboys are being forced out. This should compensate for the high cost of living, especially in Taipei. Some schools prefer American English, and there is also a demand for teachers of children. Watch out for split shifts and weekend work, or your day could be long. The major cities are severely polluted.

List of schools in Taiwan:

ELS (see p00) have branches in Taipei and Kaohsiung.
Hess Language School, 51 Ho Ping East Road, Sec 2, 1F Taipei. Tel: 7031118.

THAILAND

Minimum salary: Rates of pay vary between 6,000 Baht monthly on a "volunteer" basis, while top posts may command a salary of up to 50,000 Baht. Average for and expatriate MA qualified university lecturer is around 20,000 Baht. Private sector language schools pay 150-500 Baht per hour. Terms for full-time staff vary widely and should be verified.

Tax and health insurance: For tax purposes, teachers may have to submit their own return - awkward for non-Thai speakers. However taxation rates are generally quite low and may be free if you are on a one-year fixed contract. Health insurance is available locally, however, it is important to ensure that you are covered for dental as well as medical treatment. Booster inoculations can be done cheaply at the Pasteur Institute in Bangkok.

Visa requirements: Still under revision. Teachers should have work permits and most employers will help arrange these. Many teachers are on a 60- or 90- day non-immigrant visa and are obliged to leave the country every few months to get a new visa.

Accommodation: Rents are affordable away from Bangkok, particularly if you are willing to share. Expect to pay around 3,000 Baht monthly for a one-bedroom flat in the provinces, while in Bangkok similar accommodation will cost nearly double that amount.

English language newspapers: *Bangkok Post, The Nation* (D).

Other information: There is no body which oversees private language schools. The academic year is June-March with a break in October. University staff get 15 days holiday per year. The local English teachers association in Thailand - TESOL - is fairly active. Contact through: AUA, 179 Rajdamri Road, Bangkok 10330, or the British Council.

Thailand is developing rapidly and the growth in the middle classes has meant an increased demand for higher education. There are now English medium universities and colleges and a drive to improve teacher training. However, few posts are advertised outside the country and many schools remain poorly equipped. Many teachers are unqualified, and get employment (well paid by local standards) whilst "passing through" on their travels. Bangkok is hot, noisy and polluted with real traffic problems, but shopping is excellent. Electrical goods are expensive. Cleanliness and respect means a lot to Thais, who are Buddhist.

Bangkok is the main centre for EFL. Chiang Mai in the north also has some EFL work, including at the Chiang Mai University. World Teach and VSO also recruit for Thailand.

List of schools in Thailand

ECC, 430/19-20 Chula 64, Siam Square, Bangkok 10330. Tel: 2551856.
The English Language Schools, 26/3, 26/9 Chonphol Lane 15, Bangkok 10900. Tel: 25110439.
The Company, 28 Suhkumvit Soi 24, Bangkok 10110. Tel: 2587036.
LCC Language Institute, 8/64-67 Ratchadapisek-Larprao Road, Bangkhaen, Bangkok 10900.

VIETNAM

Lifting of US sanctions may soon change the economic climate of Vietnam. However, at the moment, opportunities are almost comletely restricted to volunteering or teacher training, although demand for English is very strong.

THE REST OF ASIA AND THE EAST

Teaching opportunities elsewhere in Asia and the east are generally limited to voluntary or aid work (see p79), mainly because these countries are either too poor to afford to pay privately for non-native teachers, the political situation is prohibitive, or because English is the official language anyway. However, there are possibilities in the following countries:

Indian sub-continent

English is the official language, though mainly spoken only by by the elite ruling classes. There are some private schools and British Council centres in India and Bangladesh, but apart from these limited (mainly teacher training) opportunities, most work is on a volunteer basis. VSO are active in Bangladesh, Bhutan, Pakistan and Nepal (see p79).

MALDIVES

Minimum salary: 10-20 rufiya per hour in the government-subsidised private schools, slightly less in the state system.

Tax and health insurance: No tax, and medical consultation is free. A private health insurance policy is recommended.

Visa requirements: You must get a sponsor to get a work permit, but this is not usually a problem. Write, with details of your educational background, to the Ministry of Education, Male, Republic of Maldives. Tel: (960) 323836.

Accommodation: This is usually provided with your contract.

Other information: The Maldives comprise of 1,200 islands and atolls, 200 of them inhabited. The English medium school system uses British exams, so British teachers are in demand. The Maldives are a developing country and living standards for teachers are modest, but your contract may include a return air fare, and bicycles are often provided. Most work is in the capital and main island, Male.

MAURITIUS

Minimum salary: Average rates of pay are between Rs 6,000-13,000 per month for graduates.

Tax and health insurance: The taxation rate for income is levied at the rate of 30%, but this only applies for income above Rs 6,000, after the deduction of any personal allowances.

Visa requirements: It is unlikely that foreign nationals will be given permits to work in Mauritius, and a work permit is a prerequisite for all foreign nationals.

Accommodation: Accommodation is expensive and can range from anything from Rs 6,000-8,000 per month, for a furnished flat or small house or more depending on size and location.

Other information: In Mauritius, the medium of education at both primary and secondary levels is English and opportunities for EFL are restricted. There are in fact no private English language schools.

MONGOLIA

Mongolia is now a free-market economy. This opening up of the country has led to its people embracing all things western, and that also means the English language which joined Chinese, Japanese and Russian as the first foreign language in 1992. The huge demand for English far exceeds the supply of teachers. 75% of the population is under 35. Retrained Russian teachers have attempted to cope with the introduction of English in the huge secondary school sector. Projects are also being carried out with the help of the UN, VSO, the British Council, CFBT, the Peace Corps and the Bell Educational Trust. Theses are mo stly in ESP and teacher training.

Although it is the size of western Europe, its population is just two million, and it is considered the world's most remote country. Transport is scarce and food supplies unreliable. At present only ministry officials and senior bankers speak any English, and there is a severe shortage of paper and English textbooks. Many aid and charitable organisations are already moving in. For information contact: Mongolian Embassy, 7 Kensington Court, London W8 5DL, UK. Tel: 071 937 0150.

Papua New Guinea

English is an official language in Papua New Guinea - education is all in English. However, with over 800 language groups, English is only loosely the second language. Jobs exist mainly in the secondary sector, and few are purely EFL posts. Teacher training is fairly advanced. Salaries are not high, although taxes are.

Visa requirements: Teachers must secure a job before applying for a working visa. The employer has to lodge an application with the authorities in Papua New Guinea and the prospective employee must apply to the immigration department of any Papua New Guinea High Commission.

Other information: The locals are excellent linguists. Although a beautiful country, their High Commission in London say it·is not a suitable destination for "those of nervous disposition", and some areas are controlled by bandits.

VSO and the UN also recruit volunteers to work in Papua New Guinea (see p79).

Addresses:

University of Papua New Guinea, Allude for teacher training.
Papua New Guinea University of Technology, Lae for tertiary EFL.

Sri Lanka

Minimum salary: 10,000 rupees per month.
Tax and health insurance: Free for the first year, although private health insurance is recommended.
Accommodation: 3,000 rupees per month in a shared flat.
Visa requirements: Enter on a tourist visa. Your employer will arrange a work permit.
English language newspapers: *The Island, Daily News* (D).
Other information: English has become important in Sri Lanka, where the government are trying to diffuse the political and cultural tension between the Tamils and the Sinhalese, who each have their own languages.

Native English speakers are in demand and for those working for international organisations in the capital, such as the British Council and the Colombo International School, living standards are high.

Most work outside Colombo is on a volunteer basis (see p79). The civil war is confined to the north and east of the country and violence is declining. Coursebooks are hard to obtain - take your own.

Addresses:

International English Language Services (PVT) Ltd., 292/1 Galle Road, Colomdo 4. Tel: (94) 1 590707.

A warning

Because of the cultural, economic or political troubles in some countries, it is advised that you proceed with great caution should you decide to work in them. Conditions change around the world all the time and the following list is inevitably not exclusive. However, if you obtain employment in the following countries, it is advisable to contact your embassy first. (See also relevant country guides):

Algeria, Burma, East Timor, Egypt (certain parts only), El Salvador, Georgia, Guatemala, Iran, Iraq, Lebanon, Liberia, Libya, Mozambique, Papua New Guinea, Peru (certain parts only), Somalia, Sudan, Yemen, former states of Yugoslavia, Zaire.

NORTH AFRICA
AND THE MIDDLE EAST

For the past 20 years a significant demand for EFL training has been sustained in much of North Africa and the Middle East, despite political and religious unrest, and war. Oil is still the driving force behind economic development in the area -English and the petro-dollar are the language of the oil business. Visitors should be aware of the political and religious environment. Women, in particular, have to restrict their lifestyle in some states, which may offer work permits only to men. Good qualifications and previous experience of living in a Muslim country will improve employment prospects. Teachers often leave the Gulf states with significant savings, thanks to contractual bonuses and low taxation.

ALGERIA

The British Council Algiers reports that English has grown in popularity due to a reaction against French. English is now a primary school option. There has been a great deal of civil unrest recently with the rise of Islamic Fundamentalism. Consult your Foreign Affairs department before taking a post.

BAHRAIN

Minimum salary: Salaries range between BD 520-580 (CTEFLA or equivalent), and BD 580-700 (DTEFLA/MA).
Tax and health insurance: No tax is charged and basic health cover can be obtained locally for approximately BD 125 per annum, and many recognised western insurance companies are established in Bahrain. More comprehensive health cover is recommended for those who are not 100% fit. The health facilities available are more than adequate.
Visa requirements: Visas are not required for British nationals born in the UK. Those not born in the UK might have to get their employers to obtain a NOC (no objection certificate), before entry into Bahrain, although usually they can get a 3- or 5- day visa on arrival and the employer can sort out the arrangements in this period. Work permits are required and are obtained by the employer soon after the employee's arrival. In order to obtain a work permit, new employees must have a medical check-up in a certain health centre in Bahrain soon after arrival.
Accommodation: Varies from BD 140-300 per month for a studio or a 1/2 bedroom flat.
Other information: There is not a vast amount of EFL work in Bahrain. Some companies and ministries have language units within training departments (including the Ministry of Education). The University has an ELC, and there are a number of private institutes which teach English.

Bahrain is a very easy, relaxed place to live. There is plenty of nightlife (including alcohol), although the salaries are not as good as in the neighbouring countries and the cost of living is higher. Bahrain is one of the most pro-Western of the Gulf states.

List of schools in Bahrain

ACCESS, Tel: 722898.
The British Council, Tel: 26555.
IPE, Tel: 290028.
Polyglot Schools Ltd., Tel: 271722.

EGYPT

Minimum salary: Rates of pay vary greatly, but normally range between LE10-27 per hour, while the British Council pays LE 30,000-40,000 per annum. Other schools often pay less but may pay a dollar supplement.
Tax and health insurance: Teachers do not currently pay local tax. It is advisable to take out your own insurance policy in addition to your employer's provisions, particularly those who are employed on a part-time contract.
Visa requirements: Work permits are required and these are normally arranged by the school after arrival. A visa can be obtained from ports of entry.
Accommodation: A two-bedroom flat costs around LE 800-1,000 per month, or LE 300-400 for a good quality shared flat - less outside Cairo. In some cases accommodation may be provided free with your contract.
English language newspaper: *Egyptian Gazette* (daily).
Other information: Although salaries may seem rather low, Egypt is a very cheap country and teachers are able to manage a reasonably good standard of living on this type of wage. One of the most pro-Western Middle Eastern countries, English is widely spoken and there are a number of private language schools around Cairo, which usually

recruit internally. Despite problems with Islamic Fundamentalists, English is still popular, particularly amongst wealthy Egyptians.

List of schools in Egypt

American University in Cairo, Room 108, Division of Public Service, Falaki Street, Cairo.

ILI, 2 Muhammad Bayumy Street, Heliopolis.

ILI School (KG), Ziziniah, Alexandria.

International Centre for Idioms, (behind Wimpy Bar), Dokki.

International Language Institute Soafeyeen (ILI), 3 Mahmoud Azmi Street, Madinet El Sohafayeen, Embaba, Cairo.

International Language Learning Institute, Pyramids Road, Guiza.

Living Language College, Heliopolis.

IRAN

There has been a resurgence in the demand for English in Iran, with a huge growth in candidates sitting Cambridge exams. Although the government is becoming more and more moderate, work possibilities for westerners remain limited unless you are a Muslim.

English Language newspaper: *Teheran Times* (D).

ISRAEL

Minimum salary: The average rate of pay is 40 NIS per class contact hour.

Tax and health insurance: 20-25%.

Visa requirements: Jews are eligible for automatic citizenship and work permits. For non-jews of any nationality, your employer should arrange visas and permits.

Accommodation: At least $300/month for a shared flat

Other information: The recent liberalisation of Eastern and Central Europe has led to a large influx of immigrants, most of whom are keen to assimilate by learning English as well as Hebrew. It is becoming harder to obtain a work permit for Israel because of rising unemployment. However, the demand for English is high and there are many private language schools that are prepared to take on unqualified native English speakers.

ISRAELI OCCUPIED (PALESTINIAN) TERRITORIES

Minimum salary: The average rate of pay is 35 NIS per class contact hour.

Tax and health insurance: No taxation. Take out medical insurance.

Visa requirements: Teachers working for the British Council do not normally get a working visa, but generally get a tourist visa which must be renewed every three months.

Accommodation: In East Jerusalem it is expensive and rent for an ordinary flat for one month cost approximately $500. For a shared flat the going rate is about $300/month - less in Gaza and Nablus.

Other Information: The British Council is the only well-known English language school. Teachers are advised to expect to work under pressure, as circumstances are very stressful. Interestingly, demand for English has increased recently, as it is seen as potentially liberating, but the "intifada" has crippled the economy.

JORDAN

Minimum salary: At the British Council, the basic teacher's salary is currently JD 784 per month, plus increments for relevant qualifications and experience and a JD 200 housing allowance.

Tax and health insurance: Taxation rates are very informal and a teacher earning a salary at the above rate would pay JD 93 per month in tax.

Visa requirements: Entry visas are required for Jordan. To work there legally it is necessary to have both work and residence permits.

Accommodation: Accommodation is often hard to come by and sharing seems to be the best option.

English language newspaper: *The Jordan Times* (D).

Other information: Opportunities for TEFL are limited, although a few private schools are in need to teach English examination syllabuses. Traditionally one of the more tolerant and stable Middle Eastern countries, Jordan's economy is recovering after Gulf War setbacks.

List of schools in Jordan

American Language Center, Amman. Tel: 659859.

British Council, First Circle, Jebel Amman, P.O. Box 634, Amman 11118.

Yarmouk Cultural Centre, Amman. Tel: 671447.

KUWAIT

Minimum salary: KD 650-700 per month. Most expatriates manage to save well over half their salary.

Tax and health insurance: At present, all salaries are tax free. However, with the present national budget imbalance, there has been talk of foreign nationals being taxed at a future date. Similarly, at present medical treatment in Kuwaiti governmental clinics and hospitals is free for British nationals, but the government is currently considering the imposition of charges for non Kuwaitis. Some teachers take out private health insurance but several big EFL employers arrange financial support for medical expenses.

Visa requirements: Once in Kuwait, a series of medical tests are required before a full working visa, or residency as it is known in Kuwait, is granted. This includes a compulsory HIV test. Prospective teachers may choose to have a test in their home country, as any HIV+ cases are immediately deported, with no attempt at counselling or such like. Unlike some other Gulf countries, you cannot enter Kuwait without a "sponsor" who is responsible for obtaining your visa. It is not possible to come on a visitor's visa to search for employment. Airlines will not allow anyone to fly into Kuwait without presenting firm evidence of having obtained a visa.

Accommodation: In virtually all cases, the employer provides accommodation free of charge for expatriate EFL staff in Kuwait, although this may involve sharing with one or more colleagues. Such accommodation may or may not include free water and electricity - an important point worth clarifying in advance. Accommodation is also furnished.

English language newspaper: *Kuwait Times* (D), *Arab Times* (D).

Other information: As most EFL teacher come on one- or two- year contracts and leave without renewing, there is a constant demand for EFL staff in Kuwait. This has increased since the invasion brought home to many Kuwaitis the need to learn to speak more English themselves and to start their children learning as early as possible. It should be noted that EFL staff with experience of teaching young learners, age 6+ are particularly in demand.

Kuwait is a very small, relatively Islamic country with limited possibilities for social and recreational activities. Most EFL teachers come to amass capital rather than expecting or hoping to play a full part in the life of the country. It could be an excellent career move if one intended to study for a distance qualification, such as an MA. The government is keen to promote English and ties with the west. It is the working language of many Kuwaiti companies. ILC Hastings and English Worldwide recruit for Kuwait.

List of schools/organisations in Kuwait

American International School. Tel: 5318175.
ELU, The Kuwait Institute of Banking Studies, PO Box 1080, Safat 13011 (ESP teachers only).
Fahaheel English School. Tel: 3711070.
Gulf English School. Tel: 5629215.
Kuwait English School. Tel: 5629356.
Language Centre, PO Box 2575, Safat 13026.
Pitman Secretarial and Business Studies Centre. Tel: 2544840.

LIBYA

Despite trade sanctions, the economy is healthy. Although the British Council warns teachers to "proceed with caution", oil and private companies occasionally recruit teachers. Contact AFMENCO (UK) Ltd, 39 Marsh Green Road, Exeter EX2 8PN.

MOROCCO

Minimum salary: Terms and conditions vary widely and full-time contracts are not common, with teachers tending to be paid on a hourly basis. This ranges from 6,000-10,000 dirhams per month for 24-25 contact hours, with the hourly rate in the region of 50-120 dirhams, depending on qualifications (current exchange rate is 13.5 dirhams to the £ Sterling).

Tax and health insurance: The taxation rates are complex, by depending on the monthly income, tends to vary between 17-30%. Tax may be deducted at source, but in some cases teachers are expected to pay their own. A private health insurance policy is recommended.

Visa requirements: Entry visas are not required by British nationals, who are entitled to stay for up to three months without a residence permit. Employers generally arrange work permits for their expatriate teachers and original copies of your birth certificate, degree, and teaching qualification will be needed. Other nationals should apply well in advance to their local Moroccan embassy, or alternatively contact Ministere de l'Emploi, Quartier des Ministeres, Rabat, Morocco.

Accommodation: Usually unfurnished and a flat in one of the main towns will cost between 1500-3000 dirhams a month. If acquired through an agent, a fee of one month's rent is charged.

Other information: Qualified teachers should easily find employment. It is however, much easier to find employment from within the country than by postal application. Transport is good in the main cities and, despite high levels of inflation, eating out is inexpensive. In general the cost of living is relatively cheap however items of clothing and footwear tend to be more expensive. Morocco is currently liberalising its exchange regulations and foreign residents may now transfer 50% of their salaries in addition to payments into pension funds and foreign social security. A knowledge of French is useful.

List of schools in Morocco

American Language Center, 4 zankat Tanja, Rabat. 9 other centers.
The British Council Language Centre, 36 rue de Tanger, B.P. 467, Rabat
Business and Professional English Centre, 74 rue Jean Jaures, Casablanca.
ILC, Rabat. Tel: 70-97-18.
The London School of English, 10 ave. des Far, Casablanca.

OMAN

Minimum salary: 600-700 rials per month.
Tax: None
Visa requirements: Employer's sponsorship required for a permit, which can take some time.
Accommodation: Usually provided; if not, 250 rials per month.

English Language Newspaper: *Oman Daily Observer* (D), *Times of Oman* (D).

Other information: It is a popular destination, but less well paid than its neighbours. Most jobs are in Muscat. Conditions are relatively good for women and you can buy alcohol.

Contact **CFBT** (see p64) or the **English Language Teaching Dept.**, Ministry of Education, PO Box 3, Ruwi.

QATAR

Minimum salary: $22,000 pa-a low salary and a huge bonus.
Tax and health insurance: Free.
Visa requirements: UK nationals can enter on a tourist visa. Employer's sponsorship is required for a work permit.
Accommodation: Free or at minimal, subsidised rate.
Other information: This tiny Gulf state offers some of the best salaries in the area.

SAUDI ARABIA

Minimum salary: Salaries vary widely, but good employers will pay around 9,000 Saudi Riyals per month at the mid point of their salary scales, with actual starting salary depending on qualifications. Packages will vary however, from between SR 5,000-10,000 per month. Some employers will offer a 13 month bonus and all will offer a gratuity payment of half a month's salary for each completed year of service.
Tax and health insurance: There is no taxation or other deduction from gross salaries. Employers will normally provide health insurance as part of the employment package. If not, cover would be required for all normal medical requirements as clinics and hospitals are private. An HIV negative certificate is required to obtain an entry permit.
Visa requirements: Most foreign teachers will require a visa, which will only be issued when the formal application is backed by documentation from a sponsoring organisation. At least four weeks should be allowed for the issue of the visa, but it may take longer. Tourist visas are not issued for Saudi Arabia, and you cannot go there in order to seek work.
Accommodation: The housing market is volatile and prices are currently rising steadily. For a single prerson, expect to pay between SR 20,000-40,000 per year, and a married couple would probably need to spend between SR 60,000-100,000. Expatriates tend to live on compounds. The quality of accommodation is particularly important for families, since women are very restricted and cannot drive or generally work. Many employers will provide an allowance equivalent to anything up to three months' salary, while some may provide accommodation free with the contract.
English language newspaper: *Arab News* (D).
Other information: There are relatively few language schools, but a great number of Saudi-based companies which have large in-house English language training programmes. These provide the major employment opportunities in Saudi Arabia for EFL teachers.

The Saudi environment is very demanding, both climatically and culturally. The cost of living is relatively low, and teachers can save a considerable proportion of their salary. Employment opportunities for women are substantially more limited than for men.

It is not really recommended for families, or for periods of about more than three years. Couples will have the best opportunities of meeting people locally - otherwise male and female students are strictly segregated. If you are offered work as a couple (and you must be married), ensure that you can both obtain work permits - women are often refused these even with a job offer. Women are also prohibited from driving.

Despite the drawbacks, many teachers love working in Saudi and find the desert landscape uniquely beautiful. Others find the prospect of being able to earn enough to retire early or set up their own business more than compensates for a few years in an alien but fascinating culture.

List of schools in Saudi Arabia.

The British Council, Direct Teaching Operation, PO Box 58012, Riyadh 11594.
Education, End of Jareer Street, Malaz, Riyadh.
English Language Centre, King Adulaziz University, PO Box 1540, Jeddah 21441.
Girls' College of Arts - General Presidency for Female Institute for Languages and Translation, c/o King Saud University, PO Box 2465, Riyadh 11451.
Institute of Public Administration, PO Box 205, Riyadh 11411.
King Fahd University of Petroleum and Minerals, English Language Centre, Dhahran 31261.
Riyadh Military Hospital-Training Division, PO Box 7897, Riyadh 11159.
Saudi Arabian Airlines - Saudia cc:452, PO Box 167, Jeddah 21231.
Saudi Language Institute, PO Box 6760, Riyadh 11575.
SCECO - East Central Training Institute, PO Box 5190, Damman 31422.
Yanbu Industrial College, PO Box 30436, Yanbu Al Sinaiyah 21477.

SYRIA

Minimum salary: Salaries can be expected to be in the region of SL 20,000 per month.
Tax: Not applicable.
Visa requirements: A visa can be obtained from any Syrian Embassy, but the foreign teachers will need a sponsor. Upon arrival in Syria, a resident permit can be obtained, and only after that can a work permit be secured.

Accommodation: For reasonable accommodation in a one- or two-bedroom flat, you can expect to pay approximately SL 20,000-50,000 per annum.

List of Schools in Syria

Al Razi, Damascus. Tel: 457301.
American Language Center, Damascus. Tel: 2247236.
Dimashk al Lughawi, Damascus. Tel: 454615.

TUNISIA

Minimum salary: It is possible to find work on either a part-time basis paid hourly or on a full-time contracted basis. Average pay depends on the school and ranges from 400-1000 dinars per month.
Tax and health insurance: Under the state health scheme (CNSS), a contribution of 6.25% is made (employer adds 18%), and 1.75% for non-compulsory health cover (COMAR). Here the employer adds 6.25%. Many teachers do, however, take out private health insurance and it is recommended. The tax rate lies between 10-15%, dependent on level of income.
Visa requirements: EC nationals usually enter Tunisia on a three-month tourist visa which is given on arrival. The employer will then put in an application for a work permit and this involves a considerable amount of paper work and organisation. Original degree certificates and original birth certificates are required. While your permit is being processed you will probably receive a temporary work permit or a letter from your employer saying that you work for them, which is also sufficient for temporary identification. The official work permit is normally valid for 1-2 years, depending on your contract.
Accommodation: Many teachers choose to live in the expatriate belt of coastal suburbs where rents for two bedroom flats are around 250-300 dinars per month. In the less fashionable areas rents are cheaper.
Other information: Tunisia is one of the Arab world's most liberal nations and has a rich, cultural heritage. Although officially classed as a developing country, this is not apparent in the cosmopolitan and predominantly European capital. Tunisians are on the whole highly motivated to learn English which is slowly replacing French in business dealings within the capital. As most Tunisians speak French as a second language, a knowledge of French is more or less essential for survival. Much teaching takes place in the evenings and while general English is the mainstay, an increasing amount of work is being done in companies off site. Most of the EFL activity is in the capital, although small, private language schools are springing up in the provinces.

List of schools in Tunisia

English Language Training Centre, British Council, 47 Avenue Habib Bourguiba, Tunis.
IBLV, 47 Avenue de la Liberte, Tunis.

UNITED ARAB EMIRATES

Minimum salary: c. $22,000
Tax and health insurance: Free
Accommodation: Usually provided, otherwise expensive.
Visa requirements: Tourist visa issued readily. Employer's sponsorship required for work permits.
English language newspapers: *Emirates News, Gulf News, Khaleej Times* (D).
Other information: With the growth of tourism, there is a growing demand for both male and female EFL teachers. Both Abu Dhabi and Dubai are cosmopolitan, but relaxed, cities, without the restrictions normally associated with the Gulf.

List of organisations

Abu Dhabi National Oil Co. (ADNOC), PO Box 898, Abu Dhabi.
ECS Ltd., PO Box 25018, Arab Monetary Fund Building, Abu Dhabi. Tel: 971-2-344246, Fax: 328534 - employs over 350 teachers.

YEMEN

Minimum salary: 200,000 rilas/month. You may get a hard cureency supplement.
Tax: None
Visa requirements: It is usually easy to obtain a tourist visa from your local Yemen embassy. Application for a work permit can be made before or after entering the country.
Accommodation: Usually free with contract.
Other information: Not being an oil state, conditions in Yemen are very different to the other Gulf states. It is a traditional Arab country with a recent history of political instability.

SUB SAHARAN AFRICA

BOTSWANA

Minimum salary: Salaries for a graduate teacher with a PGCE begin at around 22,000 Botswana Pula (P) per year, but this varies according to qualifications and experience (current rate of exchange approx. P2.5 = $1).

Tax and health insurance: Tax is about 8-10% depending on income.

Visa requirements: Tough entry restrictions are in place requiring an entry visa or permit to be obtained merely to visit Botswana. Visitors can usually obtain a permit valid for a maximum of only thirty days -but only if they have a return ticket and evidence of sufficient financial support. All non-national teachers in the private sector require work permits from the Department of Labour, which are valid for only a limited period and must be renewed. Since employers are required to give preference to Botswana nationals, work permits are becoming increasingly difficult to obtain. For those employed in the public teaching sector, a combined residence and work permit is generally issued by the Immigration Department.

Accommodation: Most state schools subsidise accommodation and it is normally charged at a rate of 15% of salary. There is an acute shortage of housing and, in Gaborone in particular, teachers can expect to spend the first few months in a hotel while waiting for a house or flat to be allocated. There is a wide range of housing each with its own rental scale and a two-bedroom flat, for example, costs P400-P650 as Government housing, while renting a similar flat privately would cost between P1,500-P2,500 per month.

Other information: The demand for EFL teachers in Botswana is fairly low, given that English is the official language and medium of instruction in schools. However, native English speakers are in demand as teachers of English as a formal subject within the curriculum. Since most teachers are employed through the Teachers for Botswana Recruitment Scheme (TBRS), administered by The British Council in Manchester and the Department of Teaching Service Management in Botswana, these are the key sources to contact for further up-to-date information and advice on teaching in this country. Qualified teachers are recruited twice a year for two year contracts throughout Botswana.

CAMEROON

Minimum salary: Average rate of pay CFA 400,000 per month plus any allowances.

Tax and health insurance: Tax is charged at an average rate of 10%. Health problems are generally associated with malaria, typhus and stomach ailments, and, although there are good clinics and pharmacies, a private health insurance policy is advisable.

Visa requirements: Visa and work permits are required for all non-nationals.

Accommodation: Accommodation is reasonable and a furnished two-bedroom flat will cost between CFA 120,000-150,000 per month.

Other information: Teaching institutes tend to rely on Cameroonians or locally available native English speakers. Prospects are not great in the short term, due to the current economic crisis and unstable political situation. Teachers wishing to teach in the Cameroon should contact the Embassy and the British Council before doing so for an update on the social and political situation. A knowledge of French is desirable.

List of schools in the Cameroon

The American Cultural Centre, BP 817, Yaounde. Tel: (237) 23 14 37.
The British Council, Ave. Charles de Gaulle, BP 818, Yaounde. Tel: (237) 21 16 96.
The Presidency Bilingual Centre, BP 7239, Yaounde. Tel: (237) 22 18 11.

KENYA

The ODA have eight English resource centres in Kisii, Bubngoma, Embu, Kwale, Nyahururu, Garissa, Eldoret and Migwnani as part of the Secondary English Language Project (SELP). The British Council has a DTO in Nairobi specialising in business communication, and support a biannual ELT newsletter. Prospective teachers should contact the National Association of Teachers of English.

LESOTHO

There are no specialised EFL schools in Lesotho.

Visa requirements: Visas are not required by UK nationals for visits of less than 30 days. Visitors intending to stay longer should make an application for extended stay to the Director of Immigration and Passport Services in Maseru. This can normally be done after arrival.

Other information: Two official languages are taught and used in schools - English and Sesotho. English is widely understood, particularly in urban areas. Lesotho is a relatively healthy country, free from many of the diseases found in tropical Africa such as malaria, bilharzia and meningitis, and medicines are freely available. Post and telecommunications are fair, and it is possible to make direct international calls to most countries, although there are few public call boxes.

NAMIBIA

Most opportunities are in teacher training. Education has been conducted in English rather than Africaans since Namibia won independence in 1990. Try contacting the Namibian Ministry of Education. See also Volunteering, p79.

SOUTH AFRICA

Minimum salary: 1,800 rand per month, R20 per hour.
Visa requirements: You must have employment before you can obtain a work permit. This can be done within the country.
Accommodation: R400 for a flat, less for a furnished room.
Other information: The economic is in decline with 40% (largely black) unemployment. Language schools are flourishing to cater mainly for Europeans on study holidays. 35% of native whites speak English as a first language. State education is poor in black towns and is often funded by the ODA. English is the official language of the ANC and is much in demand.
Addresses:
Bloemfontein School of Languages, Bloemfontein.
Cape Town School of English, Claremont 7700. Cape Town. Tel: (021) 61 7635. Same address for information on South African Federation of English Language Schools.

SWAZILAND

Opportunities for EFL teachers in Swaziland are limited. There are no private sector language schools, however there is an international school which employs expatriate teachers called Waterford Kamhlava United World College - P.O. Box 52, Mbabane. Currently about 20% of secondary school teachers are non-Swazis, and most of these come from other African countries, though there are one or two foreign EFL teachers. Details of employment opportunities can be obtained from: The Teaching Service Commission, P.O. Box 39, Mbabane. The University of Swaziland has an Academic Communications Skills Unit, and offers rather better terms and conditions than the Ministry. There are a few European expatriate staff on local contract. Details from: The Registrar, University of Swaziland, Private Bag, Kwaluseni.

UGANDA

Uganda is an English speaking country, in which English is the medium of education. It does not therefore have English language schools. There are a number of private schools however which may offer opportunities. We have no salary guidelines at present.
Tax and health insurance: You should consider taking out health insurance which covers emergency repatriation to your home country.
Visa requirements: All foreigners now require an entry visa to visit Uganda, with single entry visas costing about $30, and multiple entry visas lasting six months costing $50. As for work permits, your employer should lodge an application for a work permit before your arrive. It takes time and bonds or a deposit air ticket may be required. You should register with the appropriate Consul soon after arrival.
Accommodation: Supply in the housing rental market has improved tremendously over the last year, and many new houses have been completed and are currently available for immediate letting. Most houses are unfurnished and a furnished house may cost $200-300 extra to furnish. Typical average monthly rents for an unfurnished two-bedroom house will be from $400 to well over $1,000 in the major urban areas.
Other information: Security risks do exist, so sensible precautions are necessary and carry some ID with you at all times.

ZIMBABWE

Minimum salary: Starting salary for a graduate with a teaching diploma is $1,600 per month.
Tax and health insurance: Tax is charged at a rate of 25-30% on such a salary and Public Services Medical Aid Insurance cost $25 per month.
Visa requirements: All teachers whether in private or state schools, are controlled by the Ministry of Education (P.O. Box 8022, Causeway, Harare) from whom a Temporary Employment Permit (TEP) must be obtained. This is granted for two years initially, and may be renewed annually up to a maximum of five years. It is a Catch 22 situation as you require a TEP to get a job, but a TEP is for a specific appointment to a specific school, and may not be transferable. Some recruitment is carried out by the Zimbabwe High Commission in London.
Accommodation: A rural school will provide one room in a share house for $20 per month. A one-bedroom flat in Bulawayo costs $300-500 per month and in Harare between $500-1,000 a month.
Other information: Teaching posts in Zimbabwe are not easy to obtain. As English is the medium of instruction throughout the educational system (officially at least), specialised EFL appointments do not exist.

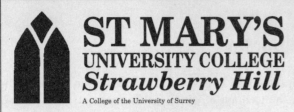

ST MARY'S
UNIVERSITY COLLEGE
Strawberry Hill
A College of the University of Surrey

MA, APPLIED LINGUISTICS & ELT
MA, LINGUISTICS IN EDUCATION
DIPLOMA IN
LINGUISTICS & EDUCATION

Whether you are:
- **Teaching ELT as a foreign or second language**
- **Training teachers**
- **Involved in ELT administration**
- **A native or non-native speaker**

Courses look at theory and practice of ELT
Assessment based on coursework and dissertation
- no written examination -

These courses are offered on a full and
part-time basis.The part-time courses run two
evenings a week from 6-8pm
**Accommodation guaranteed for overseas
students**

For further information please contact:
The Registry, St Mary's College,
Strawberry Hill, Twickenham TW1 4SX
081-892 0051 ext 249 081-744 2080 (Fax)

 Diploma in TEFL

Aims: [a] to provide an understanding of the principles of teaching and learning English as a foreign and second language together with an ability to apply language description and analysis to the professional task; [b] to provide teaching observation and practice, and classroom methodology workshops suitable for the candidate's individual level of experience in the TEFL profession; [c] to develop relevant skills in the description and analysis of English grammar, vocabulary and pronunciation both at basic and at higher levels of language structure; [d] to enable candidates to develop a topic of their own personal interest in the composition of a 5,000 word project.

Objectives: each candidate will have sufficient knowledge, skills and the confidence to teach a full range of learners of English from beginning to advanced and will have reached a level of professional ability above that of the RSA Diploma in TEFLA.

Programme: Principles and Methods of Language Teaching; Teaching Observation and Practice; Practical Workshops; Description, and Phonetics, of English; Applied Linguistics.

Fee: only 75% of standard university fee. Courses begin every October. Optional extra courses in computing and practical phonetics; writing centre (all free).

Further information and application papers from: The Secretary, English Language Studies, UWCC, PO Box 94, Cardiff CF1 3XB. Fax: (0222) 874242; Tel: (0222) 874243

Certificates, Masters and Research courses also available.

TESOL
at
MANCHESTER UNIVERSITY

First Certificate in Teaching English to Speakers of Other Languages (TESOL)

Diploma and M.Ed Courses in TESOL
M.Ed in Educational Technology and TESOL

Also degrees by research: M.Phil, PhD

Modes of attendance to suit the applicant: full-time, part-time, distance, summer

Diploma, M.Ed and research degrees can be started at the beginning of any term

Contact:
The Secretary, CELSE,
School of Education, Manchester University,
Oxford Road, Manchester M13 9PL

Tel: 061-275 3467; Fax: 061-275 3480

PROFESSIONAL DEVELOPMENT

In order to progress through the hierarchy of EFL, you need a mixture of experience and training, so there is a wide range of courses available; from specialised weekend courses to Masters degrees and PhDs. Once you are on the first rung of the ladder, this section you how to choose courses that will ensure your steady climb to the top.

SO, YOU WANT TO DO A FURTHER QUALIFICATION?

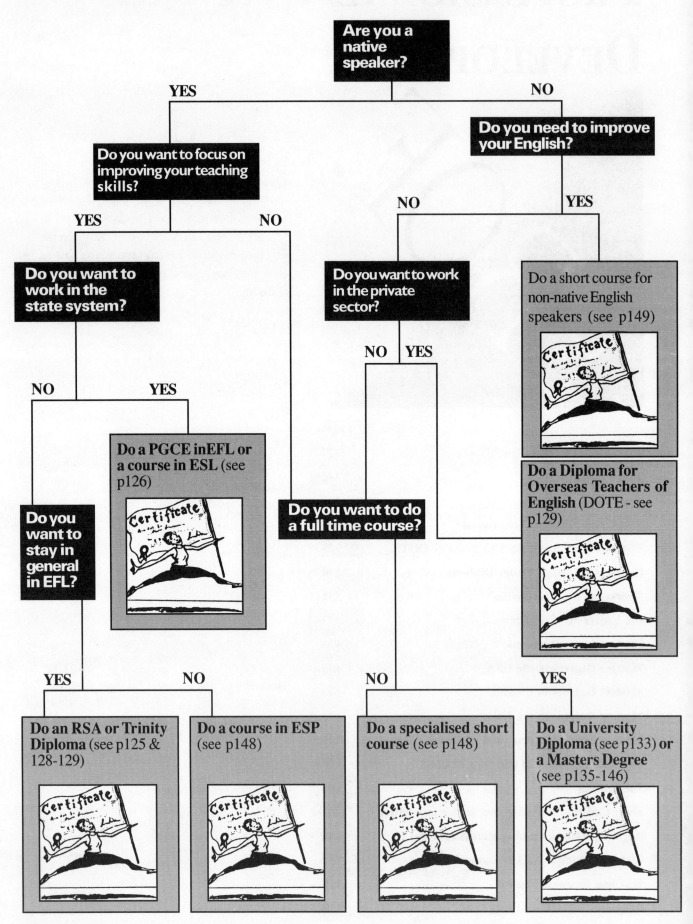

Are you a native speaker?

YES / NO

Do you need to improve your English?

Do you want to focus on improving your teaching skills? (YES / NO)

NO / YES

Do you want to work in the state system? (YES)

Do you want to work in the private sector?

Do a short course for non-native English speakers (see p149)

NO / YES

NO / YES

Do a PGCE in EFL or a course in ESL (see p126)

Do a Diploma for Overseas Teachers of English (DOTE - see p129)

Do you want to stay in general in EFL?

Do you want to do a full time course?

YES / NO

NO / YES

Do an RSA or Trinity Diploma (see p125 & 128-129)

Do a course in ESP (see p148)

Do a specialised short course (see p148)

Do a University Diploma (see p133) or a Masters Degree (see p135-146)

YOUR CAREER PATH

Everyone has different career objectives, which may rely upon qualifications, so here are the most popular options.

Although its emphasis is on successful classroom methods, Teaching English as a Foreign Language is still an academic discipline and it is important that you take time out to continue studying and researching as your career develops. Academic qualifications will definitely be a factor in obtaining high profile jobs, especially in the public sector.

Let's suppose you start with a university degree and a Cambridge RSA or Trinity preparatory certificate, obtained by doing a short training course, as discussed in Section Two (see pages 23-62).

A Diploma

Some teachers may choose immediately to study for a recognised EFL diploma, for example, the Cambridge\RSA or Trinity Diploma. This exam contains both written papers and a practical, two lessons, each with a different class, taught by you, observed by an examiner and marked accordingly. Many teachers prefer to have practical teaching experience for up to a year before entering for a Diploma. A diploma course may take up to three months' study.

A distance learning RSA Diploma has also been offered for many years by International House. However, to take the examination you will need to be registered with a recognised school.

A diploma is a recognition of your practical application of the theory and practice of Teaching English as a Foreign Language. You will probably have to have it if you wish to continue in classroom teaching beyond two years.

Experienced teachers with two years or more classroom experience behind them may proceed directly to the Diploma in Education, specialising in EFL. This is also a one year University degree course, equivalent to the general Postgraduate Diploma in Education (DipEd) which quantifies teachers in other subjects to teach in secondary schools.

The Master of Arts (MA)

Academically, EFL is an application of linguistics and many teachers choose to do a one year MA in Applied Linguistics. As part of your MA course you will have to do research for a short

dissertation, This may allow you to pursue areas of special interest, for example the use of media or the use of video in ELT. If this is the case, you should look for colleges that have a special interest in this area, such as the University of Westminster or the Language Centre at Brighton Polytechnic.

Doctorate in Philosophy (PhD)

Either as a manifestation of your academic interest or because you intend to undertake a university teaching career, you may wish to study for a doctorate. Doctorates involve researching and writing a dissertation on your chosen area of research and can last from between two years (full time research) and what sometimes seems like a lifetime (part time). The subject for your doctoral research must be agreed by a University at the outset and a research supervisor will be assigned to you. Some Universities, London is one, offer a one year MPhil (Masters in Philosophy) which counts towards the full doctorate. This might be appropriate for a practising teacher who has done the Diploma and wants to approach doctorate work without doing the MA.

English for Specific Purposes (ESP)

If you have some EFL teaching experience, you can do a course in ESP. A specialist background, such as in business, will make you particularly suitable to teach ESP, which is teaching English towards a specific objective. If your students want to be doctors or pilots, they will need specific English for this, so ESP is job rather than exam orientated. ESP courses analyse the needs of such students, looking at syllabus design and materials development. See p148 and pages 149-157 for course details.

English for Academic Purposes (EAP)

EAP courses are generally run for non-native English speakers who wish to attend anglophone higher educational establishments. Courses give students the language skills to understand lectures, write essays, etc. Probably the best way into EAP is to do a related short course and apply for a support service position with a university in a non-anglophone country. This will give you the academic background. If you succeed in this competitve field, senior university positions and their respective salaries will follow.

Academic qualifications will definitely be a factor in obtaining high profile jobs, especially in the public sector.

A specialist background, such as in business, will make you particularly suitable to teach ESP.

English as a Second Language (ESL)

In the United States ESL refers to teaching English to all foreign students in the country. In the UK, Australia, Canada and New Zealand ESL or E2L refers to teaching English to immigrants. Unlike general EFL students, immigrants' main needs are how to integrate into the country's educational system, work environment and general social culture. ESL is taught to children and adults, with courses often run by state schools and colleges.

A move into ESL can offer EFL teachers the opprtunity to stay in their native country.

A move into ESL can offer EFL teachers the opprtunity to stay in their native country in a job with a clearer career structure. Although levels of pay are not particularly high, ESL teaching may, perhaps, offer more social satisfaction.

In the UK the National Association for the Teaching of English and Other Community Languages to Adults (NATECLA) has been campaigning for more bilingual and non-native teachers in ESL, particularly those who speak the languages of the Indian sub-continent, Vietnamese, Turkish, Arabic or Greek. Courses in ESL in the UK include the RSA/Cambridge Certificate in TESL for Adults and their Diploma in Further Adult and Community Education.

International Equivalence

If you intend to work in another country in the national education system it is important to check that your qualifications are comparable to the qualifications in the country in which you intend to work. For example, in some countries a British MA is considered equivalent only to a first degree. If you intend to settle down in a foreign country for the duration of you career and work within the national education system, you should seriously consider studying for the teaching qualifications that pertain in that system. It could avoid all kinds of problems.

Go East!

You will have a better opportunity for many EFL jobs if you have travelled.

You will have a better opportunity for many EFL jobs if you have travelled. The reason is simple - if you are working with foreign students, experience of their cultures and countries will enrich you and the institution you are working for. If you have the opportunity of spending a couple of years teaching in a country outside Western Europe, it will be an employment advantage.

Publish and be saved!

All academic progress in enhanced by publishing and EFL is no exception. EFL lives on the interchange of ideas between teachers and several magazines and journals are devoted to making this happen.

You don't have to be a university researcher to carry out your own classroom research. In recent years academics have stressed the importance of teachers carrying out informal research into what works and doesn't work for their students. Teachers can carry out their own classroom research into methodology or materials and write up the results for any one of a number of journals such as ELTJ (English Language Teaching Journal), PET (Practical English Teaching), MET (Modern English Teacher) or local journals. Also there is the opportunity to present your observations and research at conferences, which can in turn be the source of more seminar work or even of publishing contracts. More details of journals and conferences are on p168 "Keeping in Touch".

EFL is an astonishingly varied career. As well as travel throughout the world, it offers opportunities in children's and adult education, in the corporate sector and at university, as well as in publishing and the media. So grab it with both hands, decide where you want to go and go there!

STARTING AGAIN

Many teachers in the State educational system retire early or decide at a late stage to begin a new career in EFL. Similarly an increasing number of people retiring early or made redundant in other careers are looking into EFL as a possible alternative. Some healthy retired people have chosen to spend their early retirement years doing voluntary work in with VSO (Voluntary Service Overseas) or other charity organisations (see p79).

It's important to stress two things. First, in the UK and USA competition for jobs is fierce at the moment. Second, EFL teaching is different from school teaching in that the stress is not so much on imparting information as on helping learners to develop a skill.

For these reasons, whatever your background and qualifications, retraining as an EFL teacher is essential before you go into the classroom. A 4-week preparatory certificate course will help you find out if you are suited to the hands-on teaching approach required, but don't be put off if you find it personally quite testing and that you are not totally successful immediately! Not everybody excels in a new discipline in four weeks. As for new teachers, a diploma will be an essential part of you job-seeking armoury and you may choose to do the twelve-week course first. It's not cheap but immensely worthwhile. Regard this as an investment in a new and fulfilling career.

HOW WILL QUALIFICATIONS HELP ME?

I am an experienced native English speaking teacher of EFL but I have no qualification. What should I do?
It is a good idea to get a qualification. You do not necessarily need to do a certificate course, which is the course most teachers of EFL will initially take. If you want to work in the private sector and you have more than two years' experience, you could do an RSA or Trinity Diploma (see p 125). Note, however, that some centres may prefer you to do the RSA Certificate before they will let you do the Diploma. If you want to work in the state system, you must achieve Qualified Teacher Status.

Does any qualification guarantee a job?
There is a popular myth that if you do a Masters degree, you will automatically get a better job. This is not necessarily true. Although jobs which require MAs generally pay well, there are not many of them around and far too many teachers with MAs chasing them. There is, however, a shortage of experienced teachers with diplomas.

I do not have any EFL qualifications. Can I do a teachers' course?
Yes - not having any previous qualifications is not a bar to entry if you have some teaching experience. If you have two years' experience you can do a Masters degree or a diploma. A recent report showed that 50% of people taking Masters courses had no EFL qualifications.

Is a university diploma equivalent to an RSA or Trinity Diploma?
It can be equivalent if it contains teaching practice, but generally it is a completely different qualification (see p131).

Are MAs much the same price?
The cost of MAs does vary from country to country. In general,

MAs in Australia and Canada are relatively cheap. In the EC, most countries have comparable costs. MAs for overseas teachers - i.e. non-residents - are more expensive. Be warned also that if you are a British teacher who has been overseas for a long time, you could be classed as an overseas teacher in the UK.

Are all MA courses similar?
Not really. Because some universities are inevitably better equipped with staff and materials in some fields, MA courses at such universities will also be stronger in those fields (see p135,141,145).

I am interested in computers/ literature/drama. What should I do?
There are courses that focus on a specialised area of teaching (see p148 - 157).

How can I pay for any further training that I do?
If you are an EU citizen, you may be eligible for a Career Development Loan - ask your college. If you do a course in Australia, you have automatic, limited work rights, whatever your nationality. In the US and Canada you can only legally work on the college campus.

Can I do a further training course while I am working?
Yes. You can do an RSA Cambridge or Trinity Diploma while you are working. Also, some MAs can be taken as distance learning courses (although these tend to suit only experienced teachers) and others can be taken on a modular basis.

I want to train to get into management. What should I do?
You could do an MBA (Masters in Business Administration). Many EFL teachers are now turning to this qualification as a way of either getting into management within EFL,

or of broadening out of EFL into general management (see p77 and p125). Bristol University, in conjunction with International House, run a management stream. West Sussex University also run a management course. Some other British MAs also incorporate management training elements. IATEFL (the International Association of Teachers Of English as a Foreign Language) has a Special Interest Group (SIG) dedicated to management (see addresses p168).

I want to teach English as a Second Language (ESL) in the UK. What should I do?
Many EFL teachers change to ESL as an opportunity to have a clearer career structure. It also offers the means to remain teaching in your native country in the primary or state sector (see p148).

I want to teach English for Specific Purposes (ESP). What is the best thing to do?
Teaching English in specific specialised subjects such as English for banking is a growing area. If you have a specialist background you could be in demand (see p148 and p157). Training courses in ESP, although not obligatory, are a common requirement for teaching ESP.

I am a primary specialist. Which is the best course for me?
There are various short courses that incorporate such experience (see p149 - 156).

Will I automatically get more money if I am better qualified?
Unfortunately not. There is no incremental system as such within the private EFL sector. Only state schools and major employers, such as the British Council, have a rigid incremental system.

RSA CAMBRIDGE DIPLOMA (DTEFLA)

College	Course length	FT/ PT	Fees	Start dates	Entry requirements	Contact	Comments	Max no of students
Anglo School, London	16 wks	PT	£755	Oct	CTEFLA + 2 yrs exp	John Sheperd		14
Bell Language School, Cambridge	30 wks	PT	£895 + exam fee	Oct	2 yrs exp	Sue Sheerin		15
The Bell Language School, Norwich	10 wks	FT	£1,300 + exam fee	Mar	2 yrs exp	Sarah Knights		15
The Bell Language School, Essex	10 wks	FT	£1,300 + exam fee	Mar	2 yrs exp	Robin Davis		15
CILC, Cheltenham	9 wks	FT	TBA	TBA		Gillian James		12
City of Liverpool Community Coll	1 yr	PT	£850	Sep	As per UCLES	Diana Lane	Own teaching practice needed	10
Colchester Institute	10 wks	FT	£600 + exam fee	Jan	Degree + 2 yrs exp	Simon Haines		12
Eastbourne School of English	8 mnths	PT	£880	Oct	Degree + CTEFLA + some exp	Dorothy S Rippon	Practising teachers	12
University of Edinburgh	10 wks	FT	On appl	Mar, Oct	Degree/Teaching Qual + exp	Sec, Inst of Appl Lang Studs		8
GLOSCAT, Cheltenham	36 wks	PT	£600	Sep	On appl	Beth Grant		12
Greenhill College, Harrow	9 mnths	PT	£450	Oct	Substantial TEFL exp	Judith Haigh	2 days per week	10
Hammersmith & West London Coll	1 yr	PT	£405 + exam fee	Sep	CTEFLA + 2/3 yrs exp	Course Director	Apply before June	15
Hilderstone Coll, Broadstairs	9 mnths	PT	£850 + exam fee	Oct	High level educ + 2 yrs exp	Valerie Horne		12
International House, London	8 wks / 8 mnths	FT / PT	£1200 + exam fee	Mar / on appl	Degree + CTEFLA + 2 yrs exp			12
Intl. Lang. Centres, Hastings	8 wks	FT	£1200 + exam fee	Mar, Oct	CTEFLA + 2 yrs exp	Adrian Underhill	Accom. Service available	12
ITTC, Bournemouth	8 wks / 8 mnths	FT / PT	£1,037 + exam fee	Oct, Feb, Apr	Degree + 2 yrs exp	Louise Earel-Jones		15
Lancashire College, Chorley	10 mnths	PT / DL	£1,200 + exam fee	Oct	Degree + 2 yrs exp	Mr Yeoman/ Mrs Wood	Residential college	16
Mid-Cheshire College, Northwich	1 yr	PT	£200	Sep	Degree + 2 yrs exp	Peter Main		18
Moray House, Edinburgh	3 mnths	FT	£1,335	Jan	Degree or equiv + 2 yrs exp	The Registrar		15
Northumbria Uni, Newcastle	1 yr	PT	£590 + exam fee	Oct	Degree/Teaching Qual or equiv	Dept Office Hist & Crit Studs	Flexible exit and entry pts	15
Richard Language Coll, Bournemouth	1 yr	PT	TBA	Sep		Director of Studies		14
Skola Teacher Training, London	8 wks / 10 mnths	FT / PT	£1,200	Jul	CTEFLA + 2 yrs exp	Lyndel Sayle	8 wks London; DL exams O'seas	15
Stevenson Coll, Edinburgh	31 wks	PT	£800	Oct	Degree + some exp	David Gibson		-
UTS Oxford Centre, Oxford	8 mnths	PT	£1,200 + exam fee	Oct	CTEFLA + Degree + 2 yrs exp	Mark Bartram		14
Waltham Forest College, Essex	1 yr	PT eves	£350 + exam fee	Sep	Currently in EFL + 2 yrs exp	Course Tutor	Apply from May	12

TRINDIP

College	Course length	FT/PT	Fees	Start dates	Entry requirements	Contact	Comments	Max no. of students
Aberdeen College	Various	PT	£165	Various	2 yrs exp	Anne Bain		
Chichester School of English	1 yr	PT	£660 + exam fee	Oct	TEFL Cert + 2 yrs exp	Director of Studies		20
Farnborough College of Tech	1 yr	PT	£460 + moderation fee	Sep	Native and non-native speakers	A Ashwell	Career advice given	16
ITS English School, Hastings	1 yr	PT	£1,250	Aug	2 yrs exp	John Palim		6
Oxford House College, London	1-3 yrs	DL	£1,000	Anytime	TEFL Cert + 2 yrs exp	Chris Polatch	DL + 2 week "London Block".	-
St Brelade's College, Jersey	9 mths	DL	£920 + exam fee	Jan, Sep	2 yrs exp	Mr Brown Miss Pastorelli	Incl. 4 wk residential block	12
Sheffield Hallam University	4 wks 40 wks	FT DL	£1200 £900	Aug	Degree + CTEFLA or teaching exp	Gill King		40
South East Essex College	Varies	FT PT	on appl	On req	On appl; Interview	Marketing		-
Surrey ACE Serv, Woking	4 terms	PT	£390	Oct	Degree + 2 yrs exp			16

DOTE1

College	Course length	FT/PT	Fees	Start dates	Entry requirements	Contact	Comments	Max no. of students
Bilkent University, Turkey	20 mths	FT	TBA	Oct	Min 2 yrs exp	Head of TT		12
British Council, Athens	9 mths	FT	on appl	Sep	TEFL qual + 2 yrs exp	Martha Cavoura		16
British Council, Thessaloniki	1 yr	PT	TBA	Oct	CPE + 500 hrs teaching	Camilla Ralls		16
Eastern Mediterranean University, Turkey	18 mths	PT	N/A	Sep	Degree + 2 yrs exp	Edward Casassa		10
Klubschule Migros, Switzerland	2 yrs	PT	SFR 7850	Sep	Practising teacher & Cambridge Prof	Peter Holland	Special Prospectus	18
Study Space, Thessaloniki	9-18 mths	PT	varies	Oct, Jan	2 yrs exp + CEELT II + interview	Chrissie Taylor	Practising teachers only	8

OTRINDIP

College	Course length	FT/PT	Fees	Start dates	Entry Requirements	Contact
ECS Abu Dhabi	8 mths	PT DL	On req	Oct	Degree or equiv; 3 yrs exp	Kate MacFarlane
ECS Dubai	8-10 mths	PT DL	On req	May, Oct, Mar, Sep	Degree or equiv; 3 yrs exp	Charles Boyle
RELC, Singapore	On appl	FT PT	On req	On appl		SEAMEO Lang Centre

College	Course length	FT/ PT	Fees	Start dates	Entry requirements	Contact	Comments	Max no of students
Australian TESOL Centre, NSW	8 wks	FT	$2,990	Feb	Degree or equiv + 2 yrs exp	Gloria Smith		12
Bilkent Univ., Turkey	9 mths	PT	$1,000	Oct	2 yrs exp	Head of TT Unit		12
British Council, Athens	9 mths	PT	on appl	Sep	CTEFLA + 2 yrs exp	Martha Cavoura		16
British Council, Cairo	8 mths	PT	1,200 LE	Nov	BC staff only	Charles Napier		8
British Council, Hong Kong	12 wks	PT	HK$ 20,000	Sep	Degree, CTEFLA + 2 yrs exp; Eng prof	Rebecca Ho		
British Council, Lisbon	8 mths	PT	N/A	Oct	As per UCLES	Julie Tice		18
British Council, Milan	9 mths	PT	2.2 m ITL	Oct	2 yrs exp	David Gibbon	On Friday	14
British Council, Naples	9 mths	PT	2.69m ITL	Sep	CTEFLA + 2 yrs exp	F C de laMotte	Practising teachers	6
British Council, Riyadh	1 yr	PT DL	on appl	Sep	Standard IH reqs	Senior Teacher		4
British Council, Singapore	9 mths	PT DL	S$4500	Sep	Teaching Qual; 2 yrs exp; Eng Prof	Rose	Teaching Adults OR Youngsters	18
British Council, Thessaloniki	1 yr	DL	on appl	Oct	Degree + 2 yrs exp	Camilla Ralls		10
British Institute of Florence	9 mths	PT	2.3 m ITL	Oct	CTEFLA pref.	School Director		12
British Institute in Paris	30 wks	PT	FR 14150	Oct	Practising teacher; several yrs exp pref	Eng Dept Sec TEFL	Incl teaching practice	12
British Language Centre, Madrid	2 mths 8 mths	FT PT	£1200 approx	Oct, Jul	Degree + CTEFLA pref	Alastair Dickinson	Help with accomm	15
British School of Milan	8 mths	PT	2.1m ITL	Oct	Degree + substantial exp	Rafaela Aldinucci	Need exp at all levels	16
Cambridge School, Verona	9 mths	PT	2.1 m ITL	Oct	Degree, CTEFLA + 2 yrs exp pref	Anne Parry		£18
Elcra-Bell, Geneva	30 wks	PT DL	SFR 5,000	Sep	As per UCLES	Sean Power		£10
International House, Barcelona	8 wks 6 mths	FT PT	240000 PTS	Jul Oct	Degree or equiv + 2 yrs exp	Jenny Johnson	Help with accomm	£18
International House, Budapest	8 mths	PT	on appl	Oct	CTEFLA + 2 yrs exp	Head of TT	For teachers in Budapest	12
International House, Lisbon	8 wks	FT	£960	July	CTEFLA + 2 yrs exp	Kathryn Gordon	Interview	12
International House, Madrid	8 mths	PT	250000 PTS	Oct	CTEFLA + 2 yrs exp	Steven Haysham		15
International House, Rome	8 mths	PT	2.4m ITL	Oct	As per UCLES	Director		14
International House, Vienna	9 mths	DL	1500	Oct	Training Qual + 2 yrs exp	Head of Training		5
Language Centre of Ireland, Dublin	8 mths	PT	IR £850	Oct	Pre-course interview	Tom Doyle		14
Languages Intl, Auckland, NZ	9 mths	PT	NZ$ 4,000	Sep	On appl	John McMahon		12

UK UNIVERSITY COURSES

Pre-experience certificates, post-experience certificates, diplomas and Masters degrees.

There are too many EFL teacher training courses offered by universities to list here, but the following information describes courses leading to certificates, advanced certificates and diplomas. Remember that there are many new universities, as changes in legislation have enabled British polytechnics to run degree courses and become universities

Pre-experience certificates

The term 'certificate' generally refers to a short course between three and six months in length. Most certificates in the UK are initial teacher training courses open to native and non-native speakers. It is possible to take a university certificate in most Anglophone countries instead of the more widely known RSA Cambridge or Trinity Certificates (see p27). However, if you take a university course, make sure it includes teaching practice with foreign students and not just peer teaching with other teachers on your course. Many employers will not recognise such a qualification unless it includes teaching practice.

Post-experience certificates

These are usually called 'advanced certificates' and last three to six months. They are designed for people who either have experience but no previous qualifications, or who have training and need further qualifications without having the time to do a full Masters degree. Recently there has been a growth in advanced certificates for experienced teachers wishing to specialise in ESP or teacher training, for example.

Postgraduate diplomas

These are usually a year in length, and are for experienced native or non-native English speakers. They are not automatically seen as equivalent to the RSA Cambridge or Trinity College Diplomas (see p27) unless they include teaching practice with EFL students.

The advantage of such courses is that they have easier entry requirements to the Masters programmes, and they should be more practical and less academic - although this is not always the case. The disadvantage of such courses is that too many universities offer exactly the same courses for diplomas or Masters. Either check the contents of the course carefully, or make sure that you opt for a course that allows you to move over from a diploma to a Masters if you do well enough.

There is also an infinite variety in academic level between one diploma and another. This is partly because there is no validation scheme for diplomas in the UK. Universities validate their own degrees, and while control of degree awards such as Masters are strictly regulated by mastership committees, diploma status seems to be more easily conferred. In effect a diploma is any course that is not a Masters, although the British Association of Applied Linguistics (BAAL) is trying to rectify this.

Masters degrees

Teachers of EFL/ESL in the United States generally hold an MA in TESL or Applied Linguistics as a minimum qualification, largely because there is no widely recognised equivalent to the RSA or Trinity Certificates (see p27). The only problem with this system is that many MA courses offer theoretical tuition with too little practical guidance. For this reason, teachers are not adequately prepared to teach in the classroom. It is therefore vital to check the Masters degree has a solid teaching component.

Elsewhere, teachers of EFL tend to take a Masters degree as a way up the careers ladder (see p141 - 144). Remember that there are now a great number of EFL teachers who hold a Masters degree, far more than there are jobs that require them. For this reason, it may be more useful to do the RSA or Trinity College Diplomas (see p125).

For details of university courses, see p132 - 134.

If you take a university course, make sure it includes teaching practice with foreign students.

Make sure that you opt for a course that allows you to move over from a diploma to a Masters if you do well enough.

College	Course Title	Course length	FT/ PT	Fees	Start dates	Entry requirements	Contact	Comments
Aston University	Cert in Principles of ESP	12 wks	FT	£1,882	Oct, Jan, Apr	Degree + 3 yrs exp	Sec, Lang Studs Unit	
	Advanced Cert in Principles of ESP	6 mths	DL	£1,100	Jan	Degree + teaching exp	Sec, Lang. Studs Unit	EFL exp. not necessary
Canterbury Christ Church College	Cert. TEFL	10 wks	FT	£332 EC £1715 non EC	Sep, Jan	Degree + relevant exp	Steven Bax	
College of St Mark & St John, Plymouth	Cert in TESP	1 term	FT	£2,600	Jan, Apr	Teaching Qual or 3 yrs exp	Director, Intl Ed Centre	
Edinburgh University	Advanced Cert in ELT	1 yr	DL	£1,150	May	Higher Ed + 3 yrs exp	Ian McGrath	2 wk res in July. Help with accomm.
	Advanced Cert in ELT	10 wks	FT	£1,200	Oct, Mar	Higher Ed; 3 yrs exp; Eng comp	Ian McGrath	Intensive
University of Essex	Cert. TEFL	10 wks	FT	£1,075	Oct	Degree + some exp	D Meyer	
Goldsmith's College, London	Cert. in Lang Teaching to Adults	1 yr	PT	£350	Oct	Degree or equiv; Good English	L Arthur	Apply early
University of Liverpool	Cert TEFL/ ESP	6 wks 6 mths	FT PT	£920	Jul Jan	Degree	Gill Richardson	Accomm available
Manchester University	First Cert. in TEFL	4 wks 4 mths	FT PT	675	Jul Feb	Degree	Debbie Cash	Apply early
Portsmouth University	Cert. TEFLA	1 yr	PT	£510	Oct	Uni entrance level	Course Secretary	Tues + Sats
	PostGrad Cert Appl Linguistics + TEFL	1 sem 2 sems	FT PT	£2270 EC £5057 non EC £645 PT	Oct	Degree or Teaching Qual or equiv + exp	Dr Paul Rastall	
Salford University	Advanced Cert. in EFL	3 mths	FT	£380	Oct, Jan, Apr	EFL exp preferred	Rob Langley	
University of Strathclyde	Cert. of Further Studs in Ed- TEFL	10 wks	FT	£1,500	As req	Teaching Qual + 2 yrs or 5 yrs exp	Paul Curtis	Modular & flexible course.
University of Surrey	Cert TESOL	1 mth	FT	600	July	N/A	Secretary	Incl practice; accomm avail
University College Swansea	Cert. TEFL	4 wks	FT	£730	8 per year	Degree + native speaker	Director, TEFL Training	Member of BATQI
University of Wales, Cardiff	Cert. TEFL	10 wks	FT	£750	Oct	Degree or equiv	Ms C Wilkinson	Incl Teaching practice
	Cert. in Applied Lings for ELT	10 wks	FT	£753 EC £1850 non EC	Jan	Degree + some exp	Dr P Tench	Teaching practice avail

College	Course Title	Course length	FT/PT	Fees	Start dates	Entry requirements	Contact	Comments
Aston University	Dip TE/TESP	6 mths 12 mths	FT DL	£1,385 EC £3529 non EC	Oct, Jan	Degree + 2 yrs exp	Sec, Lang Studs Unit	CTEFLA useful
University of Brighton	Dip TEFL	1 yr 2 yrs	FT PT	£900 £540	Oct	Degree + exp or Initial TT	Zamy Alibhai	
Bristol University	Dip/ MEd TEFL	1 yr 2-5 yrs	FT PT	£2,000 EC £5700 non EC	Sep, Oct, Jan	On application	Arlene Gilpin	Gd research & training
Canterbury Christ Church College	Dip TEFL	1 yr 2 yrs	FT PT	£220 EC per module £5046 non EC	Oct	Degree or Cert + relevant exp	Steven Bax	
University of East Anglia	PostGrad Dip ELT & App Lings	8 mths	FT	£2,260 EC £5550 non EC	Sep	Degree or EFL training	Dr Jeremy Fox	No exp required
University of Essex	Dip TEFL	9 mths	FT	£2,260 EC £5550 non EC	Oct	Degree + 2 yrs exp	D Meyer	
University of Hull	Dip Applied Lang & New Tech	9 mths 21 mths	FT PT	£2,260 EC £5550 non EC £630 PT	Oct	Degree pref.	Language Centre	
Leeds University	Advanced Dip in ELT	1 yr	FT	£2,200 EC £5700 non EC	Oct	Degree + 3 yrs exp or 5 yrs exp	Hywel Coleman	
Liverpool University	Dip ELT	1 yr 1-4 yrs	FT PT	£4,400	Oct, Jan, Apr	Degree + 2 yrs exp; Non-native 6.5 IELTS	Gill Richardson	Foundation theme + 4 mods
London Guildhall University	LCCI Dip in TE for Business	2x3 wks	FT	£1390 + exam fee	July	Degree, EFL Qual + 1yr Bus Eng teaching exp	David Scarborough	Awarded by LCCI
Manchester University	Dip TESOL	1yr 1-6 yrs	FT PT DL	£2,260	Oct, Jan	Degree + 2 yrs exp	Debbie Cash	
University of Newcastle upon Tyne	Dip Advanced Ed Studies	1 yr	FT	£2,260 EC £5550 non EC	Oct	Teaching Qual + 2 yrs exp	The Director	Day-time course
University of Northumbria at Newcastle	PostGrad Dip TEFL	2 yrs	PT	£590 + exam fee	Oct	Degree or Teaching Qual or equiv	Office of Historical & Crit Studies	
University College of North Wales, Bangor	Dip/MA Linguistics	1 yr	FT	£2,260 EC £5550 non EC	Oct	Degree in rel subject	Secretary	
	Dip/MA Theoretical Lings	1 yr	FT	£2,260 EC £5550 non EC	Oct	Degree in rel subject	Secretary	
	Dip/MA Ling Research	1 yr	FT	£2,260 EC £5550 non EC	Oct	Degree in rel subject	Secretary	
University of Portsmouth	PostGrad Dip Appl Linguistics & TEFL	2 sems 4 sems	FT PT	£2270 EC £5057 non EC £645 PT	Oct	Degree or equiv + Teaching Qual + exp	Dr Paul Rastall	
University of Reading	Dip ELT	9 mths 1-3 yrs	FT PT	£3300 EC £5500 non EC	Oct, Jan, Apr	Degree + Teaching Qual + 3 yrs exp	Course admin CALS	
Sheffield University	Dip Modern English Lang & Linguistics	1yr 2yrs	FT PT	£2,260 EC £5550 non EC £565 PT	Sep	Degree or equiv	Secretary	

UK University Diplomas

College	Course Title	Cours length	FT/ PT	Fees	Start dates	Entry requirements	Contact	Comments
University of Stirling	PostGrad Dip TESOL	9 mths	FT	£2,260 EC £5450 non EC	Sep	Degree + 2 yrs exp	Mrs C Tytler, CELT	
University of Strathclyde	Dip Prof Studies in Education (TEFL)	24 wks	FT	£4,500	on appl	Qual + 2 yrs exp or 5 yrs exp	Paul Curtis	Modular, award-bearing course
University of Wales, Cardiff	Dip TEFL	9 mths	FT	£1,695 EC £4160 non EC	Oct	Degree or equiv + exp	Ms C Wilkinson	Teaching practice avail
University of York	Dip Linguistics & ELT	9 mths	FT	£2,260 EC £5550 non EC	Oct	Degree or Teaching Qual + exp	Sec, Grad admissions	Taught course with project

MAs in the USA and Canada

North America is famous for its choice of Masters' programmes. Here is a selection.

A Masters is a considerable investment for an EFL teacher, so it is important when choosing where to go that you try and find the one that suits you best. While most programmes offer a general overview, as with any other course, the subjects that they teach best are those in which their staff are interested and trained.

Decide what you are particularly interested in (for example testing or teaching young children) and find a course that excels in this area. This is often easier said than done - the universities are notoriously reluctant to admit their strengths and weaknesses. We have asked staff, former students and experts throughout north America to nominate the courses that they think are outstanding in certain fields.

In the United States an MA is normally considered the minimum qualification necessary to teach EFL. In Canada, on the other hand, most programmes ask for some experience. With so many Masters courses in TEFL/TESL related subjects on offer, it is very hard to know which is the most appropriate course for your needs. But if you have not taught before, make sure your course has a teaching practice component - one which only deals with theory will not equip you to deal with classroom problems. There are too many masters programmes to discuss, but the following is a list of fields for which particular centres have been recommended.

EFL (which in North America refers to teaching overseas) is a strong feature at the School for International Training, Florida State University, the Universities of Hawaii, San Francisco and South Florida (which gives special preference to teachers with Peace Corps experience).

East Michigan, Indiana, Iowa State, Stony Brook and UCLA all offer exchange programmes, while Teachers College of Colombia University, New York has a campus in Japan and a summer school in Spain. The University of Illinois at Urbana Champain offers the opportunity of an internship in Madrid. Saint Michael's College, Vermont, with students from all over the world, offers a good balance between theory and practice. The Monterey Institute of International Studies in California has a good international feel.

Classroom observation is a feature at the University of Hawaii and at Teachers College New York, which also emphasises **methodology** and **pedagogy,** as does the School for International

Training, the Universities of San Francisco and Minnesota. Encouraging reports on methodology are also coming out of Harvard, which is most famous for its work in **linguistic theory.**

Theoretical linguistics is strong at the University of Pittsburgh, UCLA, Colorado at Boulder, Ball State, Illinois at Chicago and, in Canada, at Concordia and Victoria. Southern California is particularly strong in **second language acquisition.** The University of Illinois at Urbana Champain leads the field in **world variants of English.** Harvard and MIT also have worldwide reputations for **pure linguistics.**

Cross cultural training is another strong point in many American schools and a particular interest at the University of Colorado in Denver, where the Master of education (MEd.) is in **Language, literacy and cultural studies.** Brigham Young University in Utah also does a lot of work in this field, as does the School for International Training at Brattleboro. **Grammar** fiends should also head for Brattleboro.

ESP in America often means English for Academic Purposes, since the majority of people on American ESP courses are going on to further studies in the country. The University of Michigan at Ann Arbour is strong in this field. **EAP writing** is an area in which many American programmes excel. The Universites of Massachusetts, Southern California and Hunter College New York have strong reputations in this field, while the University of Alabama gives particular emphasis on **rhetoric** and **composition.** In Canada, Carleton University is renowned for its work on **writing** both in its Linguistics department and at the Centre for Applied Language Studies. **EAP reading** is a speciality of San Francisco State, while **materials development** is excellent at the University of Pittsburgh.

Testing is good at the University of Hawaii, which is also strong on **research.** UCLA, Georgetown and Michigan are also strong on testing (the last two boast their own examinations which offer an alternative to TOEFL).

Bilingualism is a speciality of many Canadian programmes, with Concordia and McGill, both in bilingual Quebec, taking a lead in the area. The University of British Columbia is doing pioneering work in the area of **content-based instruction.**

For addresses, see p172-177.

Teachers College of Colombia University, New York has a campus in Japan and a summer school in Spain.

Bilingualism is a speciality of many Canadian programmes,

College	Course Title	Course Length	FT/PT	Fees	Application Dates	Entry Requirements	Contact
Adelphi University	TESOL	3 sems	FT	$252 per credit hour	any sem	degree	B. Robbins
University of Alabama	TESOL	6 sems	FT	$1,004 ps inst. $2,258 ps outst.	any sem	-	C. Davies
American University	Linguistics, TESOL	4 sems	FT/PT	$451 per credit hour	any sem	-	J. Schillinger
University of Arizona	ESL	4 sems	FT/PT	$289 per unit ps	any sem	good degree	D. Adamson
Arizona State University	TESL	30 sem hrs	FT/PT	on application	any sem	degree	J.W. Ney
Azusa Pacific University	M.Ed ESL	4 sems	FT/PT	$220 per unit	any sem	degree	M. Mardock
Ball State University	Linguistics, TEFL / TESOL	3 sems	FT/PT	$1,140 ps inst. $2,680 ps outst.	any sem	degree + 2 yrs exp.	L.M. Davis
Biola University	TESOL / Applied Linguistics	4-5 sems / 4 sems	FT/PT	$240 per semester unit	Aug	degree	H.C. Purnell
Boston University	M.Ed	3 sems	FT/PT	$7,975 ps	any sem	degree	S.J. Molinsky
University of California, Davis	Applied Linguistics	3-6 qrts	FT/PT	$0 pq inst. $895 pq outst.	May	degree	DoS
University of California, Los Angeles	TESL	6 qrts	FT	$969 pq inst. $3,535 pq outst.	Jan	good degree	C.O. Kramer
California State University, Dominguez Hills	English, TESL option	2-4 sems	FT/PT	c.$500 ps	any sem	degree + 1yr foreign lang. study	A. Yamada
California State University, Fresno	Linguistics, TESL/TEFL	3-4 sems	FT/PT	$549 ps inst. $3,501 ps outst.	Feb,Aug	-	V. Samiian
California State University, Fullerton	MS Ed with TESOL	30 sem units	FT/PT	$554 ps inst. $800 ps outst. (1-6 units)	Mar	degree + 2yr foreign lang. study	N. Baden
California State University, Long Beach	Linguistics, TESL/TEFL	3-4 sems	FT/PT	c.$500 ps	Aug	good degree	S.B. Ross
California State University, Northridge	Linguistics (TESOL Track)	2 sems + thesis	FT/PT	$564 ps inst. $438 ps outst. (7+ units)	Feb,Sep	good degree	F. Hallcom
California State University, Sacramento	English, TESOL option	3 sems	FT/PT	$530 ps inst. $246 pu outst.	any sem	degree	F. Marshall
University of Colorado at Boulder	Linguistics	3-4 sems	F/T	$1,260 ps inst. $4,806 ps outst.	Sept	degree, knowledge of foreign lang.	A. Bell
Colorado State University	English, TESOL	4 sems	FT/PT	$1,069 ps inst. $3,419 ps outst.	Mar	degree	DoS

US Masters Degrees

College	Course Title	Course Length	FT/PT	Fees	Application Dates	Entry Requirements	Contact
University of Delaware	Linguistics, concentration ESL	3 sems	FT/PT	$1,610 ps inst. $4,195 ps outst.	Jul,Dec	degree	I. Vogel
East Carolina University	M.Ed English, TESOL	3 sems	FT/PT	$676 pyr inst. $5,730pyr outst.	Mar,Jun,Oct	good degree	C.W. Sullivan
Eastern Michigan University	TESOL	5 sems	FT/PT	$89.50 pchr inst. $212 pchr outst.	Apr,Aug,Dec	degree + 1yr foreign lang. study	J. Aebersold
Florida International University	MS in TESOL	33 sem hours	FT/PT	$800 ps inst. $2,400 ps outst.	any sem	degree	C.U. Grosse
Fordham University at Lincoln Center	MS Ed, TESOL	2.5 sems	FT/PT	$352 per credit	any sem	degree + 2yrs teaching exp.	A. Carrasquillo
University of Georgia	MEd, TESL	4 qrts	FT/PT	$692 pq inst. $1,840 pq outst.	any qrtr	on application	C.J. Fisher
Georgia State University	MS, TESL	4 qrts	FT/PT	$625 pq inst. $2,000 pq outst.	Feb,May,Aug, Nov	under grad. degree in relevant area	P. Byrd
University of Hawaii at Manoa	ESL	4 sems	FT/PT	$860 ps inst. $2,620 ps outst.	any sem	degree + 1 other lang.	C. Chaudron
Hofstra University	MS, TESOL	3 sems	FT/PT	$3,816 ps	any sem	good under grad. prospects + 1 other lang.	N. Cloud
University of Houston	Applied Linguistics	3 sems	FT/PT	$1,848 ps (12 hrs)	Nov,Apr,Jun	good degree	S.C.Pena
Hunter College of the City University of New York	TESOL	5 yrs max.	FT/PT	$95 pc inst. $189 pc outst.	Mar,Oct	degree + working knowledge of 1 other lang.	D.R.H. Byrd
University of Idaho	ESL	4 sems	FT/PT	$177 ps inst. $1,100 ps outst.	any sem	good degree	DoS
University of Illinois at Chicago	Linguistics, TESOL	2 sems + the following summer	FT/PT	$1,827 ps inst. $4,298 ps outst.	Jul,Nov	degree	E. Judd
University of Illinois at Urbana-Champaign	TESOL	4 sems	FT/PT	$1,418 ps inst. $3,894 ps outst.	Mar,Oct	degree + working knowledge of 1 other lang.	E.G. Bokamba
Illinois State University	MA in Writing + TESOL	4 sems	FT/PT	$1,827 ps inst. $4,298 ps outst.	Jan,Mar,Oct	degree	W. Woodson
Indiana University	TESOL	3 sems	FT/PT	$1827 ps inst. $4298 ps outst.	Feb,Sep	degree	H.L. Gradman
Inter American University of Puerto Rico, San German	TESL	variable	PT	$110 pc	Jul,Dec	degree or equiv.	Associate Director
Inter American University of Puerto Rico, Metropolitan	ESL	2yrs	FT/PT	$110 pchr	any sem	good under grad. prospects	DoS
University of Iowa	Linguistics, TESL focus	4 sems	FT/PT	$1,158 ps inst. $3,372 ps outst.	Mar	on application	C. Ringen
University of Kansas	Applied Linguistics	2 yrs	FT/PT	$1,003 ps inst. $2,860 ps outst.	Jun,Nov	degree + working knowledge of 1 other lang.	F. Ingemann
University of Maryland, College Park	MEd TESOL	4 sems	FT/PT	on application	Mar,Nov	good degree	W.E. DeLorenzo
University of Miami	MSEd TESOL	4 sems	FT/PT	$576 pc	Apr,Jul,Nov	acceptable GPA or GPE	S. Fradd

College	Course Title	Course Length	FT/PT	Fees	Application Dates	Entry Requirements	Contact
MIchigan State University	TESOL	4 sems	FT/PT	$5,000 inst. $10,000 outst.	Feb	degree or equiv.	S. Gass
University of Minnesota	ESL	2 yrs	FT/PT	$1,084 inst. $2,168 outst. (7-15 credits)	Mar	degree	DoS
University of Mississippi	TESOL	3-4 sems	FT/PT	$990 ps inst. $1,581 ps outst.	any sem	degree	A. Schrade
Monterey Institute of International Sudies	TESOL	3 sems	FT/PT	$5,650 ps	any sem	degree	R. Larimer
Nazareth College	MSEd (TESOL)	2 yrs	FT/PT	on application	any sem	good degree	DoS
University of Nevada, Reno	TESL	4 sems	FT/PT	$66 pc inst. $1,800 ps outst. + credit fees	Jan,Jul	degree	TESL Coordinator
University of New Mexico	MEd TESOL	3 sems	FT/PT	$785 ps inst. $2,639 ps outst.	Apr,Jul,Nov	degree teaching exp. pref.	R.H. White
College of New Rochelle	MEd, TESL	3-4 sems	FT/PT	-	any sem	degree + teaching cert.	L. Lyman
State University of New York at Albany	MS, TESOL	3 sems	FT/PT	-	any sem	degree	R.L. Light
State University of New York at Buffalo	MEd TESOL	3 sems	FT/PT	$1,600 ps inst. $3,258 ps outst.	Feb	degree + knowledge of a foreign lang.	D. Rissel
State University of New York at Stony Brook	Applied Linguistics ——— TESOL	2-3 sems	FT/PT ——— FT/PT	$1,075 ps inst. $3,258 ps outst.	Mar	degree + 2 yrs foreign lang. study	DoS
Northern Arizona University	TESL	4 sems	FT/PT	$764 ps inst. $2,316 ps outst.	Feb	degree	Applied Linguistics Faculty
University of Northern Iowa	TESOL ——— TESOL/Moder Languages	3-4 sems	FT/PT	$1,076 ps inst. $2,746 ps outst.	AprJul,Nov	degree	TESOL Coordinator
Notre Dame College	MEd, TESL	2-5 yrs	PT	$216 pchr	any sem	degree + other language exp.	B. Arnbjornsdttir
Nova University	MS TESOL	1.5 yrs	FT/PT	$170 pshr	throughout year	on application	DoS
Old Dominion University	Applied Linguistics	1 yr	FT/PT	$148 pchr inst. $375 pchr outst.	Jul,Nov	degree	J. Bing
University of the Pacific	ESL	2 yrs	FT/PT	$7,080 ps	Apr,Dec	degree	J. Milon
Pennsylvania State University	TESL	4 sems	FT/PT	$2,423 ps inst. $4,846 ps outst.	Jul,Dec	degree	P. Dunkel
Portland State University	Applied Linguistics, TESOL	6-7 qtrs	FT/PT	$1,151 pqrt inst. $1,827 pqrt outst	Jan,Apr	degree	J.R. Nattinger
University of Puerto Rico	TESL	2yrs	FT/PT	$55 pc inst.	Feb	degree, Spanish +English	DoS
Rhode Island College	MEd, ESL	2 sems + 1 summer	FT/PT	$100 pshr inst. $202 pshr outst.	any sem	degree + teaching qual.	DoS
University of Rochester	MEd, TESL	3 sems	FT/PT	$400 pchr	Feb,Nov	on application	DoS

College	Course Title	Course Length	FT/ PT	Fees	Application Dates	Entry Requirements	Contact
Saint Michael's College	TESL	3 sems	FT/PT	$176 pc	any sem	degree	Dos
University of San Francisco	TESL	3-4 sems	FT/PT	$432 pc	Jul,Dec	degree	D. Messerschmit
San Jose University	TESL	3 sems	FT/PT	on application	Aug,Jan	degree + foundation	Thom Huebner
School For International Training	MA TESOL	1 yr or 2 summers	FT	$17,000 inc.	Aug,June	degree	DoS
Seton Hall University	ESL	3 sems	FT/PT	$346 pc inst.	May,Jul,Nov	degree	W.E. McCarton
University of South Carolina	TEFL	4 sems	FT/PT	$1,404 ps inst.	any sem	degree	A. Mosher
University of South Florida	Applied Linguistics, TESL	4 sem	FT/PT	$66 pchr inst. $191 pchr outst.	Apr,Aug	degree	C. Cargill
Southeast Missouri State University	English, TESOL emphasis	2-3 sems	FT/PT	on application	any sem	degree	A. Heyde-Parson
University of Southern California	Applied Linguistics	4 sems	FT	$319 pu inst.	Mar	on application	W. Rutherford
Southern Illinois University at Carbondale	EFL/ESL	3-4 sems	FT/PT	$68 pc inst. $205 pc outst.	May/Apr	degree	P.J. Angelis
	Applied Linguistics	4-6 sems					
University of Southern Maine	MS.Ed Literacy Education, ESL	3 sems	FT/PT	$90 pchr inst. $254 pchr outst.	Mar,Oct	on application	M. Wood
University of Southern Mississippi	Teaching of Languages, TESOL	3 sems	FT/PT	$1,054 ps inst. $ $1,785 ps outst.	May,Aug,Dec	degree	W. Powell
Syracuse University	TESL	3 sems	FT/PT	$381 pchr	any sem	degree	J.D. Marcero
Teachers College of Columbia University	Applied Linguistics	1 yr	FT/PT	on application	any term	degree	J.A. Kleifgen
	TESOL			-	Apr,Jul,Dec		DoS
Temple University	MEd, TESOL	3 sems	FT/PT	$219 pc inst. $248pc outst.	any sem	on application	G. Moskowitz
University of Texas at Arlington	Linguistics	2-4 sems	FT/PT	$25 pchr inst.	May,Sep	degree	G. Underwood
University of Texas at Austin	Applied Linguistics TESOL	3 sems	FT/PT	on application	any sem	good degree	G. Underwood
University of Texas at San Antonio	TESL	2-3 sems	FT/PT	$20 pchr inst. $136 pchr outst.	Mar,Jun,Oct	degree	C.W. Hayes
University of Texas Pan American	ESL	1 yr	FT/PT	$38 pchr inst. $ $136 pchr outst.	Apr,Jul,Nov	degree	L. Hamilton
University of Toledo	MAEd ESL	4 qrts	FT/PT	$90 pchr inst. $194 pchr outst.	any qrt	degree	D.W. Coleman
United States International University	TESOL	4-5 qrts	FT/PT	on application	any qrt	degree + interview	E. Butler Pascoe

US Masters Degrees

College	Course Title	Course Length	FT/ PT	Fees	Application Dates	Entry Requirements	Contact
University of Utah	Linguistics	6 qrts	FT/PT	$550 pqrt inst. $1,500 pqrt outst	any qrt	degree	M. Mixco
Universtiy of Washington	MAT ESL	6 qrts	FT/PT	$1,129 pqrt inst. $2,824 pqrt outst	Jan,Apr	degree + intro course	DoS
Washington State University	English, TESOL	4 sems	FT/PT	$1,694 ps inst. $4,236 ps outst	Feb,Oct	degree, foreign lang. recommended	DoS
West Chester University	TESL	5 sems	FT/PT	$146 pshr inst. $186 pshr outst.	any sem	degree + other lang.	D.L. Godfrey
Western Kentucy University	English, ESL	33 sem hrs	FT/PT	$790 ps inst. $2,230 ps outst.	Jul	degree	R.D. Eckard
University of Wisconsin, Madison	Applied English Linguistics	2-4 sems	FT/PT	$1,512 ps inst. $4,542 ps outst.	any sem	good degree	C.T. Scott
University of Wisconsin Milwaukee	MS Curriculum, Instruction, ESL	2 yrs	FT	$1,534.15 for 12+ credits	Feb,Sep	degree	D.E. Bartley

Canadian Masters Degrees

College	Course Title	Course Length	FT /PT	Entry Requirements
Concordia University	MA Applied Linguistics	33 credits+thesis	FT/PT	2 yrs experience+good GPA
McGill University	M.Ed	36 credits	FT/PT	2 yrs experience
Ontario Institute for Studies in Education	MA	8-12+thesis	FT	degree in related area+good GPA
	M.Ed	8 courses	FT/PT	
Simon Fraser University	MA	33 credits+thesis	FT/PT	degree
	M.Ed	coursework, no thesis	-	
University of Alberta	M.Ed	33 credits+thesis	FT	degree + 1 yr exp. + teaching cert
University of British Columbia	MA TESL	1 yr min.	FT/PT	degree + experience
	M.Ed TESL			
University of Calgary	MA	2 yr + 1 yr resid.	FT	degree + good GPA in Ling. & Ed.
	M.Ed	1-2 yrs	FT/PT	experience
University of Victoria	MA Applied Linguistics	24 units + thesis	on app.	degree + good GPA

MAs in the UK

Which Masters is best for you?

Masters degrees in Britain are usually full-time courses for experienced teachers. The main reason for a British teacher to do a Master of Arts (MA) or Master of Education (MEd) in ELT, linguistics or TEFL is not to get a better job (there are too few posts), nor to be a better teacher (the diploma is better - see p125), but to study more deeply in a field that interests you. Before you start out, you need to know which area you want to specialise in.

Most MAs are run by the EFL unit or the language centre of a University. By talking to staff members and former students about the courses in the UK, we have compiled a list of recommended courses for particular areas of interest. The first question to ask is, how much linguistic theory do I want? The main complaints about MAs are that it was too theoretical, or that it was not theoretical enough. So before you contemplate doing a course, decide if you want a heavy academic element or if you are looking for something more practical.

Those teachers looking to MAs to get them out of general EFL will be pleased to see an increasing number of courses in specialist areas:

Linguistic theory: Masters in Linguistics, such as those at the SOAS, University College London, Reading University's Linguistics Department and Westminster University are the most theoretical. **Applied Linguistics** MAs tend to be more academic than those in EFL/ELT/ESOL, etc. Birkbeck, Edinburgh, Essex, Exeter, Kent, Lancaster and Royal Holloway Universities are strong in this field.

Research is strongly featured at the Universities of Cambridge (where the MPhil is largely research-based), Liverpool, Sheffield and Birkbeck. Cambridge and Essex are also strong on **psychological processing.**

Discourse analysis is emphasised at the Universities of Aston, Nottingham, Liverpool, Stirling and Birmingham, which is also strong on **lexicography,** as is Exeter. The related field of **Text and Description** is a speciality at the University of Kent.

Teaching related courses are strong at the practically based MA at London's Institute of Education, and the Universities of Manchester, Leicester, Wales (Cardiff), Thames Valley, York, Durham and Portsmouth (which also offers teaching practice).

Methodology is strong at the Universities of Birmingham, Stirling, Newcastle, Durham, Canterbury Christchurch College and the Institute of Education.

CALS, Reading is proud of its work in **Oral-Aural skills,** a field that Cambridge and Lancaster universities are also strong in - although these concentrate on theoretical input. Exeter is also strong in **writing skills.**

Teaching young learners is a growing field which Warwick, Moray House and the School of Education all specialise in.

ESL (or English for Immigrants) is strong at St Mary's Strawberry Hill, the Institute of Education and Birmingham University's MA in TEF/SL. Thames Valley University offer a special course in **Language in the Multi Cultural Community.** **Literature** teachers can opt for the specialist courses at the Universities of Aberdeen, Nottingham and Strathclyde. It also features strongly at Southampton.

Adult literacy is a speciality of the University of Lancaster and the Institute of Education.

ESP (English for Specific Purposes) is covered in the Masters at the College of St Mark and St John and at the Universities of Warwick and Aston, which offers a distance-learning programme and validates an MSc run by the British Council in Athens. Southampton, Essex and Liverpool universities also have good reputations in this field.

Teacher training MAs are available at Moray House and College of St Mark and St John. The programmes at Warwick and Southampton also place a lot of emphasis on this area. The University of Bristol/IH London offer teacher training as one of two study streams.

Management is the other main option at Bristol and there is a special MEd in ELT Management available at the West Sussex Institute of Higher Education. Management options are also availableat the Universities of Birmingham, Reading, Warwick, Edinburgh and Lancaster.

Testing is traditionally strong at the universities of Leeds, Edinburgh and Lancaster, while Manchester, Liverpool and the Centre for Applied Language Studies (CALS) at Reading also have growing reputations in this field.

Materials design is highlighted at the Universities of Birmingham, Lancaster, Liverpool, Thames Valley, Canterbury Christchurch and Bangor, while Newcastle offers an MA in **Software design for EFL.**

Computer Assisted Language Learning (CALL) is available at the Universities of East Anglia and Essex. And for the video buff, the University of Brighton offers an MA in **Media Language Learning.**

See pages 172 - 177 for addresses.

The first question to ask is, how much linguistic theory do I want?

Those teachers looking to MAs to get them out of general EFL will be pleased to see an increasing number of courses in specialist areas.

College	Course Title	Course length	FT/ PT	Fees	Start dates	Entry requirements	Contact	Comments
Aston University	MSc TE/TESP	1 yr 19-22 mths	FT DL	£2260 EC £6165 non EC £4200 EC PT £5000 non EC	Oct Jan	Degree + 3 yrs exp	Sec, Lang Studs Unit	CTEFLA useful
University of Cambridge	MPhil Eng & Appl Lings	9 mths	FT	£8,770 EC £11815 non EC	Oct	Good Degree + 4 yrs exp	Susan Rolfe	
Canterbury Christ Church College	MA Eng Lang Education	1 yr	FT	£1,310 EC £5225 non EC	Oct	Degree + 3 yrs exp	A Holliday	
College of St Mark & St John, Plymouth	MEd English Lang Teaching	1 yr	FT	£2,650 EC £5320 non EC	Oct	Degree or equiv + 3 yrs exp	Dir, Intl Ed Centre	Non-grad route via BPhil (Ed)
	MEd Eng Lang Teacher Training	1 yr	FT	£2,650 EC £5320 non EC	Oct	Degree or equiv + 3 yrs exp	Dir, Intl Ed Centre	Non-grad route via BPhil (Ed)
	MEd TESP	1 yr	FT	£2,650 EC £5320 non EC	Oct	Degree or equiv + 3 yrs exp	Dir, Intl Ed Centre	Non-grad route via BPhil (Ed)
University of Durham	MA Applied Linguistics/EL	1 yr	FT	£2,200 EC £5550 non EC	Oct	Degree + 3 yrs exp	Peter Grundy	
University of East Anglia	MA ELT & Appl Lings	8 mths	FT	on appl	Sep	5 yrs exp	Dr Jeremy Fox	For exp EFL teachers
University of Edinburgh	MSc Applied Linguistics	12 mths 2 yrs	FT PT	£2,350 EC £5980 non EC	Oct	Degree + relevant exp	Say Oliver	
University of Essex	MA ELT	9-36 mths	FT PT	£2,260 EC £5550 non EC	Oct	Degree + 3 yrs exp	Susan Barrington	
	MA Applied Linguistics	9-36 mths	FT PT	£2,260 EC £5550 non EC	Oct	Degree	Susan Barrington	
	MA Descriptive & Appl Lings	9-36 mths	FT PT	£2,260 EC £5550 non EC	Oct	Degree	Susan Barrington	
University of Exeter	MEd Language Teaching	1 yr	FT	on appl	Oct	Degree + Teaching Qual	Further Prof Studs Sec	Written assessment
University of Hertfordshire	MA Lings & Applications	10 mods	PT	£88 per module	Sep	On appl	On appl	
University of Hull	MA Appl Lang & New Tech	1 yr 2 yrs	FT PT	£2,260 EC £5550 non EC £630 PT	Oct	Degree pref	Language Centre	
University of Kent at Canterbury	MA Applied Linguistics	12 mths	FT	£2,340 EC £5912 non EC	Oct	Degree or equiv	Robert Veltman	Examined on coursework & dissertation
University of Lancaster	MA Linguistics for ELT	1 yr	FT	£2,260 EC £5550 non EC	Oct	Min 3 yrs exp	Dorothy Barber	
	MA Language Studies	12 mths 2 yrs	FT PT	£2,260 EC £5550 non EC	Oct	Degree pref but not essential	Dorothy Barber	

See pages **159-162** for reference advertising

and pages **172-177** for addresses

College	Course Title	Course length	FT/ PT	Fees	Start dates	Entry requirements	Contact	Comments
University of Leeds	MA Linguistics	1 yr	FT	£2,200 EC £5320 non EC	Oct	Degree + min 2 yrs exp	PostGrad Admissions	Modular option avail
	MEd TESOL	11 mths 2-5 yrs	FT PT	£5,550	Oct, Apr, Jan	Degree + Prof Qual + 3 yrs exp	Higher Degrees Officer	Wide range of modular options
University of Leicester	MA Applied Lings &TESOL	1 yr	FT	£2,260 EC £5550 non EC	Oct	Degree + 2 yrs exp pref	Julie Thomson	Overseas : 6.5 IELTS/ 5.5 TOEFL
Liverpool University	MA Lang Teaching & Learning	1 yr	FT	£2,260 EC £5550 non EC	Oct	Degree + 2 yrs exp	Gill Richardson	Incl dissertation. Overseas: 6.5 IELTS
	MEd Lang Teaching & Learning	2-4 yrs	PT	£67 EC £550 non EC per module	Oct, Jan, Apr	Degree + 2 yrs exp; Overseas: 6.5 IELTS	Gill Richardson	Incl 20,000 word dissertation
London University Birkbeck Coll	MA Applied Linguistics	2 yrs	PT	£1,032 EC £1484 non EC	Oct	Degree + exp pref	Malcolm Edwards	Apply early
London University Inst of Education	MPhil/PhD ESOL	2-3 yrs 3-10 yrs	FT PT DL	on appl	All year	Degree	Sec, ESOL Dept	Apply early
	MA TESOL	1 yr 1-4 yrs	FT PT DL	£2,260 EC £5550 non EC	Oct, Jan, Apr	Degree + Qual in Education	Dr Guy Cook/ Anita Pincas	DT by Computer Networking
University of Luton	MA Materials Preparation for TESOL	1yr	FT	£2,260 EC £5520 non EC	Oct	Teachers, Trainers & Curr. developers	Vicki Vidal	
	TEFL Module	1 sem	FT PT	£110	Oct	Uni entrance level or Interview	Vicki Vidal	Various modules
Manchester University	MEd TESOL	1 yr 1-6 yrs	FT PT DL	£2,260 EC £5700 non EC	Jun Oct, Jan	Degree + 3 yrs exp	Debbie Cash	
	MEd Educ Tech & TESOL	1 yr 1-6 yrs	FT PT DL	£2,260	Oct, Jan	Degree + 3 yrs exp	Debbie Cash	
Moray House, Edinburgh	MA TESOL	11 mths 1-4 yrs	FT DL	£2950 EC £5725 non EC; DL fees on appl	Oct Open	Degree or equiv + 3 yrs exp	Registrar	Modular; optional exit pts
University of Newcastle-upon-Tyne	MEd TESOL	1 yr	FT DL	£2,260 EC £5550 non EC	Oct	Degree + Teaching Qual + 4 yrs exp	Director	Day-time courses
University College of North Wales, Bangor	MA Linguistics	1 yr	FT	£2,260 EC £5550 non EC	Oct	Degree	Secretary	
	MA Linguistic Research	1 yr	FT	£2260 EC £5550 non EC	Oct	Degree	Secretary	
	MA Theoretical Linguistics	1 yr	FT	£2,260 EC £5550 non EC	Oct	Degree	Secretary	

See pages **159-162** for reference advertising and pages **172-177** for addresses

College	Course Title	Course length	FT/PT	Fees	Start dates	Entry requirements	Contact	Comments
University of Portsmouth	MA Applied Lings & TEFL	1 yr 2 yrs	FT PT	£2270 EC £5057 non EC £645 PT	Oct	Degree or equiv + Teaching Qual + some exp	Dr Paul Rastall	
University of Reading CALS	MA TEFL	12 mths 1-6 yrs	FT PT	£3,515 EC £5500 non EC	Jan, Jul, Oct	Degree + TEFL Training + 3 yrs exp	Course Admin. CALS	
St Mary's University Coll, Strawberry Hill	MA Applied Lings & ELT	2 yrs	PT	£1,560	Oct, Jan, Apr	Degree + relevant exp	Ann Brumfit	Route via Cert & Dip
	MA Linguistics in Education	1 yr	FT	£2,200	Oct	Degree + teaching exp	Dr Mike Connelly	Coursework + dissertation
Sheffield University	MA Applied Linguistics	1 yr 2 yrs	FT PT	£2260 EC £5550 non EC £565 PT	Jan, Sep	Degree + teaching exp	Secretary	Modular
	MA Modern Eng Lang & Lings	1 yr 2 yrs	FT PT	£2260 EC £5550 non EC £565 PT	Sep	Degree	Secretary	Introductory week in Sep
University of Southampton	MA (Ed) Lang in Education	1 yr 2 yrs	FT PT	£2260 EC £5550 non EC £620 PT	Oct	Degree + 2 yrs exp or equiv	Asst Registrar	
	MA Applied Lings for Lang Teaching	12 mths	FT	£2,260 EC £5550 non EC	Oct	Degree + 2 yrs exp	Asst Registrar	
University of Stirling	M/Ed TESOL	1 yr	FT	£2,260 EC £5450 non EC	Sep	Prof Qual	Mrs Tytler CELT	
University of Strathclyde	DPhil TEFL or Linguistics	variable	FT PT DL	£1130-£5700	on appl	Higher Degree pref	Paul Curtis	
	MPhil TEFL/Linguistics	variable	FT PT DL	£1130-£5700	on appl	First Degree	Paul Curtis	Research Degree
University of Surrey	MA Applied Linguistics	27 mths	DL	£5,000	Oct, Mar	Degree + teaching exp	MA Course Admin	Optional Modules
University of Sussex	MA Applied Linguistics	1-2 yrs	FT PT	on appl	Oct	Degree or equiv	Dr Max Wheeler	
Thames Valley University	MA ELT	1 yr 2yrs	FT PT	£2260 EC £5047 non EC £2200	Oct	Degree + relevant exp	Barbara Boniface	
	MPhil/PhD	1-3 yrs	FT PT DL	£2260 EC £5550 non EC £1130 PT	Oct, Jan, Apr	Degree + 2 yrs exp	Dr N Coupland	
University of Wales, Cardiff	MEd TEFL	12 mths	FT PT	£2,260 EC £5550 non EC	Oct	Degree or equiv + 2 yrs exp	Dr P Tench	in conj with School of Education
	MA Appl English Lang Studs (TEFL)	12 mths	FT	£2,260 EC £5550 non EC	Oct	Degree or equiv + 2 yrs exp	Dr P Tench	
University of York	MA Linguistics & ELT	12 mths	FT	£2,260 EC £5550 non EC	Oct	Degree + substantial teaching exp	Dept Sec, Grad Admissions	Coursework + Dissertation

MASTERS DEGREES IN AUSTRALIA AND NEW ZEALAND

Australia and New Zealand provide great opportunities for studying with a difference. Here we look at the Master's programmes on offer.

Australia

Although the fees for overseas students have recently gone up in Australia, the country still remains one of the cheaper places to do a Masters degree in Teaching English to Speakers of Other Languages (TESOL) or Applied Linguistics. Add to that the Australian government's work rights scheme, whereby all full time students are allowed to work part time, and it is not surprising that the country's ever growing number of Master's programmes are popular with overseas students. This is true especially with those students living and working in the Pacific basin area. Most programmes require experience and/or Qualified Teacher Status (QTS), in other words a teaching qualification for the state sector of their country, such as the Post Graduate Certificate of Education (PGCE) in the UK. The majority of programmes in Australia can be taken either full time or part time.

For those unable to get to Australia, there is a **Distance Learning Programme** available from Macquarie University. With their vast experience of teaching immigrants, the Australians excel particularly in the field of English as a Second Language (ESL or E2L) and the related area of literacy studies. Extremely good work is also being done in **theoretical linguistics, testing** and **curriculum design.**

ESL and **linguistics** is a particular speciality at the University of Sydney, while the Canberra College of Advanced Education runs the M. Ed in TESL, which is strong on **curriculum design.**

Students also favour of the **research** element on the MA in TESOL at Sydney's University of Technology. **Research** is also a feature of the M.Ed at La Trobe University. Monash University's MA in TESOL is recommended for its **theoretical** content. Monash also has a large number of overseas students, for whom thiscourse is particularly suitable.

The MA in Applied Linguistics at the Australian National University is considered strong in the areas **of linguistic literature, sociology** and **anthropology.**

All full time students are allowed to work part time.

Macquarie University's MA in Applied Linguistics has a particular emphasis on **cross-cultural studies** and **ESL.** It is an ideal course for teachers with experience in **teacher training, translation** and **sociolinguistics,** although it is not designed for students interested in pure linguistics.

New Zealand

New Zealand has a small, but growing number of Master's courses. Most students are language graduates, although teachers with extensive practical experience will be considered if they have a degree in another field or have the Diploma in TESL.

Victoria University of Wellington run the MA in Applied Linguistics, which covers **language learning theory, literary linguistics, curriculum development and English as an international language.** The University of Auckland currently runs the Diploma of English Language Teaching, but may shortly introduce an MA in TESOL.

Contact the University of Otago, Massey University, Waikato University and Lincoln University for details of their courses.
See the information grids on p146 and p147.

Teachers with extensive practical experience will be considered if they have a degree in another field.

AUSTRALIAN MASTERS

College	Course Title	Course length	FT/ PT	Entry requirements	Contact	Comments
Australian National University, Canberra	M.Litt Appl Lings	6 sems	FT PT	Degree or equiv	Dr Tim Shopen	20000 word dissertation
Bond University, Queensland	MA Appl Lings	3 sems	FT	Degree	Prof Lian	Poss by ext studs
University of Canberra	MA TESOL	2 yrs	FT	Grad Dip or equiv; IELTS 6.5	Director, TESOL Centre	Overseas students
Deakin University, Toorak Campus Victoria	MEd TESOL	1½ yrs	FT	Teaching Qual	Alex McKnight	
Edith Cowan University, Perth	MEd TESOL	2 yrs	PT	Degree	Bernard Hird, Educ Fac	
Griffith University, Queensland	MA Appl Lings	On appl	FT PT	On appl	Gary Birch	
Macquarie University, Sydney	MA Appl Lings	1 yr 2 yrs	FT PT	Degree or rel exp	Sue Rea-Young	Avail by ext studs
University of New England	M Litt, Lings Major	2 yrs	PT	1-2yr prelim course or Lings Major	Jeff Siegal	Avail by ext studs
University of New South Wales	MEd TESOL	8 sems	FT PT	Degree + 2 yrs exp; Eng prof	David Smith	
	MA Applied Linguistics	1 yr 2 yrs	FT PT	Degree or equiv	PostGrad Section	
University of Queensland	MA Applied Linguistics	1 yr 2 yrs	FT PT	Degree + 3 yrs exp	Dr M Wales	
University of South Australia, Adelaide	MEd TESOL	1½ yrs	FT PT	Degree; TESOL Qual; 2 yrs exp	Graham Ross	Normally by ext studies
University of Sydney	MA Applied Lings TESOL	2-3 sems	FT PT	Degree; Teaching Qual; 3 yrs exp	Diane Ferari	
	MEd TESOL	8 sems	FT PT	Degree; 2 yrs exp; Eng prof	Pamela Riley	Modular basis
University of Technology, Sydney	MA TESOL	1 yr	FT	Degree; Dip TESOL; 3 yrs exp	Anita Auxins	Modular
University of Wollongong, New South Wales	MEd TESOL	1 yr 2 yrs	FT PT	Teaching Qual; TESOL/TEFL exp	Beverley Derewianka	Poss by ext studs

NEW ZEALAND DIPLOMAS AND MASTERS

College	Course Title	Course length	FT/ PT	Entry requirements	Contact	Comments
Auckland College of Education	Dip TESOL	On appl	On appl	On appl	Roly Golding	For Prim & Sec teachers
Auckland University	Dip Eng Lang Teaching	1 yr 2 yrs	FT PT	Degree; Teaching Qual; 2 yrs exp	Marilyn Lewis/ Jackie Greenwood	
Victoria University, Wellington	Post Grad Dip TESL	On appl	On appl	On appl	On appl	On appl
Univesity of Waikato, Hamilton	PostGrad Dip 2nd Lang Teaching	On appl	On appl	On appl	On appl	On appl

College	Course Title	Course length	FT/PT	Entry requirements	Contact	Comments
Australian Catholic University, Victoria	Grad Dip Education	1 yr 2 yrs	FT PT	3 yrs Teaching Qual	Mary Fisher/ Diane Cullen	
Australian National University, Canberra	Grad Dip Appl Lings	6 sems	FT PT	Degree or equiv	Dr Tim Shopen	Choice of sem units
Avondale Lang Centre, New South Wales	BEd Primary/ Secondary Educ	4-10 yrs	FT PT	Uni entrance level; English prof	Registrar	Avondale is a Christian institution
Bond University, Queensland	Grad Dip TESOL	2 sems	FT	Degree or equiv	Prof Lian	Poss by ext studs
University of Canberra	Grad Dip TESOL	1 yr	FT	Degree + Eng prof	Director	Incl teaching practice
Curtin University of Tech, Perth	Grad Dip TEFL	1 yr 2 yrs	FT PT	Degree + exp	Dr Don Yeats	Provides strong theoretical background
Deakin University, Toorak Campus Victoria	Grad Dip Educ/TESOL	1 yr 2 yrs	FT PT	Dip Teaching or equiv + 1 yr exp	Alex McKnight	Recognised by Victorian Ministry of Ed & Trg
Edith Cowan University, Perth	Grad Dip Arts & Lang Studs	1 yr 2 yrs	FT PT	Degree or equiv	Dr Graham McKay	Incl teaching practice
Macquarie University, Sydney	PostGrad Dip Lang Education	1 yr 18 mths	FT PT	Degree or equiv; 1 yr exp	Anne Burns/ Sue Rae-Young	
Monash University, Victoria	Grad Dip TESOL	1 yr	FT PT	Degree or 3 yrs training + 3 yrs exp	Marie-Thèrese Jensen	
University of Northern Territory	Grad Dip Applied Lings	1 yr 2-4 yrs	FT PT	Teaching Qual + 1 yr exp	Prof Frances/ Rob Amery	May be taken by ext studies
Phillip Inst of Tech, Victoria	Grad Dip Ed Studies TESOL	1 yr 2 yrs	FT PT	Degree/ Teaching Dip	Mr Lawford	
University of Sydney	Dip TEFL	1 yr		Degree; 2 yrs exp; Eng prof	Pamela Riley	Mainly for non-native speakers
University of Tasmania	Grad Dip Educ Studies	1 yr 2 yrs	FT PT	Degree; Teaching Qual; 2 yrs exp	Val Walsh	Teaching Adults

SPECIALISING

Short courses focusing on particular areas of EFL are a UK speciality. While universities in the USA and Australia run more general summer schools, often as part of a Masters programme, these countries do not have the range and variety of short courses on offer in the UK. This should help you to choose a short course that suits you.

These courses offer a convenient way of studying an area of teaching that interests you without the commitment in time and money of a full-blown academic course, however, few of these courses lead to recognised qualifications. Unlike the United States, the UK does not operate a credit system which would allow you to count such courses towards another qualification, such as an MA. Some non-native English speaking teachers might get credits from their country's state system on completing the course (check with your local Ministry of Education), but most native English speaking teachers will not.

The main reason for doing such a course is that it should interest you, rather than because it leads directly to better money or job opportunities, however, more and more employers are recognising the importance of specialist EFL teachers. Business English teachers are in great demand in northern Europe, for example. If you are not sure what area of specialisation to go into, the best advice is to concentrate on an area in which you already have some experience or knowledge. Established EFL teachers with experience of another field, combined with the knowledge gained during a short course, can command premium salaries.

Where can I do a short course?
A whole range of institutions offer short courses, from universities to private language schools (see p149-156). Language schools in the UK play a more important role in teacher training than in most other anglophone countries. With the advent of programmes like the EC's Lingua, teacher training is likely to become an even greater part of EFL in the UK.

Who are they for?
Most of the courses in this section are aimed at experienced teachers. Some courses, particularly Refresher courses, are designed specifically for non-native English speaking teachers - refer to the details in the information grids on the following pages. Generally, non-native English speaking teaching courses will include some work on language. In fact the Cambridge Examination in English for Language Teachers (CEELT) concentrates entirely on language in a classroom context (see p157).

What do they cover?
There are courses available on almost everything. Some are more general, such as on ELT methodology or refresher courses for non-native English speakers. Others look at specific areas. Two of the most rapidly growing areas are Primary EFL and English for Specific Purposes.

What to look for
Before you choose a course, it is important to ask yourself the following questions:

1) What do I know about the institution offering the course?
What is their general approach? Some courses are very academic, others are practical or humanistic. The biggest number of complaints we receive about courses is that they are either too theoretical or not theoretical enough! In a short course, it is often difficult to strike a good balance of approach.

2) How well known is this institution for its work in this field?
Beware of institutions that offer courses in subjects that they either do not actually teach, or for which they do not have trainers with the right background. This is very important especially in a boom area like primary EFL where the demand for courses is greater than the number of specialist trainers available. If you want to find out more about the background to the staff on the course, do not be afraid to ask.

3) How many trainers actually work on the course?
For courses that last longer than a week or two, it is better if you have more than one trainer. This will mean you get a variety of outlooks on the subject.

4) Is the course relevant to my teaching situation?
Check that if, for example, you teach literature to 12-15 year-olds, the course deals with teaching literature to this age group.

5) How much experience does the course presuppose?
Most of the courses require teaching experience, but specialist experience is important too (see the information grids on the following pages).

6) Is my English good enough for such a course?
For a non-native English speaker, this is a vital question. Be brutally honest, particularly about your listening and speaking skills - or you will not benefit from it. Many of the courses listed on the following pages are designed for non-native speakers.

7) How can I get involved in running a short course?
IATEFL run a Special Interest Group (SIG) in short courses, as do the TESOL Teacher Education Interest Group (see p168-169). The British Council and International House also run courses worldwide.

College	Course Title	Course length	FT/PT	Fees	Start dates	Entry requirements	Contact	Comments	Max. no. of students
Abon Language School, Bristol	Refresher	25 hrs	FT	£275	Jun, Jul, Aug	Non-native teacher	Heather Crispin	Help with accomm	10
Anglia Polytechnic Univ, Cambridge	Refresher	2 wks	FT	£475	Aug	Non-native speaker teachers	Jan Fisher		15
Anglo European Study Tours, London	Secondary Teachers' Course	2 wks	FT	£450	throughou year	Secondary teachers	Dir of Studs	incl accomm	12
	Primary Course	2 wks	FT	£450	throughou year	Primary teachers	Dir of Studs	incl accomm	12
AngloLang Scarborough	Eng in Britain	2 wks	FT	£580	Jun, Jul, Aug	Teaching Qual; Non-native	Mrs Winspear	incl accomm	15
	General Refresher	2 wks	FT	£580	Jun, Jul, Aug	Teaching Qual; Non-native	Mrs Winspear	incl accomm	15
	Britain Today	2 wks	FT	£580	Jun, Jul, Aug	Teaching Qual;	Mrs Winspear	Fee incl full accomm	15
Anglo World, Oxford	Refresher	2-4 wks	FT	£540 approx	Jun, Jul, Aug		Simon Barnes	incl accomm	15
BBC Summer School, London	Short	3 wks	FT	£950	Jul, Aug	Non-native teachers	Secretary	residential	15
BEET Language Centre, Bournemouth	Refresher Course	1-8 wks	FT	£143 per week	Jan, Feb, Jul, Aug	non-native teachers	Lindsay Ross		14
Birkbeck College, London	EAP	22 hrs	PT eves	£146	Jan, Mar, Jun	Non-native University entrance level	Language Centre		16
	Academic Writing Workshops	5 eves	PT	£75	on appl	University entrance level	Language Centre		16
British Council, Cardiff	Lang & Cultural Identity	2 wks	FT	£1650	Sep	EFL Managers; senior teachers; trainers	Colin Evans	accomm optional	
British Council, Edinburgh	Hands-on Teacher Training	2 wks	FT	£1850	Sep	exp teachers; trainers	Ian McGrath	accomm optional	
British Council, Hastings	Facilitatio styles for TT	3 wks	FT	£1400	May	ELT teachers; trainers	Adrian Underhill	accomm optional	
British Council, Lancaster	Directions in Appl. Linguistics	3 wks	FT	£990	Aug	Academics	John McGover	accomm optional	
British Council, Leeds	ELT in large classes	2 wks	FT	£1690	Sep	ELT teachers; teacher trainers; administrators	Prof Hywel Coleman	residential only	
British Council, Liverpool	Devloping Lang Learning Mats	2 wks	FT	£1480	Sep	teacher trainers; materials writers	Geoff Thompso	residential only	
British Council, London	Teaching Young Learners	3 wks	FT	£1120	Apr	Teacher Trainers	Jean Brewster/ John Clegg	accomm optional	

College	Course Title	Course length	FT/ PT	Fees	Start date	Entry requirements	Contact	Comments	Max. no. of students
British Council, Uni of Newcastle	Exploring Spoken English	18 nghts	FT	£1395	July	Teachers at Secondary level	Don Salter/ Veronica Brock		
British Council, Nottingham	Literature in ELT	3 wks	FT	£1590	Aug	Teachers & Teacher Trainers; Mats Designers	John McCrae/ Ron Carter	residential only	
British Council, Oxford Univesity	Extending Teachers' Experise	3 wks	FT	£1395	July	Teachers	Katie Gray		
British Council, Warwick	Literary Translation	1 wk	FT	£1120	Dec	Teachers; Translators	Prof Susan Bassnett	accomm optional	
British Council, Aberdeen Univ	Literature & Langaue	18 nghts	FT	£1395	July	Overseas Teachers of English; Lit & Lang teachers	Richard Ellis		
British Council, Brighton Univ	Video, Audio & Comps in teaching	18 nghts	FT	£1395	July	Exp Teachers	Prof Brian Hill		
British Council, Chester College of Higher Ed	Methodology, Mats & Resources	18 nghts	FT	£1395	Aug	Teachers; teacher trainers esp. ESP/EAP	Dr Gillian Porter Ladousse		
British Council, College of St Mark & St John	Teaching ESP	18 ngths	Ft	£1395	Aug	Exp teachers	Jean floyd/ Ray Williams		
British Council, Durham University	Contemporary Approaches to ELT	18 nghts	FT	£1395	July	Teachers	Kathy Keohane/		
British Council, Dyffryn Conference Centre, Cardiff	Training the Trainer	18 nghts	FT	£1395	July	Exp teachers and teacher trainers	Maggy McNorton		
British Council, Fitzwilliam College Cambridge	Intro to teacher training	18 nghts	FT	£1395	July	Trainee teacher trainers	Keith Morrow		
British Council, Lancaster University	Teaching & Testing	18 nghts	FT	£1395	July	Native & Non-native speaker teachers	Alan Waters		
British Council, Leeds University	Teaching Young Learners	18 ngths	Ft	£1395	July	Non-native speaker teachers; 3 yrs exp	Lynne Cameron		
British Council, Leeds University	Communicativ Approaches	18 nghts	FT	£1395	July	Teachers; Teacher Trainers	Niall Henderson		
British Council, Lisbon	various short courses	various	PT	on appl	Oct, Jan, Apr	Non-native speaker Teachers	Julie Tice		10
British Council, Milan	ITC Teachers' Course	12 wks	PT	330000 ITL	Oct	Teachers exp in Italian Schools	Jacqui Robinson		16

College	Course Title	Course length	FT/ PT	Fees	Start dates	Entry requirements	Contact	Comments	Max. no. of students
British Council, Milan	Lang & Practical Ideas classroom	12 wks	PT	4050 ITL	Oct	Primary teachers	Bhasi Panikker		16
		25 wks	PT	5700 ITL	Oct	Sec Teachers	Bhasi Panikker		16
British Council, Moray House Inst	Training in ELT	18 nghts	FT	£139	June	Teachers, Mngrs; Teacher Trainers	Mike Wallace	incl accomm	
British Council, Nottingham University	Invigorating Coursebooks	18 nghts	FT	£1,39	July	Teachers; TTs; Writers	Gaynor Ramsey	incl accomm	
British Council, Oporto, Portugal	Drama & Music	5 wks	PT	8800 Esc	on appl	Trainers; Teachers	Pauline Sibbald	1½ hrs per week	15
	Lang improvement	10 wks	PT	1750 Esc	on appl	Non-native speaker teachers	Mike Kirby	1½ hrs per week	15
	TEFL Intro in Primary	10 wks	PT	1750 Esc	on appl	Portuguese EFL teachers	Mike Kirby	1½ hrs per week	15
	Grammar & Meaning	10 wks	PT	1750 Esc	on appl	All speaker teachers	Pauline Sibbald	1½ hrs per week	15
	Various Workshops	1½ hrs /week	eves	600 Esc /eve	every fortnight	All speaker teachers	Pauline Sibbald		42
British Council, Unis of Oxford & Strathclyde	British Cultural Studies	18 nghts	FT	£139	July	Secondary level teachers	Dr Martin Montgome	Fee incl accomm & social acts	
British Council, Rome	Various	10-20 wks	PT	on appl	Oct	Practising Italian State Teachers	Nancy Rossi		14
British Council, University of Stirling	Professional Development	18 nghts	FT	£1,39	July	Teachers/Teach Trainers	Ian McGrath	incl accomm	
British Institute of Florence	Teachingthe Young Learner	7 mnths	PT	on appl	Oct-May	FCE or above		2 hrs/week	
British Language Centre, Madrid	Pre-diploma Course	3 wks	PT	£175 appro	Jan	Exp in ELT	Alastair Dickinson	Prep for DTEFLA	12
Cambridge Centre for Langs, Cambridge	Refresher Course	3 wks	FT	£935	July	Practising Teachers	David Ball	incl accomm, lunch & CEELT prep	12
Carleton University, Canada	Dip in EFL	4 wks	FT	CA$ 750	Aug	EFL Cert or equiv	Prof Ian Pringle	Non-native teachers	12
CELT Athens	Lang Awareness	120 hrs	PT	£600	Oct	CPE or Equiv; non native	Course Tutor	Interview	
CILC, Cheltenham	Overseas Teachers	2 wks	FT	on appl	TBA		Gillian James		
Colchester Eng Study Centre	Teachers' Course	3 wks	FT	£615	Jul, Aug	Non-Native Speaker	Jenny Gray	Accomm £65 per week	13
College of St Mark & St John, Plymouth	Principles & Practices of ELT	1 term	FT	£260	Jan, Apr	Qual Teacher; 3 yrs exp	Dir, Intl Ed Centre		15
	Short ELT Courses	2-3 wks	FT	£360 +	Mar, Jul, Aug	Qual exp Teacher	Dir, Intl Ed Centre		15

College	Course Title	Course length	FT/ PT	Fees	Start dates	Entry requirements	Contact	Comments	Max. no. of students
College of St Mark & St John, Plymouth	Teachers' Development	3 wks	FT	£540	July	min 1-2 yrs exp	Ross Lynn	incl social excursion	
	Teaching Young Learners								
	TESP								
Concorde Intl, Canterbury	Teacher Development	2 wks	FT	£650 approx	Jul, Aug	on appl	Colin Stone	inl accomm For Non-native	12
Coventry TESOL Centre	Intensive TEFL for Overseas Teachers	2 wks	FT	£200	July	min 1 yr exp	Christophe Fry	Refresher Course for overseas teachers	15
Devon School of English, Paignton	Refresher Course	2 wks	FT	£480	Jul, Aug	Teaching exp	Joan Hawthorne	Course can be tailored	12
Eastbourne School of English	Refresher Course	2 wks	FT	£360	Jan, Jul, Aug	Practising overseas teachers	Principal	Family accomm avail	12
Eastern Mediterranean University, Turkey	Short Course	1 day	PT	N/A	all year	Degree & 1 yrs exp	Edward Casassa	Other Unis will contribute	20
Edinburgh Language Foundation	TEFL for Eng Teachers	2 wks	FT	£360	all nyear	Upper/Inter English	Mrs B Holmstrom		12
	CALL	2 wks	FT	£360	all year	Upper Inter English	Mrs B Holmstrom		12
	Teaching ESP	2 wks	FT	£360	throug year	Upper Intemediate English or above	Mrs B Holmstrom		12
English Experience, Folkestone	TT (Accelerated Learning)	2 wks	FT	£911	Jul, Oct	Teaching exp	Mark Fletcher	Fee incl accomm	12
English Language Inst, British Colombia Uni, Vancouver	Eng for Eng Teachers	4 wks	FT	CA$ 1100	July	Practising teachers	Corinne Janow	accomm avail	15
Eurocentre, Bornemouth	Refresher Course	2-4 wks	FT	£187 week	Jan, Jul	Non-native teachers	Ray Bell	Can be tailored	
Filton College, Bristol	Various	on appl	on appl	on appl	on appl	teachers	Helen Bowen		
GEOS, Hove	Refresher Course	2-4 wks	FT	£400 -£750	Jan, Jul, Aug	FCE English; 1-2 yrs exp	School Secretary	For Overseas Teachers; accomm avail	12
Goldsmith's College, London	Various	1 term	PT	£55	Sep, Jan		L Arthur	Pre-service & early service	20
Hammersmith & West London Coll	Overseas Teachers'	4 wks	FT	£295	July	Post FCE English	Course Director	Leads to CEELT exam	15
Hilderstone College, Broadstairs	Intl Teachers' Course	2 wks	FT	£526	Jul, Aug	Overseas teachers	Pat Biagi	Fee incl accomm	12

College	Course Title	Course length	FT/ PT	Fees	Start dates	Entry requirements	Contact	Comments	Max. no. of students
Hilderstone College, Broadstairs	Language Intensive	2 wks	FT	£526	July	Overseas Teachers	Intl Students Office	Fee incl accomm	12
	Lang & Practical Ideas	2 wks	FT	£526	Jul, Aug	Overseas Teachers	As above	Fee incl accomm	12
	For Primary School Teachers	2 wks	FT	£526	July	Overseas Teachers	As above	Fee incl accomm	12
Hull College	Refresher Course	4 wks	FT	£480	July	Proficiency English + exp	Tina Cole	Option to take CEELT	15
inlingua, Cheltenham	D.S course	5 days	FT	£275	Mar, Dec	DTEFLA	D. Lewis		6
	Introduction Seminar	5 days 2 days	FT FT	£155 £75	all year	CTEFLA	D. Lewis		10
IH, Budapest	various	6-20 hrs	PT	(£3,56	all year	CTEFLA	Head of TT		12
International House, Hastings	Advanced English for Teachers	2 wks	FT	£360+	Jan, Jul, Aug	by application	Adrian Underhill	Poss Oxford Uni/ ARELS exam	12
	Brush up your English	2 wks	FT	£360+	Mar, Jun, Jul, Aug	on appl	Adrian Underhill	For non-native teachers. Accom avail	12
	Methodology 2	2 wks	FT	£360+	Feb, Mar, Jul, Aug	on appl	Adrian Underhill	Non-native teachers. Accomm avail	12
	Methodology 1	2 wks	FT	£360+	Jun, Jul, Aug	on appl	Adrian Underhill	Non-native speakers. Accomm avail	12
	Humanistic Approaches	4 days	FT	200	Jan	on appl	Adrian underhill	Accomm avail	12
	Teaching & Learning Vocabulary	5 days	FT	200	Jan	on appl	Adrian Underhill	Accomm avail	12
	Designing & Creating Materials	5 days	FT	200	Jan, Jul	on appl	Adrian Underhill	Accomm avail	
	Mod Eng Lit & Culture	2-4 wks	FT	£220+	Jan, Jul, Aug	on appl	Adrian Underhill	incl accomm	
	Facilitating Teacher Dvlpmt	5 days	FT	£200+	Nov	on appl	Adrian Underhill	Accomm avail	12
	People Skills	5 days	FT	£200+	Oct	on appl	Adrian Underhill	Accomm avail	12
	Presence & Performance	5 days	FT	£200+	Sep	on appl	Adrian Underhill	Accomm avail	12
	6 Category Intervention Analysis	5 days	FT	£200+	Jan, Jul	on appl	Adrian Underhill	Accomm avail	12
	Self-Directed Learning	5 days	FT	£200+	Jan	on appl	Adrian Underhill	Accomm avail	12

College	Course Title	Course length	FT/ PT	Fees	Start dates	Entry requirements	Contact	Comments	Max. no. of students
International House, Hastings	Close Encounters	5 days	FT	£200+	Mar, Aug	on appl	Adrian Underhill	Accomm avail	12
	Dramatic Improvements	5 days	FT	£200+	Apr, Aug	on appl	Adrian Underhill	Accomm avail	12
	From Teacher to Facilitator	5 days	FT	£200+	July	on appl	Adrian Underhill	Accomm avail	12
	Sound Foundations	5 days	FT	£200+	Jan, Oct	on appl	Adrian Underhill	Accomm avail	12
	Skills of TT	2 wks	FT	£400+	Feb, Aug	on appl	Adrian underhill	Accomm avail	12
	Communicative Lang. Teaching	2 wks	FT	£360+	Feb	on appl	Adrian Underhill	Accomm avail	12
	Advanced 6 Category Intervention Analysis	5 days	FT	£200+	Sep	on appl	Adrian Underhill	Accomm avail	12
	TEFL to Young Learners	5 days	FT	£200+	Sep	on appl	Adrian Underhill	Accomm avail	12
International House, Lisbon	TEFL to Young Learners	2 wks	FT	£280	Sep	CTEFLA + 1 yr exp	Kathryn Gordon		15
International House, London	IH Cert TEFL	4 wks	FT	£775	all year	CPE	TT Dept	Apply early	
	Language Development		FT	£580	Jul, Aug	IH Lang Test	TT Dept	Apply early	
	Methodology Refreshers	2 wks	FT	£340	Jun, Feb	IH Lang Test	TT Dept	Selection process	
	Short courses for teachers	2-3 days	FT	£124 £176	Jul, Aug	IH Lang Test	TT Dept	full list of courses on appl.	
	Language & Classroom Skills for Primary teachers	2 wks	FT	£340	Jul, Aug, Sep	IH Lang Test	TT Dept	Selection process	
	Teaching Literature	2 wks	FT	£340	Jul, Aug, Sep	IH Lang Test	TT Dept	Selection process	
	Background to Britain	2 wks	FT	£405	July	IH Lang Test	TT Dept	No Methodology	
	Teaching Business English	2 wks	FT	£405	Sep, Nov	IH Lang Test	TT Dept	selection process	
	Educational Mnagmt	2 wks	FT	£615	Aug	IH Lang Test	TT Dept	selection process	
	TT Skills & Approaches	2 wks	FT	£615	Aug	IH Lang Test	TT Dept	selection process	
	Pre Lang Teaching Skills	4 wks	FT	£580	all year	IH Lang Test	TT Dept	Post CFC lang work	

College	Course Title	Course length	FT/ PT	Fees	Start dates	Entry requirements	Contact	Comments	Max. no. of students
International House, Rome	Teaching Young Learners	5 days	FT	550000 ITL	June	CTEFLA	Director	Intensive	12
International Language Academy, Cambridge	Lang Improvement & Methodology	2 wks	FT	£350	all year	Practising Teachers	Nick Kenny		15
ITS English School, Hastings	Overseas Teachers'	2 wks	FT	£295	July	Non-native Teachers	John Palim		6
Lake School of English, Oxford	Practical Refresher	5 days	FT	£210	Mar, Jun, Sep	CTEFLA or equiv	Susan Kay	Between Cert and Diploma	14
	Comm Activity Workshops	1 day	FT	£55	Twice\ wk	CTEFLA or equiv	Susan Kay	Practical	25
Leeds University	Training Teachers for ELT	3 mths	FT	£2,850	Jan	Degree or equiv + 5 yrs exp	Course Dir	Develops training skills	20
Liberty English Centre, Brazil	Refresher Course	3 wks	FT	$100	on appl	Cambridge Proficiency	O. Belloso Riberiro		20
Living Lang Ctr, Folkestone	Refresher Course	3 wks	FT	£900 approx	Jul, Aug	High level English	Bridget Peacock	Fee incl accomm	12
Lydbury English Centre, Shropshire	Personal Lang Development	1 wk	FT	£250+	on appl	Intermediate English + exp	DJ & RA Baker	Content negotiable	8
Milner Intl Coll, Perth	Short Course	on appl	FT PT	varied	on appl	on appl	Warren Milner	Tailored to clients	
Oxford Academy	Refresher	3 wks	FT	£210	Jan, Jun, Aug	Non-native Teachers	Anthea Bazin	Accomm avail	
Oxford House School of English	Summer Seminars	10 days	FT	£490	Jul, Aug	Non-native speaker Teachers	Brenda de Martino	Fee incl accomm.	N/A
Pilgrims, Canterbury	Refresher Courses	1 wk 2 wks	FT	£465 c.£900	Jul, Aug Sep	N/A	Marianne Carter	Fees incl accomm	N/A
Pitman, London	Overseas Teachers	3 wks	FT	£337	Aug	Advanced Eng	Jane Townsend		
	Adv Lang Courses	2 wks	FT	£301	Aug	Advanced Eng. Practising Teacher	Jane Townsend		10
Polyglot Lang Services, London	Teaching ESP	1 wk	FT	£245	Feb, Jun, Sep, Dec	1 yr exp	Secretary		8
Portsmouth University	Refresher	2 wks	FT	£395	July	Teaching exp	Mrs Bailey	eligible for LINGUA funding	15
Reading University	English through Theatre	3 wks	FT	£980	July	Theatre & language studies	Course administrat		20
	Language Methodology	3 wks	FT	£980	July	Practising Teachers	Course administrat	Incl accomm	20
Richard Lang. College, Bournemouth	Refresher	1 wk	FT	N/A	as required	on appl	DoS		14

College	Course Title	Course length	FT/ PT	Fees	Start dates	Entry requirements	Contact	Comments	Max. no. of students
St Giles, Highgate	Refresher	2 wks 4 wks	FT	£295 £580	Aug Jan	Practising EFL Teachers	Patricia Samuels		12
St Giles, Eastbourne	Foreign Teachers of English	3 wks	FT	£490	July	Non-native speaker Teachers	Accomm avail. CEELT I option		12
St Giles, San Francisco	Foreign Teachers of English	2 wks	FT	$595	Feb, Jun, Dec	Cambridge Proficency level	Claudia Schuster		12
Salisbury School of English, Wiltshire	Teachers' Secondary or Primary	2 wks	FT	£275	Jul, Aug	Practising Non-native Teacher.	Registrar	extra lang tuition avail	
Skola Teacher Training, London	Practical Update	on appl	FT	£400	all year	Exp Non-native speaker Teachers	Lyndel Sayle	Observation incl	2
Strathclyde University	TEFL to Young Learners	2 wks	FT PT	£280	Once per term	Teaching Qual & native speaker competence	Paul Curtis	Focus 8-14 yr olds	15
Study Space, Thessaloniki	Refresher	15 wks	PT	85000 Drs	Jun, Sep	Teaching experience	Chrissie Taylor	Modular	7
	ESP How to Teach	15 wks	PT	varies	Sep, Oct	2 yrs exp	James Arnold	Focus Bus/ Medical Eng	5
Surrey Language Training Ltd, Farnham	Overseas Course	2 wks	FT	600	July	Relevant Teaching exp	Ronald Micallef		12
Sussex University Language Centre	ELT Refresher	8 days	FT	260	Mar	ELT exp	Margaret Khidhayir	Non-native teachers	12
Suzanne Sparrow, Plymouth	Refresher	1 wk	FT	270	Aug	1 yr ELT exp	P J Clarke	all teachers	8
Swan School, Oxford	Overseas' Teachers	2-4 wks	FT	£490-£780	through year	O'seas English teachers	Registrar		12
Thames Valley University	as req	as req	FT PT	as req	as req	on appl	Linda Williams	Tailor-made	as req
University of Bristol	Attachments	2 wks-6 mths	FT DL	on appl	as req	Senior ELT professionals	Pat O'Brien	Tailor-made	20
	Task Based Lang Learning	1-2 wks	FT	£320 pw	July	Practising Eng teachers	Marilyn Mackenzie	Fee incl accomm & social events.	
UTS Oxford Centre	ESP Teacher Training	1-4 wks	FT	£300 pw	all year		Mark Bartram		
Westminster College, London	Practical Teacher Training	10 wks	PT	650	Jan, APr, Sep	Overseas Teachers	G Raman	incl teaching practice	16
YES Educational centre, Sussex	Refresher	2-3 wks	FT	£138 pw	on req	Degree and/or Teaching Qual	John Blackwood	Adaptable content	6

College	Course length	FT/ PT	Fees	Start dates	Entry requirements	Contact	Comments	Max no of students
Basil Paterson College, Edinburgh	2 wks	FT	on appl	Jul, Aug	Practising overseas EFL teachers	Mary Beresford-Peirse		14
BEET Lang Centre, Bournemouth	4 wks	FT	£840	Jul, Aug	Practising/trainee EFL teachers			14
Bilkent University, Turkey	10 mths	PT	TBA	Oct	CEELT I level	Head of TT Unit		15
Brasshouse Centre, Birmingham	1 mth	FT	£250	Jul, Aug	FCE/ CPE level	Deborah Cobbett	Also poss 1:1	10
British Council, Lisbon	varied	PT	TBA	Oct, Jan, Apr	Teaching exp & Eng competence	Julie Tice		10
British Council, Naples	1 yr	PT	1.1m ITL	Sep, Jan	BC Scale level 5/6	F C de la Motte		15
British Council, Rome	20 wks	PT	N/A	Oct		Nancy Rossy		14
British Council, Thessaloniki	135 hrs	FT PT	N/A	Oct, Jun	CPE	Camilla Ralls		16
British Institute of Florence	9 mths	PT	940000 ITL	Oct	FCE level 1 or CPE level 2 pref	School Director		10
Cambridge Exams, Finland	8 mths	PT	FM 380-42	Sep	Finnish Matric.	Bernard A. Jones		25
Canterbury Christ Church College	2 wks	FT	£337	July	Relevant experience	Ms Hammersley	Help with accomm	14
Chichester School of English	2 wks	FT	£330	July	FCE/TOEFL 500	Dir of Studs	Also tailor -made courses	20
City of Bath College	3 wks	FT	£372	Aug	Non-native speaker teachers	EFL Section		12
City of Liverpool Comm College	3 wks	FT	£420	July	Upper Intermediate English	Diane Lane		10
Clarendon College, Nottingham	3 wks	FT	TBA	Jun	Good FCE pass	Linda Taylor		15
Eastbourne School of English	2 wks	FT	£360	July	FCE	Dorothy Rippon	Accomm avail	12
Eastern Mediterranean Uni, Turkey	6 mths	PT	N/A	Sep	Degree + 1 yrs exp	Edward Casassa	In-house only	20
GLOSCAT, Cheltenham	2 wks	FT	£300	Jul, Aug	Good level of English	Paul Burden		12
Hammersmith & West London Coll	3 mths	PT	£250	Sep, Jan, Apr	Post-FCE level	Course Dir	Leads to CEELT exam	20
Hendon College, London	6 mths	PT	£360	Sep, Jan	As per UCLES	Dina Brook		15
International House, London	Open to students following language development course (see Short Courses)							
Liberty English Centre, Brazil	1 yr	PT	$200	Mar, Jul	CCSE level 3/4; CPE pass for CEELT II	Ophelia Belloso Riberiro		8
Richmond Adult & Comm College, Twickenham	3 mths 6 mths	PT	£180,27	Sep Jan	Min A/B pass at FCE	Hugh Burney	Apply early	16
St Giles, Eastbourne	3 wks	FT	£490	July	Intermediate English	Reynold Elder		12

CAMBRIDGE CEELT COURSES

College	Course length	FT/ PT	Fees	Start dates	Entry requirements	Contact	Comments	Max no of students
SBCI, Brazil	1 yr	PT	$1000	Feb	Cambridge First Cert	Linda Ruas		15
School House, Goiania, Brazil	6 mnths	PT	$500	Feb, Aug	Post SCE/ Post CAL	Maria Brown	On demand	14
Skola Teacher Training, London	3 wks	FT	£470	Jul, Aug	Teaching exp & English prof	Lyndel Sayle		15
Study Space, Thessaloniki	15 wks	PT DL	40000 Drs	Feb	Proficiency exam & interview	Chrissie Taylor	Once a week	8
University College Cork, Ireland	4 wks	FT	IR £560	Aug	Practising or trainee teacher	Goodith White	Accomm avail	12
Waltham Forest College, London	varied	FT PT	on appl	on appl	FCE/ CPE; Degree/ rel exp	CEELT Course Tutor	CEELT I & II	10
Westminster College, London	12 wks	PT	£154	Jan, Apr, Sep		Georgie Raman		-

TEACHING ENGLISH FOR BUSINESS

College	Course length	FT/ PT	Fees	Start dates	Entry requirements	Contact	Comments	Max no of students
AngloLang, Scarborough	2 wks	FT	£580	Jun, Jul, Aug	Teaching Qual; Eng prof	Mrs L Winspear	Fee incl accom	15
British Council, Hong Kong	30 hrs	FT PT	HK$ 1500	TBA		Tim Gore		
University of Edinburgh	2 wks	FT	on appl	Aug	2 yrs exp	Inst Appl Lang Studs Sec	Intensive	8
Inlingua, Cheltenham	3 days	FT	£100	Mar, Dec	CTEFLA + 1 yr exp	Dagmar Lewis	Intro to Teaching Bus Eng	10
International House, Budapest	1 wk 2 wks	FT	£150 £250	on appl	CTEFLA or equiv	Head of TT		12
International House, Hastings	5 days 2 wks	FT	£194 £367	Jan Aug	Practising teachers	Adrian Underhill	Accomm service	12
International House, Lisbon	1 wk	FT	£80	Sep	CTEFLA + 1 yr exp	Kathryn Gordon	TE to Professionals	15
International House, London	2 wks 8 wks	FT PT	£615 £715	Aug, Nov Oct	Degree + CTEFLA + 2 yrs exp		Teaching Eng for Business	-
Language Institute, Athens	25 hrs	FT PT	£165	on appl	Teaching Qual	Clare O'Dononghue// Jennifer Smith	Intro Bus Eng course	12
London Guildhall University, Lang Servs Centre	2 wks	FT	£370	July	Practising Teacher	David Scarborough	Practical Workshop	15
	1 day	FT	on appl	As req	Locally set	David Scarborough	Seminars arranged in UK & overseas	-
	2-3 wks	FT	£1,390	July	Degree + Teaching Qual + 1 yr exp	David Scarborough	LCCI Awarded Dip TEB	15
Lydbury English Centre, Shropshire	1 wk	FT	£250	As req	Experienced teachers only	DT and RA Baker	Run alongside Bus Eng trainers	-
Regent Lang Training Capital Exec Centre, London	5 days	FT	£425	Mar, Jul, Sep, Dec	Degree + Teaching Qual + 1 yr exp	Helen Mattacott	LCCI validated Cert TEB	10
	5 days	FT	£350	Mar, Jul, Sep, Dec	Degree + Teaching Qual + 1 yr exp	Helen Mattacott	Course participation only	10

CENTRE FOR APPLIED LANGUAGE STUDIES

For more information please write to:

The Course Administrator,
Centre for Applied Language Studies,
University of Reading,
Whiteknights,
PO Box 218,
Reading,
Berks RG6 2AA

Tel: (0734) 318511/2

MA in TEFL

The Centre for Applied Language Studies offers experienced teachers a course of continuous or discontinuous study leading to an MA in the Teaching of English as a Foreign Language.

Module One is now available on the following dates:

1994
July 4th to September 9th
October 10th to December 16th

1995
January 16th to March 24th
July 10th to September 17th
October 9th to December 15th

Diploma in ELT

A modular course for qualified teachers of English as a foreign/second language and/or for teachers with at least three years' experience. Other applicants with relevant backgrounds can also be considered. Entry is usually in October but it is also possible to join the course in January or May.

Module One
1994 October 10th to December 16th

Module Two
1995 January 16th to March 24th

Module Three
1995 May 2nd to July 6th

University of Reading

UNIVERSITY OF essex

Department of Language and Linguistics offers 9/12/24/36-month MA programmes and 3/5-year PhD programmes in

Applied Linguistics
Descriptive & Applied Linguistics
English Language Teaching
Language Acquisition

+ 8 other modular MA/MSc/PhD programmes.

The Department has achieved the maximum 5-star rating for its research in all three official reviews of UK universities, and has a category A rating from the ESRC. It has more than 40 members of staff (including 6 professors).

The EFL Unit offers:

DIPLOMA in Teaching English as a Foreign Language [D.T.E.F.L.]
A modular nine month course for experienced graduate teachers, a chance of combining CTEFL and CTESP, or CTEFL with a dissertation, and having additional courses of its own.

CERTIFICATE in English for Teaching English [C.E.T.E.]
An English course for Classroom management, communicative activities, teaching techniques & materials, plus the Cambridge Examination in English for Language Teachers. (Spring Term)

CERTIFICATE in Teaching English as a Foreign Language [C.T.E.F.L.]
A ten-week course for experienced qualified teachers wishing to improve their knowledge of basic disciplines. (Autumn Term)

CERTIFICATE in Teaching English for Specific Purposes [C.T.E.S.P.]
An intensive ten-week course (Summer Term) for experienced graduate EFL teachers concerned with ESP teaching.

For further information, write to: D Meyer, A 25, Department of Language and Linguistics, University of Essex, Wivenhoe Park, COLCHESTER, CO4 3SQ, Essex, England

West Sussex Institute of Higher Education

Courses for teachers, advisors & administrators

● MA/ADVANCED DIPLOMA ELT MANAGEMENT for DOS, advisors, ELT administrators, inspectors and senior teachers.

Now in new modular format.

● BA (Ed) IN-SERVICE (ESOL) for overseas teachers with classroom experience

● SPECIALIST INTENSIVE SEMINARS IN ELT

● LANGUAGE SKILLS FOR TEACHERS OF ENGLISH

● COURSES FOR OVERSEAS TEACHERS OF YOUNG CHILDREN

● SHORT COURSES IN ELT - ELT MANAGEMENT THROUGHOUT THE YEAR

● SUMMER PROGRAMMES FOR ELT TEACHERS, OVERSEAS UNDERGRADUATE STUDENTS *June-September 1994*

TESOL Section
The Dome
Upper Bognor Road
Bognor Regis
West Sussex
PO21 1HR
Tel: (0243) 829291
Fax: (0243) 841458

The Department of
Applied Linguistics
The Institute for Applied
Language Studies

Degree, Certificate and Short Courses

MSc in Applied Linguistics
- core courses in general, descriptive and applied linguistics
- a range of 25 options presented by the Department and the Institute

Certificated courses at the Institute
- UCLES/RSA Dip TEFLA
- Advanced Certificate in ELT (ACELT)
- ACELT by Distance Learning

Short Summer Courses at the Institute
- Teaching and Learning English
- CEELT Preparation Course
- Teaching English for Specific Purposes
- Teaching English for Medical Purposes
- Teaching English for Business Purposes
- Teaching Literature with EFL
- Grammar and Communicative Teaching
- Drama for English Language Teachers
- English for TEFL/Applied Linguistics

Department of Applied Linguistics 14 Buccleuch Place, EDINBURGH EH8 9LN, Scotland, UK. Tel 031 650 3864. Fax 031 650 6526.	Institute for Applied Language Studies 21 Hill Place, EDINBURGH EH8 9DP, Scotland, UK. Tel 031 650 6200. Fax 031 667 5927.

UNIVERSITY OF BRISTOL
TEFL COURSES
for teachers and teacher educators

◆ **MPhil/PhD**

◆ **Modular MEd (TEFL)**

◆ **BEd (Hons) (overseas teachers)**

◆ **Short courses**

◆ **Summer School**

For information:
Marilyn Mackenzie
School of Education
35 Berkley Square
Bristol BS8 1JA, UK
Tel: 0272 303030
Fax: 0272 251537

**MORAY HOUSE
Institute of Education
Heriot-Watt University**

 Scottish Centre for International Education

MA TESOL

■ 1 year full time

or ■ by Distance Education

or ■ a combination of attendance and distance learning

■ optional exit points at Postgraduate Certificate or Postgraduate Diploma

■ choice of specialist electives

RSA/UCLES Dip TEFLA

■

For details of these and other courses, write to:

The Director
Scottish Centre for International Education
Moray House Institute
Holyrood Road
Edinburgh EH8 8AQ   Fax No 031 557 5138

TESOL Centre

Qualify to teach English or develop your EFL career at Sheffield Hallam University's TESOL Centre. We have an international reputation for training both new and practising teachers, plus the resources of one of Britain's largest universities. Our programmes consist of distance learning followed by one month intensive courses leading to

Certificate in TESOL, Licentiate Diploma (TESOL)
Associate Diploma (TESOL), Postgraduate Diploma (TESOL)

Flexible payment scheme for fees.

*For full details write to TESOL Centre
Sheffield Hallam University, Totley Campus
Totley Hall Lane
Sheffield S17 4AB.
Telephone 0742
720911/532816.
Fax 0742 532832.*

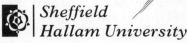 **Sheffield Hallam University**

Canterbury Christ Church College

MA IN ENGLISH LANGUAGE EDUCATION
(University of Kent)

- Twelve-month course for TEFL/TESL professionals
- Advanced qualification for teachers, trainers and administrators
- Professional development in teaching, planning, management and evaluation
- Course begins October 1994

DIPLOMA/MA IN TEFL
(University of Kent)

- Nine-month course for Diploma
- Professional qualification for EFL Teachers
- Emphasises practical skills and professional abilities
- Possibility of continuing to MA level by dissertation
- Course begins October 1994

CERTIFICATE IN TEFL

- Eleven-week practical courses
- Certificates can be used as credit for award of Diploma
- Courses begin in October 1994 and January 1995

These courses are open to teachers from all countries.

For a copy of our prospectus and an application form, please contact:

International Programmes Office, Christ Church College, Canterbury CT1 1QU
Tel: 0227 458459   Fax: 0227 781558

UNIVERSITY OF SHEFFIELD

MA in APPLIED LINGUISTICS
modular programme: one year full-time; two years part-time.

ADVANCED CERTIFICATE IN TESOL
12 weeks full-time, for non-native and native speaker teachers of English. 2 courses a year.

For further details contact:
Dr Mike Reynolds,
Department of English Language
and Linguistics, University of Sheffield,
`5 Shearwood Road, Sheffield S10 2TD.
Tel: (0742) 768555 ext. 6042.

Centre for Language in Education
(Faculties of Arts and Educational Studies)

- MA in Applied Linguistics for Language Teaching (full-time)
- MA(Ed) in Language in Education (part-time)
- Research degrees (MPhil/PhD) in Language/Literature/Applied Linguistics

These courses are recognised for the award of ESRC studentships.

Working for equal opportunities.

University of Southampton

For further details, apply to:
Mrs K Rush (CG),
Faculty of Educational Studies,
University of Southampton,
Southampton SO9 5NH, UK

Excellence in English Language Teaching

At Thames Valley University we are proud of our substantial experience of English language teaching and teacher education.

Our School of English Language Teaching has a 30 year history in a wide range of specialist areas.

You can choose from the following programmes:

MA English Language Teaching
1 year full time or 2 years part time

MA Language in the Multicultural Community
2 years part-time

MPhil/PhD

RSA/Cambridge Certificate TEFLA

We also offer a range of full time and part time programmes including degrees, intensive English, specialist courses and attachments.

You can contact us at:

Thames Valley University
School of English Language Teaching
Walpole House
18 – 22 Bond Street
Ealing
London W5 5AA

Telephone 081 231 2405
Facsimile   081 231 2900

TVU
LONDON

Aston University

Courses for your career development

MSc in TESP
1 year full-time (Oct start)

MSc in TESP or TE
22 months by distance learning (Jan start)
Centres in Spain, Turkey, Greece, France, Japan, Mexico and Abu Dhabi as well as UK
2-3 year MSc in preparation

Certificate in Principles of ESP
3 months full-time (Oct/Jan/Apr start)

Advanced Certificate in Principles of TEFL
Individually-based distance learning (Jan-Jun) plus short practical classroom component in August

Introductory Certificate in TEFL
1 month full-time (July and Aug)

Further details:

Language Studies Unit,
Aston University,
Birmingham B4 7ET, UK.
Tel: 021 359 3611 (ext. 4242/4236)
Fax: 021 359 2725
Email: lsu@aston.ac.uk

APPENDIX

This section serves as a quick reference for acronyms, recognition bodies, book suppliers, associations, publications, major events and useful addresses throughout the world.

TERMINOLOGY

As with most specialist business or academic sectors, the English Language Training industry has a number of standard acronyms, which are often interchangeable, but have specific meanings as outlined below. In order to avoid repetition and confusion, the term EFL has been used throughout this book as the general term for English for non-native speakers of the language.

EFL
English as a Foreign Language
-the general UK term, although in the US and Australia it is used to refer to teaching abroad only.

ELT
English Language Teaching or Training
-a general international term used widely by publishers.

ESL
English as a Second Language
-the general US term for any English language teaching within the country, but in the UK and Australia it refers to teaching English for immigrants.

ESOL
English for Speakers of Other Languages
-another general US term.

TEFL
TESL
TESOL
-the prefix (T) simply stands for **Teaching.**

ELICOS
English Language Intensive Courses to Overseas Students
-the general Australian term.

EAP
English for Academic Purposes
-preparation for university education using English.

ESP
English for Specific Purposes
-for example, English for Aviation or English for Computing. Often includes Business English, although this has now become a specialisation in its own right.

RECOGNITION SCHEMES

A quick guide to the major recognition bodies and related associations.

When choosing a language school, remember that there are various organisations which have been set up to monitor the standards of teaching and student welfare throughout the world. Unfortunately the recognition schemes can be confusing - Britain has several. Non membership of an organisation may not mean the school is necessarily a bad one - for example in the UK, new schools do not qualify for recognition. However, the major recognition organisations in Anglophone countries are worth contacting if you want to research a school or college.

Australia
The ELICOS (English Language Intensive Courses for Overseas Students) Association represents English language colleges. It established the National ELICOS Accreditation Scheme (NEAS). This approves schools and colleges which meet its required standards.

Canada
English teaching is largely confined to the state sector. The University and College Intensive English Programs aims to advance standards in intensive English courses at Canadian universities and colleges.

Ireland
In Ireland, standards in private language schools are maitained by the Advisory Council for English Language Schools (ACELS) under the aegis of the Department of Education. ACELS has representation from The Recognised English Language Schools Association (RELSA) and NATEFLI (National Association of TEFL in Ireland). The Association for Teacher-training in TE FL (ATT) has been set up to ensure Irish TEFL qualifications are of a similar standard to international qualifications.

New Zealand
FIELSNZ (the Federation of Independent English Language Schools) and CRELS (Combined Registered English Language Schools) represent the interests of private language schools, and member schools have been approved by the New Zealand Qualifications Authority (NZQA). NZEIL (New Zealand Education International Limited) is a cooperative venture between the New Zealand Government's Trade Development Board and the education institutes, and aims to support private schools and state colleges in providing educational services to intemational students.

United Kingdom
The situation is complicated. The British Council run an accreditation scheme for private language schools. The seven categories that are checked for recognition of these schools are: management and administration, premises, resources, professional qualifications, academic management, teaching and welfare. However, some schools are not eligible for accreditation - schools that have been running for less than two years, for example. 80% of the British Council accredited schools also join ARELS. which is the trade organisation for recognised private language schools. Smaller schools may not be able to afford to join ARELS.

Another 17 major language schools decided to set up their own association, FIRST, because they were dissatisfied with ARELS - FIRST is growing and its members are still accredited by the British Council.

The situation is further complicated by the British Council's validation scheme for state colleges and polytechnics - which can lead to courses being regulated by BASCELT (the British Association of State Colleges of English Language Teaching). Finally, universities that belong to BALEAP (the British Association of Lecturers in English for Academic Purposes) operate their own internal self monitoring programme for their courses in English for Academic Purposes. Fortunately in the future there may be a European accreditation scheme.

United States
There is no accrediting agency specifically for English as a Second Language (ESL) programmes, although some states run courses which must meet particular state requirements. In Florida, private schools are accredited by ACCET (Accrediting Council for Continuing Education and Training). The American Association of Intensive English Programs is open to organisations offering intensive courses, and aims to promote prefessional standards and the awareness of opportunities for English language study in the USA.

TESOL has developed a programme of self study for adult training courses which are based on a 'Statement of Core Standards for Language and Professional Training Programs'. The TESOL statement is accepted as the standard by the profession.

Non membership of an organisation may not mean the school is necessarily a bad one.

TESOL has developed a programme of self study for adult training courses.

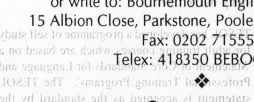

INTERNATIONAL EFL BOOK SUPPLIERS

ARGENTINA
Libreria Rodriguez, Sarmiento 835, Buenos Aires.

AUSTRALIA
AEE, PO Box 455, Cammeray, NSW 2062
The Bridge Bookshop, 10 Grafton Street, Chippendale NSW 2008
Language Book Centre, 555 Beaufort Street, Mount Lawley, Western Australia 6050.
The Language People, 207 Boundary Street, West End, Queensland, 4101.

BRAZIL
Sodilvro, Rua Sa Freire 40, CP 3655, 20930 Rio de Janeiro RJ.
Livraria Nobel SA, Rua de Balsa 559, 02910 Sao Paulo SP.

CANADA
Dominie Press, 1316 Huntingwood Drive, Unit 7, Agincourt, Ontario, M1S 3JL.

CYPRUS
Bridgehouse Bookshop, PO Box, 4527 Bridgehouse Building, Nicosia.

DENMARK
Atheneum International, Booksellers, 6 Norregade, 1165 Kobenhavn.

ECUADOR
The English Book Centre, Acacias 613, y Avenida Las Monjas, Guayaquil.

EGYPT
International Language Bookshop, Mahmoud Asmy ST, PO Box 13, Embaba, Cairo.

FINLAND
Akateeminin Kirjakauppa, Keskuskatu 1 SF-00100 Helsinki.

FRANCE
Keltic Paris, 22 Passage Dauphine, 75006 Paris.
Bradleys Bookshop, 32 PI. Gambetta, 3300 Bordeaux.
Just Books, I Rue de la Paix, Grenoble.
Decitre, 29 PI. Bellecour, 69002 Lyon.
English Books, 8 Rue Doree, 30000 Nimes.
Librairie des Facultes, 2 Rue de Rome, Strasbourg.

GREECE
The Bookstall, Harilou Trikoupi 6-10, 106 79 Athens.
Efstathiadis Group, Olympou 34, 546 30 Thessaloniki.

HONG KONG
Commercial Press, 9-15 Yee Wo Street, Causeway Bay, Hong Kong.

ICELAND
Bokabud Malsog Menningar, Laugavegi 18, 101 Reykjavik.

INDONESIA
Triad Book Centre, Jalan Purnawarman 76a, Bandung, 40116.

IRELAND
International Books, 18 South Frederick Street, Dublin
Modern Languages Ltd., 39 Westland Row, Dublin 2

ISRAEL
Eric Cohen Books, 5 Hanakin St., Ra'anana 43 464.

JAPAN
Biblos, Fl Bldg. 1-26-5 Takadanobaba, Shinjuku-ku, Tokyo 160.

JORDAN
Jordan Book Centre, PO Box 301, (Al Jubeiha) Amman.

KENYA
Book Distributors Limited, PO Box 47610, Weruga Lane, Nairobi.

KUWAIT
Kuwait Bookshops, Thunayan Al Ghanem Bldg. PO Box 2942, Safat.

MALAYSIA
STP Distributors, SDN BHD 31 Green Hall, 10200 Penang.

MEXICO
Libreria Britannica SA, Serapio Rendon 125, Col San Rafael, 06470 DF.

MOROCCO
Librairie Nationale, 2 Avenue Mers Sultan, Casablanca
American Bookstore, 4 Zankat Tanja, Rabat.

NEW ZEALAND
University Bookshop, 34 Princes Street, Auckland.

NORWAY
Olaf Norlis Bokhandel, Universitetsgt 18-24, 0162 Oslo.
Norsk Bokirnport, Postboks 784 S Ovre Vollgate 15, 0106 Oslo 1.

SWEDEN
The English Book Centre, Surbrunnsgatan 51, Box 6207, 102 34, Stockholm.

SWITZERLAND
Librairie Franckc, Neuengasse 43\Von Werdt Passage, 3001 Bem.
Elm Video and Books, 5 rue Versonnes, 1207 Geneva.

TAIWAN
Caves Books, 103 Chung Shan N Road, Sec 2 Taipei.

TURKEY
ABC Kitabevi, 461 Istiklal Cad. Istanbul.
Baris Kitabevi, Koca M. Pasa Cad,No.5914, Cerrahoasa, Istanbul.

UNITED KINGDOM
Athena Bookshop, 71-73 Old Christchurch Road, Bournemouth
BEBC London, 106 Piccadilly, London W1
Dillons University Bookshop, 82 Gower Street, London WC1.
European Bookshop, 4 Regent Place, London W1R 6BH
KELTIC, 25 Chepstow Comer, Chepstow Place, London W2 4TT.
LCL Benedict Limited, 104 Judd Road, London WC1.
Skola Books, 27 Delaney Street, London NW1 7RX.
Hudsons Bookshop, 116 New Street, Birmingham, B2 4JJ.
Bournemouth English Book Centre, 15 Albion Close, Parkstone, Poole, Dorset BH12 3LL
The English Language Bookshop, 31 George Street, Brighton, East Sussex, BN2.
Cambridge International Book Centre, 42 Hills Road, Cambridge, CB2 1LA.
Albion Bookshop, 13 Mercery Lane, Canterbury, Kent.
James Thin Ltd., Buccleuch Street, Edinburgh.
John Smith & Son Ltd., 578 St Vincent Street, Glasgow.
International Bookshop, Palace Chambers, White Rock, Hastings.
Austicks Polytechnic Bookshop, 25 Cookridge Street, Leeds LSI 3AN.
Haigh and Hockland Ltd., The Preoinct Centre, Oxford Road, Manchester.
Thornes Bookshop, Grand Hotel, Percy Street, Newcastle Upon Tyne, NE1 7RS.
Blackwells, 50 Broad Street, Oxford OXI 2BQ.
Dillons the Bookstore, William Baker House, Broad Street, Oxford OX2.
The English Book Centre, 24 Middleway, Oxford OX2 7LG.
Sherrat and Hughes, 94 Above Bar, Southampton S09.
Cactus Bookshop, 104 College Road, Stoke on Trent ST4.
Thomas C. Godfrey Limited, 32 Stonegate, York, North Yorkshire Y01.
Waterstones, *Birmingham* 24-26 High Street, B4 7SL. *Bournemouth* 14-16 The Arcade BH1 2AH. *Edinburgh*, 128 Prince's Street, EH2 4AD. *Leeds*, 93-97 Albion Street, LS1 5AP.

KEEPING IN TOUCH

How newspapers, magazines, associations, conferences and the radio can keep you company no matter where in the world you are.

Stuck in a classroom on 25 or more teaching hours a week? Feeling lonely and uninvolved? Wondering how all those intellectual vistas you marvelled at when you entered the profession have shrunk? Experienced in the widening of horizons that comes from a year at a prestigious university and then wondering where it all went when you got back to the chalkface? Read on.

Professionally and personally teachers need contact as well as new, fresh ideas. EFL is by and large an enthusiast's profession and it is well serviced with ways in which the classroom teacher can keep in touch with the profession at large. This article suggests a range of ways in which you can keep your professional awareness and personal motivation alive.

A monthly trade newspaper landing on your doorstep is simply the best way of keeping up to date.

EFL Gazette
Yes, it is produced by the sister organisation of the *EFL Guide*, but a monthly trade newspaper landing on your doorstep with news of the profession, recruitment, surveys of academic fields and different countries, as well as pedagogical articles, conference reports and materials reviews is simply the best way of keeping up to date. Love it or hate it, you'll want to read it. Specimen copies are usually available at major conferences or from 10 Wright's Lane, London W8 6TA, UK. The *EFL Gazette* is available from specialist bookshops and on subscription and costs £22 (UK), £25 (Europe) and £30 (Rest of the World) in 1994. (Visa/Mastercard telephone orders on +44 71 938 1818, Fax: +44 71 937 7534.)

Language Journals
There are a number of specialist journals which keep you up to date with developments in thinking about the English Language. One of the most popular is the easily approachable is *English Today*, a quarterly review published by Cambridge University Press, The Edinburgh Building, Shaftesbury Road, Cambridge CB2 2RU, UK.

If you are working in a third world country, it is worth finding out if there is a Peace Corps or a VSO office in the capital.

For word buffs, *Verbatim* is the answer. A monthly magazine produced by Lawrence Urdang, former editor in chief of the Random House dictionaries. There is also *Applied Linguistics* published by the International Applied Linguistics Association.

Pedagogic Journals
Three main pedagogic journals for EFL teachers are published in the UK. They are *ELTJ, MET* and *PET.*

ELTJ (the English Language Teaching Journal) is the EFL profession's journal of record. It appears four times a year and is published by Oxford University Press, Walton Street, Oxford OX2 6DP, UK. It contains articles on methodology and linguistics and also reviews of courses and teachers' books.

PET (Practical English Teaching) is a monthly magazine primarily for teachers in secondary school. It contains articles and features, mainly on methodology and is a very useful source of ideas. Its companion monthly, *JET* is for teachers in primary education. *MET (Modern English Teacher)* is a quarterly compilation of articles, also on methodology.

TESOL Matters and *Tesol Quarterly* are the journals of the TESOL association (See overpage under Associations and Conferences). They are provided as part of your membership of TESOL and reflect on developments in research and methodology .

The British Council and USIA
A very important source of information once you are in a particular country is the British Council or the American Cultural Centers. Both organisations have libraries including ELT materials and run seminars. They are useful for advice on local associations and resources. The relevant contact in the British Council is the ELO (English Language Officer). The relevant USIA contact will be the Director of the American Cultural Center. The headquarters of the British Council is Medlock Street, Manchester, UK and the US Information Agency headquarters is 301 4th Street West, Washington DC 20547.

If you are working in a third world country, it is worth finding out if there is a Peace Corps or a VSO office in the capital. These can also be a source of support.

Associations and Conferences
Ask your colleagues about local EFL organisations whose meetings you can attend.

There are two major international organisations that you should know about, one British-based and one US-based.

IATEFL (The International Association of Teachers of English as a Foreign Language) is the major British based association. It publishes its own newsletter and holds an international conference once a year (usually in April) attended by about 1000 teachers. Members also have the option to belong to special interest groups or SIGs. These hold their own seminars at various points of the year and publish their own newsletters. Membership of IATEFL costs £23 (surface mail) or £29 (airmail) and details are available from the Secretary, IATEFL, 3 Kingsdown Chambers, Whitstable, Kent. IATEFL also has a number of national affiliated organisations, mainly in central and eastern Europe.

TESOL (Teachers of English to Speakers of Other Languages) is the largest association, with over 20,000 members and national affiliates running their own local organisations in a number of countries. Like IATEFL, TESOL has a network of special interest groups. It publishes magazines: *TESOL News* and *TESOL Matters* and holds an annual international conference usually in March at a major North American city and attended by up to 10,000 teachers. Details of membership from TESOL, 1600 Cameron Street, Suite 300, Alexandria, Virginia, USA 22314.

Other regional conferences that attract an international group of teachers are the JALT (The Japan Association of Language Teachers, Central Office, Shamboru dai-2, Kaweseki 305, 1-3-17 Kaizuka, Kawasaki-ku, Karagawa 210, Japan) conference held in Japan every October or November, LABCI (Latin American British Cultural Institutes) bi-annual conference held in Latin America, the British Council Convenio for teachers of English in Italy. (NB. If you want to get really involved and present a conference paper at one of these conferences remember that the deadline for offering a presentation may be issued up to ten months ahead of the conference.)

An association for people interested in alternative approaches to language teaching is SEAL (the Society for Effective Affective Learning). SEAL attracts teachers with a special interest in Suggestopaedia, Neuro Linguistic programming and suchlike disciplines and has a newsletter and bi-annual international conference. Details from Emma Grant, SEAL, The Language Centre, University of Brighton, Falmer, Sussex BN1 9PH, UK. The US equivalent is SALT (Society for Alternative Learning and Teaching).

For teachers in Australia, a very good source of information is NCELTR (National Centre for English Language Teaching Research), School of English and Linguistics, Macquarie University, Sydney, NSW 2109.

Broadcasting and Publishing
The BBC World Service's English by Radio Department offers regular programmes for teachers such as its *Speaking of English* magazine programme, offering interviews and reviews for teachers. Schedules and details of programmes can be obtained from *BBC Worldwide* magazine, PO Box 76, Bush House, London WC2B 4PH, UK. The US equivalent is Voice of America; schedules and details from your local US embassy.

This is what is available to keep you in touch at the international level. At the national and local level there is so much more. So don't get locked in. Go out and find it!

IATEFL also has a number of national affiliated organisations, mainly in central and eastern Europe.

TESOL is the largest association, with over 20,000 members.

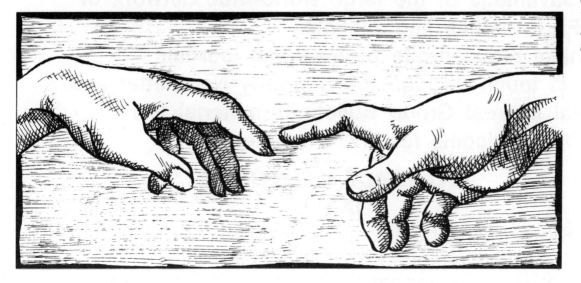

IATEFL

International Association of Teachers of English as a Foreign Language

Get in touch, Share your ideas!
Join IATEFL and you can:

- meet EFL teachers from all over the world and exchange ideas at our annual conference and other small-scale meetings and workshops
- find out more about our Special Interest Groups (13 groups from Business English to Young Learners)

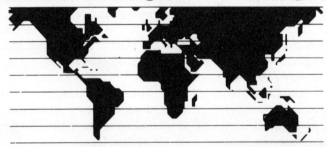

- take advantage of the large world-wide network of IATEFL Branches and Affiliates
- purchase reduced-rate professional journals
- keep in touch through the quarterly Newsletter and Special Interest Group Bulletins, (material from members welcome for all Newsletters).

Contact us now at:
IATEFL

3 Kingsdown Chambers, Kingsdown Park, Tankerton
Whitstable, Kent CT5 2DJ. England.
Telephone: (0227) 276528 Fax: (0227) 274415

CONFERENCE CALENDAR

The major international language fairs of 1994.

8-12 March   *TESOL '94 Annual Conference*
'Sharing Our Stories'
Baltimore,
Maryland,
USA

Contact: TESOL Conventions Dept.
1600 Cameron Street,
Alexandria
Virginia,
22314-2751 USA

28 March -   *Eigteenth FIPLV*
1 April   *(Federation Internationale des
Professeurs de Langues
Vivantes)*
Hamburg, Germany

Contact: FIPLV Head Office,
Seestrasse 247,
CH-8038 Zurich,
Switzerland

6 - 9 April   *IATEFL, Twenty-Eighth
International Conference*
Brighton Centre,
Brighton,
Sussex, UK.

Contact: IATEFL

22-24 April   *Languages and Culture*,
Moscow, Russia

Contact: International Where + How,
Tel: +49 228 22 30 86.
Fax: +49 228 22 26 43.

4-8 May   *Mondolingua*,
Geneva,
Switzerland

Contact: Mondolingua,
chemin du Pont-du-Centenaire 109,
CP 930-1212 Grand-Lancy 1,
Geneva,
Switzerland

21-23 July   *Language Expo*
Sydney,
Australia

30 August -   *ARELS Workshop,*
1 Sept.   Metropole Hotel,
Brighton, UK

Contact: ARELS
2 Pontypool Place,
Valentine Place,
London SE1, UK.

8-11 October   *Japan Association of Language
Teachers*
Ehime,
Shikoku Island,
Japan

Contact: Jalt '94
Jalt Central Office,
2-32-10 Nishinippori,
Arakawaku, Tokyo 116,
Japan

UNITED KINGDOM

Aberdeen College of Further Education
Dept. of English & Communication
Holburn Street, Aberdeen AB9 2YT

Abon Language School
25 St. Johns Road, Clifton, Bristol BS8 2HD

Albion Bookshop
13 Mercury Lane,, Canterbury, Kent

Anglo School
146 Church Road , London SE19 2NT

Anglo-Continental School of English
29 - 35 Wimbourne Road,Bournemouth BH2 6NA

Anglo European Study Tours
8 Colesbridge Mews, Porchester Road, London W2 6EU

Anglo Lang
20 Avenue Road, Scarborough, North Yorkshire

Angloworld, Cambridge
75 Barton Road , Cambridge CB3 9LJ

Anglo-World Oxford
108 Banbury Road, Oxford OX2 6JU

ARA
26 Hay's Mews, London W1X 7RL

ARA International
Carolyn House, Dingwall Road
Croydon CR0 9XF

ARELS (Association of Recognised English Language Schools)
2 Pontypool Place, Valentine Place, London SE1 8QF

Aston University
Language Studies Unit
Birmingham B4 7ET

BALEAP (British Association of Lecturers in English for Academic Purposes)
English Language Unit, Huw Owen Building, OCW, Penglais, Aberyswyth, Dyfed, Wales

BASCELT (Association of UK State Colleges)
Cheltenham and Gloucester College of Higher Education, Francis Close Hall, Swindon Road, Cheltenham, Glos GL50 4AZ

Basil Paterson
22-23 Abercromby Place
Edinburgh EH3 6QE

BBC English
P O Box 76, Bush House, London WC1

Bedford College of Higher Education
School of Humanities Mander Buildings Cauldwell Street, Bedford MK42 9AH

Bedford Study Centre
94-96 Midland Road, Bedford MK40 1QE

Beet Language Centre
Nortoft Road, Chorminster, Bournemouth BH8 8PY

Bell College
South Road, Saffron Walden
Essex CB11 3DP

Bell Educational Trust
The Lodge, Red Cross Lane, Cambridge CB2 2QX

Bell Language Schools
Hillscross, Red Cross Lane
Cambridge CB2 2QX

Bell Language Institute
Regent's College,
Inner Circle
Regent's Park,
London NW1 4WS

Bell School Bath
Henley Lodge, Western Road, Bath BA1 2XT

Bell School Norwich
Bowthorpe Hall,
Norwich

Berlitz School of Languages Ltd
Wells House , 79 Wells Street
London W1

Blackpool and The Fylde College
Ashfield Road, Bispham, Blackpool SY2 0HB

Bone & Company (International Ltd)
69a Castle Street, Farnham, Surrey GU9 7LP

BEBC
15 Albion Close, Parkstone, Poole, Dorset, BH12 3LL

BEBC London
International House, 106 Piccadilly, London W1V

Bradford and Ilkley Community College
Great Horton Road,
Bradford, West Yorkshire

Brasshouse Centre
City of Birmingham Education Dept.,
Brasshouse Passage
Birmingham B1 2HR

British Council
CMDT Recruitment, 10 Spring Gardens
London SW1A 2BN

Medlock Street, Manchester M15 4AA

Brooklands Technical College,
Heather Road, Weybridge,
Surrey KT13 8TT

Brudenell School of English
Larnerton House,
27 High Street,
London W5 5DF

Cambridge Centre for Languages
Sowston Hall
Cambridge CB2 4JR

Central Bureau for Exchange
Seymour Mews House,
Seymour Mews, London W1H 9TE

Central Manchester College
St Johns Centre Lower Hardman Street
Manchester

CFBT Education Services
Quality House, Gyosei Campus,
London Road, Reading RW1 5AQ

Chichester College of Technology
General Studies Westgate Fields
Chichester, W. Sussex PO19 1SB

Chichester School of English
Tutorial College 45 East Street
Chichester, W. Sussex PO19 1HX

Chippenham Technical College
Commercial & Media Studies
Cocklebury Road
Chippenham SN15 3QD

Christ Church College
Language Studies, North Hulmes Road, Canterbury CT1 1QU

Christians Abroad
1 Stockwell Green, London SW9 9HP

Cicero Languages International
42 Upper Grosvenor Road, Tunbridge Wells, Kent TN1 2ET

Clarendon College of Further Education
The Berridge Centre, Stanley Road
Fimest Fields, Nottingham NG7 6HW

Colchester Institute
Dept of Humanities, Sheepen Road
Colchester, Essex CO3 3IL

Colchester English Study Centre
19 Lexden Road, Colchester, Essex

College of Ripon and York St. John
College Road, Ripon HG4 2QX

Concorde International
Radnor Chambers, Cheriton Place, Folkestone, Kent CT20 2BB

College of St Mark & St John
International Education Centre
Derriford Road, Plymouth PL6 8BH

College of St Paul & St Mary
TEFL Unit, Francis Close Hall
Swindon Road, Cheltenham GL50 4AZ

Coventry Technical College
Meridian, Tesol Centre,
Butts, Coventry CV1 3GD

Croydon College of Continuing Education
Fairfield, College Road,
Croydon CR9 1DX

Davies School of English
56 Ecclestone Place, London SW1V 1PO

Delta School of Education
Manchester University,
Oxford Road, Manchester M13 9PL

Devon School of English
42 Palace Avenue, Paignton,
Devon TQ3 3HF

DHSS (Overseas Branch)
Newcastle upon Tyne NE 98 1YX.

Eastbourne School of English
8 Trinity Trees, Eastbourne
East Sussex BN21 3LD

East European Partnership
15 Princeton Court,
53-55 Felsham Road,
London SW16 1AZ

Eaton Hall International
Retford, Nottinghamshire DN22 OPT2

ECCTIS 2000 Ltd.
Fulton House, Jessop Avenue,
Cheltenham,
Gloucester GL50 3SH

Edinburgh Language Foundation
11 Great Stuart Street,
Edinburgh EH3 7TS

The Education Policy Information Centre
The Mere, Upton Park,
Slough, Berks SL1 2DQ

EF International
1/2 Sussex Square, Brighton BN2 1FJ

EF Schools
74-80 Warrior Square,
St. Leonards-on-Sea, Hastings

EFL Gazette
10 Wright's Lane,
London, W8 6TA

EFL Services
Avenue Farmhouse,
Elsworth, Cambridge CB3 8HY

ELC Norwich
46 Unthank Road,
Norwich NR2 2RB

Elmbridge Institute of Adult Education
The Day Centre, 19 The Green,
Esher, Surrey

ELT Banbury
20 Horsefair Road, Oxon, OX16 9AH

English and Spanish Studies
London House, High Street Kensington,
London W8

English Lang. Centre Bournemouth
163-169 Old Christchurch Road,
Bournemouth BH1 1JU

English Teaching Information Centre
The British Council,
10 Spring Gardens, London SW1A 2BN

English Worldwide
17 Concordia Wharf, Mill Street,
London SE1 2BB

Eurocentre, Bournemouth
26 Dean Pk Road, Bournemouth BH1 1H2

Eurocentre, Lee Green
21 Meadowcourt Road, London SE3 8EU

European Council of International Schools
21b Lavant Street
Petersfield Hampshire GU32 3EL

Executive Training Centre
8 St. Peter's Grove, York YO3 6AQ

Farnborough College of Technology
Manor Park Centre, Manor Walk,
Aldershot, Hampshire GN12 4JN

Filton Technical College
EFL Dept., Filton Avenue,
Bristol BS12 7AT

GEOS
55-61 Portland Road, Hove,
Sussex BN3 5DQ

Gloscat
Dept of Management & Business,
The Park Campus, 73 The Park,
Cheltenham
Glos GL50 2RR

Godmer House
90 Banbury Road,
Oxford OX2 6JT

Goldsmith's College
Lewisham Way, London SE14

Greenhill College
Lowlands
Harrow, Middx HA1 3AQ

Haigh & Hochland Ltd.
The Precinct Centre,
Oxford Road, Manchester

Hammersmith & West London College
Dept. of English Studies, Gliddon Road,
Barons Court, London W14 9BL

Harrogate Langauge Academy
8a Royal Parade, Harrogate,
N. Yorks H61 2SZ

Hart Villages Centre (Basingstoke)
Robert Mays School, West Street, Odiham,
Basingstoke RG25 1NA

Hendon College of FE
Montague Road Centre, Hendon
London NW4 3ES

Hilderstone College
English Study Centre, St Peters Road
Broadstairs, Kent CT10 2AQ

Huddersfield Technical College
New North Road, Huddersfield HD1 5NN

Hull College
Queen's Gardens, Hull HU1 3DG

IATEFL (International Association of
Teachers of English as a Foreign Language)
3 Kingsdown Chambers, Tankerton,
Whitstable, Kent CT5 2DJ

ILC Recruitment
1 Riding House Street, London W1A 3AS

ILTB (International Language Teachers)
55 Hither Green, London SE13 6TZ

Infospeed Ltd.
Infospeed House, 47 Commercial Road,
Poole, Dorset, BH14 0HU

inligua School of Languages
55-61 Portland Road
Hove, Sussex BN3 5QD

inlingua Teacher Service
Essex House, Temple Street,
Birmingham B2 5D8

Inner Track Learning
Forge House, Kemble, Glos GL7 6AD

Institute of Education
University of London, TESOL Dept.,
20 Bedford Way, London WC1 0AL

International House, Hastings
ITTI, Whiterock, Hastings,
E. Sussex TN34 1JP

International House, London
106 Piccadilly,
London W1V 9FL

International House Northumbria
14-18 Sidwell Street,
Newcastle upon Tyne NE1 4XQ

ILC (International Language Centre)
24 Polworth Gardens, Edinburgh EH11

International Language Institute
County House,
Vicar Lane,
Leeds LS1 7JH

International Language Services
36 Fowlers Road
Salisbury Wilts SP1 2QU

International Teacher Training Centre
674 Wimbourne Road,
Bournemouth BH9 2EG

ITS English School, Hastings
43-46 Cambridge Gardens,
Hastings, E. Sussex TN34 1EN

Intuition Languages
109 Shepperton Road, London N1 3DF

James Thin Ltd.
Buccleuch Street, Edinburgh

Japan Information and Cultural Cen-
tre
Embassy of Japan, 104 Piccadilly,
London W1V 9FN

JET Programme Officer
Japan Information Centre,
Embassy of Japan, 9 Grosvenor Square,
London W1H 9LB

Jordanhill College
Southbrae Drive, Glasgow G13 1PP

KELTIC Bookshop
25 Chepstow Corner,
Chepstow Place, London W2 4TT

Kirkby College of F.E.
Faculty Gen. Education,
Oman Road, Linthorpe, Middlesborough,
Cleveland TS5 5PJ

Language Matters
4 Blenheim Road, Moseley,
Birmingham B13 9TY

Language Training Services
5 Belevedere, Lansdowne Road,
Bath, BA1 5ED

LCCI
Marlow House, Station Road,
Sidcup, Kent, DA15 7BJ

LCL Benedict Ltd.
104 Judd Road, London

Linguarama Ltd
53 Pall Mall, London SW1Y 5JH/
Oceanic House, 89 High Street,
Alton, Hants GU34 1LG

Living Language Centre
Highcliffe House, Clifton Gardens,
Folkstone, Kent CT20 2EF

London Boroughs of Camden &
Westminster
3 Picton Place, London W11

London Boroughs of City of London
& Tower Hamlets,
Harford Street,
Mile End Road, London E1 4PY

London Borough of Greenwich
Riverside House, East Beresford Street,
London SE18 6DF

London Borough of Hackney
Oakway House, 41 Stamford Hill,
London N16 5SR

London Borough of Hammersmith,
Kensington & Chelsea
50 Brook Green, London W6 7BJ

London Borough of Islington
North Star House,
556-564 Holloway Road, London N7

London Borough of Lambeth
50 Acre Lane, London SW2 5SS

London Borough of Lewisham
Capita House, 47 Rushey Green,
London SE6 4AT

London Borough of Southwark
2 Camden Square, London SE15 5LE

London Borough of Wandsworth
Lavender Hill School, Amies Street,
London SW11 2JW

London Guildhall University
84 Moorgate, London EC2M 6SQ

London Study Centre
Munster House, 676 Fulham Road,
London SW6 5SA

Luton College of HE
Park Square, Luton
Bedfordshire LU1 3JU

Manchester Business School
Language Centre, Booth Street West,
Manchester M15 6PB

Manchester Central College
Lower Hardman Street,
Manchester M3 3FP

Manchester Metropolitan University
Fac of Community Studies,
799 Wilmslow Road, Manchester M20 8RR

Marble Arch Teacher Training
21 Star Street, London W2 1QB

Mid-Cheshire College F.E.
Management Dept, Chester Road,
Hertford Campus, Northwich CW8 1LJ

Millbrook College
TEFL, Bankfield Site, Bankfield Road,
Liverpool, Lancs L13 0BR

Moray House College of Education
Holyrood Road, Edinburgh EH8 8AQ

Multilingua
53 Woolbridge Road, Guildford GU1 4RF

NATFHE (National Association of
Teachers in Further and Higher
Education)
27 Britannia Street, London WC1X 9JP

NEATEFL
Newcastle College, Rye Hill
Newcastle on Tyne

Newnham Language Centre
8 Grange Road, Cambridge CB3 9DV

Nord Anglia International Ltd
Broome House, 152 Palatine Road,
West Didsbury, Manchester M20 8QH

North East Surrey College of
Technology
Reigate Road, Ewell,
Fosom, Surrey KT17 3DS

North Trafford College
Talbot Road, Stretford,
Manchester M32 0XH

NUT (National Union of Teachers)
Hamilton House, Mabledon Place,
London WC1

OCTAB (The Overseas Contract Teachers and Advisors Branch of the IPS)
The Secretary,
24 Ashford Road,
Manchester M20 4EH

Oxford Brookes University
Gypsy Lane Campus, Headington,
Oxford OX3 0BP

Oxford College
Oxpens Road,
Oxford OX1 1SA

Oxford House College
3 Oxford Street, London W1R 1RF

Park Lane College
Park Lane, Leeds LS3 1AA

Pilgrims Language Courses
8 Vernon Place, Canterbury,
Kent CT1 37G

Pitman School of English
154 Southampton Row,
London WC1B 5AX

Practical TEFL Training
PO Box 191, London SW1Z

Primary House
300 Gloucester Road, Bristol BS7 8PD

Regency School of English
Royal Crescent, Ramsgate, Kent

Regent Capital Centre
4 Percy Street, London W1 PF

Regent Schools
5 Percy Street, London W1P NFA

Regent School of English
Teacher Training, 4 Percy Street,
London W1P 9FA

Returned Volunteer Action
1 Amwell Street, London EC1R 1UL

Royal Holloway & Bedford New
College
English Dept., Egham Hill,
Egham, Surrey TW20 0EX

RSA Cambridge Exams
UCLES
1 Hills Road, Cambridge CB1 2EU

Salisbury School of English
36 Fowlers Road,
Salisbury, Wiltshire SP1 2QU

Saxoncourt (UK) Ltd.
59 South Molton Street,
London W1Y 1HH

Scarborough International School
Cheswold Hall, 37 Stepney Road,
Scarborough, W. Yorks YO12 5BN

SOAS
University of London,
Market Street, London WC1

Severnvale
Central Language Academy,
Shrewsbury SY1 1ES

Sheffield Hallam University
The TESOL Centre, Totley Hall Lane
Sheffield S17 4AB

Skill Share Africa
3 Belvoir, Leicester LE1 6SL

SLS York
Cromwell House, 13 Ogleforth,
York YO1 2JG

South Devon College of Arts &
Technology
Newton Road, Torquay,
Devon TQ2 5BY

South London College
Knights Hill, West Norwood,
London SE27 0TX

Southampton Institute of Higher Education
East Park Terrace,
Southampton, Hants SO9 4WW

Southend College of Technology
Dept of Gen Education & Science
Carnarvon Road, Southend-on-Sea
Essex SS2 6LS

Southwark College
209-215 Blackfriars Road,
London SE1 8NL

St Giles Brighton
69 Marine Parade,
Brighton, E. Sussex BN2 1AD

St Giles College, London
51 Shepherds Hill,
Highgate, London N6 5QP

St Mary's College
Strawberry Hill, Twickenham TW1 45X

Stanton School of English
167 Queensway, London N2 4SB

Studio School of English
6 Salisbury Villas, Station Road,
Cambridge CB1 2JF

Stoke on Trent College
Stoke on Trent S14 2DG

The Sudan Embassy
The Recruiting Officer, Cultural Section
31 Rutland Gate, London W7 1PG

Surrey Language Centres
Sandford House, 39 West Street,
Farnham, Surrey GU9 7DR

Swan School of English
11 Guild Street, Stratford-upon-Avon CV37

Swan School of English (Oxford)
11 Banbury Road, Oxford OX2 6JX

Trebinshun Group
Brecon, Powys, Wales LD3 7PX

Thames Valley University
St. Mary's Road, Ealing, London W5 3RE

Thomas C. Godfrey
32 Stonegate, York, North Yorkshire YO1

Thurrock Technical College
Woodview, Grays, Essex ILM16 4YR

Trinity College, London
11-13 Mandeville Place,
London W1M 6AQ

UCLES
1 Hills Road, Cambridge CB1 EU

UNIPAL
12 Helen Road, Oxford OX2 0DE

United Nations Association
UNA International Service,
3 Whitehall Court,
London SW1A 2EL

United Nations Volunteers
c/o VSO, 317 Putney Bridge Road
London SW15 2PN

University College Of Wales, Bangor
Dept. of Education,
Deinol Road,
Bangor LL57 2UW

University College of Wales, Cardiff
P.O. Box 78,
Cardiff CF1 1XL

University College of Wales, Aberyswyth
Dept of Education,
Old College, King Street,
Aberystwyth, Dyfed S723 2AX

University of Aberdeen
Dept of English, Aberdeen AB9 1FX

University of Aston
Language Studies Unit
Aston Triangle, Birmingham B4 7ET

University of Birmingham
Dept of English, P.O. Box 363
Birmingham B15 2TT

University of Brighton
Language Centre, Falmer, Brighton,
Sussex BN1 9P4

University of Bristol
School of Education, 35 Berkley Square
Bristol BS8 1JA

University of Cambridge
Dept. of TEFL, 1 Hills Road,
Cambridge CB1 2EU

University of Central England
Perry Bar, Edgebaston,
Birmingham B42 2SU

University of Durham
Elvet Riverside, 11 New Elvet,
Durham DH1 3JT

University of East Anglia
School of Modern Languages, Norwich

University of Edinburgh
Applied Ling & Lang Studies
21 Hill Place, Edinburgh EH8 9DP

University of Essex
Wivenhoe Park, Colchester CO4 3SQ

University of Exeter
School of Education, St Lukes,
Heavitree Road, Exeter EX1 2LV

University of Glasgow
English Lang Dept., Glasgow G12 8QQ

University of Hull
Language Centre, Hull HU6 7RX

University of Kent
Inst. Lang & Ling, Cornwallis Building,
Canterbury, Kent CT2 7NF

University of Lancaster
Dept of Lings & Mod Eng Lang
Lancaster LA1 L7T

University of Leeds
Overseas Education Unit
School of Education, Leeds LS2 9JT

University of Leicester
School of Education, 21 University Road
Leicester LE1 7RF

University of Liverpool
E L Unit, Mod Langs Building
P.O. Box 147,
Liverpool L69 3BX

University of London, Birbeck College
Applied Linguistics, 20 Bedford Way,
London WC1H 0AL

University of Manchester
Dept of Education, Manchester M13 9PL

University of Newcastle-upon-Tyne
St Thomas Street, Newcastle-upon-Tyne
NE1 7RU

University of Northumbria at Newcastle
Lipman Building,
Newcastle-upon-Tyne NE1 8ST

University of Nottingham
Dept of English Studies
University Park, Nottingham NG7 2RD

University of Oxford Delegacy of Local Examinations
Ewert House, Summertown,
Oxford OX2 7BZ

University of Portsmouth
Wiltshire Building, Hampshire Terrace,
Portsmouth PO2 BU

University of Reading
Dept Linguistics & Science,
Whitenights, Reading RG6 2AD

University of Sheffield
ELT Centre, Arts Tower,
Sheffield S10 2TN

University of Salford
Special Studies Unit,
Salford, Lancs, M5 4WT

University of Southampton
Dept of Education
Southampton SP9 5NH

University of Stirling
Stirling FK9 4LA

University of Strathclyde
Livingstone Tower, Richmond Street,
Glasgow G1 1XH

University of Sussex
Language Centre, Arts A,
Falmer, Brighton BN1 9QN

University of Ulster at Coleraine
Education Faculty
Cromore Road, Coleraine
Co. Londonderry NI BT52 1SA

University of Warwick
Centre for English Lang Teaching
Westwood, Coventry CV4 7AL

University of Westminster
Faculty of Languages, 9-18 Euston Centre,
London NW1 3ET

University of York
Dept of Linguistic Science & Lang Teaching Centre, Heslington, York YO1 5OD

Voluntary Services Overseas
317 Putney Bridge Road
London SW15 2PN

Waltham Forest College
Gen. Ed. Dept., Forest Road, Walthamstow,
London E17 5JB

Waverley Adult Educ Institute
Bridge Road, Godalming,
Surrey GU7 3DU

West Sussex Institute of H.E.
The Dome, Upper Bognor Road,
Bognor Regis, W. Sussex

Western Language Centre Ltd
Forge House, Kemble, Glos GL7 6AD

Wigston College of F.E.
Station Road, Wigston Magna,
Leicester LE8 2DW

Woking & Chertsey Adult Ed. Inst.
Danesfield Centre, Grange Road
Woking, Surrey GU21 4DA

Women in TEFL
42 Northolme Road, London N5 2UX

AUSTRALIA

ATESOL
P O Box 296, Rozelle
New South Wales 2039

Australian Centre for Languages
Teacher Education Institute
420 Liverpool Road, South Stratfield
New South Wales 2136

Australian College of English (C/D)
P O Box 82, Bondi Junction
New South Wales 2022

Canberra College of Advanced Education
P O Box 1, Canberra 2616

ELICAS Association
3 Union Street, Ayrmont, NSW 2009

Institute of Technical and Adult Teacher Education (D)
62 Kameruka Road, Northbridge, 2063

International College of English
230 Flinders Lane, Melbourne
Victoria 3000

La Touche University
Bundoora 3083, Victoria

Macquarie University
N.S.W. 2109

Milner International College of English
1st Floor, 195 Adelaide Terrace
Perth WA 6000

National Curriculum Resource Centre
5th Floor, 197 Rundal Mall
Adelaide 5000

Overseas Service Bureau
P O Box 350, 71 Argyle Street
Fitroy, 3065 Victoria

RMIT University
PO Box 12058
A'Beckett Street
Melbourne 3000

Sydney College of Advanced Education
Office of the Principal, Secretary & Admin
53-57 Renwick Street,
Redfern 2016
P O Box 375, Waterloo,
New South Wales

University of New South Wales
P O Box 1, Kensington, NSW 2033

University of Melbourne
Perkville, Victoria 3052

University of Sydney
NSW 2006

Western Australian College of Advanced Education
Rensen Street, Churchlands 6018
P O Box 217,
Western Australia 6018

AUSTRIA

International House
Schwedenplatz 2/6/55, Alolo, Vienna

BRAZIL

Britannia Association for Teacher Education
Rua Nascimento Silva 154
Ipanema, Rio De Janeiro

British Association for Teacher Education Brasil (Bate)
Rua Vinicius De Moraes 179
Ipanema 22411, Rio De Janeiro

Braztesol
Rua Julia da Costa 1500,
80430 Curitba PR

LAURELS (Latin American Association of Registered English Language Schools)
c/o Liberty English Centre,
Rua Aminta de Barros 1,
05980 Curitiba Paran

Sociedad Cultura Brasiliera dos Cultura Inglese
Av Graca Aranha, 327-7CP
Caixa Postal 821 Rio de Janeiro

CANADA

Canadian Council of Second Languages
151 Slater Street, Ottawa,
Ontario T1P 5NI

Canadian University Services Overseas
135 Rideau Street, Ottawa

University of Calgary
2500 University Drive NW
Calgary AB, T2N 1N4

University of Alberta
Edmonton AB, T6G 2G5

McGill University
3700 McTavish Street
Montreal QC, H3A 1Y2

University of Victoria
PO Box 170, Victoria BC, V8W 2YS

Simon Fraser University
Burnaby BC, V5A 1S6

University of British Columbia
2125 Main Mall
Vancouver V6T 125

Ontario Institute for Studies in Education
252 Bloor St. West
Toronto, Ontario, M5S 1V6

Concordia University
1455 de Maisonneuve Blvd
Montreal QC, H3G 1M8

COLOMBIA

Association Colombiana de Profesores de Lenguas
Centro Oxford,
Apartado Aereo 102420,
Unicentro, Bogota

CYPRUS

Bridge House Bookshop
PO Box 4527,
Bridgehouse Building,
Nicosia

The English Institute
c/o The English School, Nicosia

DENMARK

Association of English Teachers in Adult Education
EETAE, Toftegardsvej
24 DK 3500 Vaerlose

ECUADOR

Ecuadorian English Teachers Society
PO Box 10935, Guayaquil.

EGYPT

British Council
192 Sharia El Nil, Agouza, Cairo

International Language Institute American University
El Sahafeyeen, PO Box 13, Embaba
Cairo

FINLAND

Association of Teachers of English in Finland
Rautatielaisenkatu 6A 00520
Helsinki

FRANCE

ESIEE
Cite Descartes,
2Bd Blaise Pascal - BP99
93162 Noisy-le-Grand Cedex

International Language Centre
20 Passage Dauphine, 75006 Paris

The British Institute
11 Rue de Constantine, 75007 Paris

TESOL France
71 rue St. Denis, 75002 Paris

University Lyon 11-Formation
86 Rue Pasteur, 69007 Lyon

GERMANY

Munich English Language Teachers Association
Maistrasse 21,
8000 Muenchen 2.

GREECE

British Council
Plateia Philikis Etairias 17,
Kolonaki Square,
PO Box 3488,
Athens 10216

British Council
9 Ethnikis Amynis, PO Box 10289
541013 Thessaloniki

Efstathiadis Group
Olympu 34, 546 30 Thessaloniki

TESOL Greece
87 Academis Street, Athens

HONG KONG

The British Council
English Language Institute
Easey Commercial Building
255 Hennessy Road

HUNGARY

International House
PO Box 95, Budapest 1364

Kecsemet Association for Teachers of English
Akademia Korut, 20.1.31
Kecsemet 6000.

IRELAND

NATEFLI National Association of Teachers of English as a Foreign Language in Ireland
PO Box 1917, Dublin 2

Academy of Education
44 Lower Leeson Street, Dublin 2

Centre of English Studies
31 Dame Street, Dublin 2

Cork Language Centre International
Emmet Place, Cork

Dublin School of English
10-12 West Moreland Street, Dublin 2

English Language Education Institute
30 The Mall, Tralee, Co. Kerry

English Language Studies Institute
99 St. Stephen's Green, Dublin 2

Galway Language Centre
The Bridge Mills, Galway

Grafton Tuition
Grafton Buildings, 34 Grafton Street,
Dublin 2

International Study Centre
67 Harcourt Street, Dublin 2

Irish Tourist Board
Baggot Street Bridge, Dublin 2

Langtrain International
Torquay Road, Foxrock, Dublin 18

Language Centre of Ireland
9-11 Grafton Street, Dublin 2

Trinity College
Centre for Language and
Communication Studies, Dublin 2

University College of Dublin
Belfield, Dublin 4

KOREA

TESOL Korea
Kangnung University San-1,
Chi byon-dong, Kangnung,
Kang-won-do 210-702

ITALY

Academia Brittanica
International House,
Viale Manzoni 57,
00185 Rome

AISLI
British Institute, via Quattro Fontane 109,
Rome

British Council Naples
Via Dei Mille 48, Palazzo D'Avalos
80121 Naples

British Institute
Via S Stefano 11, 40125 Bologna

British Schools
Viale Liegi 14, Rome

Cambridge School
Via S Rocchetto 3,
37100 Verona

International House
Viale Manzoni 57, 00185 Rome

Regent School of Rome
Via Monterone 4, 00187 Rome

The British School
Via Montenapoleione 5, 20121 Milan

The Milan Training Centre
Via Fabio Filzi 27, 20131 Milano

JAPAN

The British Council
2 Kagurazaka 1, Chome Shinjuku-Ku,
Tokyo 164

International Education Service
Shin Taiso Building, 2-10-7 Dogensaka
Shibuya-ku, Tokyo 150

International Language Centre
Iwanami Building 9F, 2-1 Jimbo-Cho
Kanda, Chiyoda-Ku, Tokyo 101

International Language Centre
Shirakabe Building 7F, Shibata 114-7
Kita-Ku, Osaka

JALT (The Japan Association of Language Teachers)
Lions Mansion Kawaramachi 111
Kawaramachi Matsubara-Agaru
Shimogyo-ku, Kyoto 600

Stanton School of English
Ikebukuro School
(Academic Division)
5F West Building, Higashi Ikebukoro
Toshima-Ku, Tokyo 170

KUWAIT

The British Council
P O Box 345, Safat

International Language Centre
Military Language Institute
P O Box 3310, Salmiya 22034

LUXEMBOURG

Association Luxembourgeoise des Ensiegnants d'Anglais
BP 346, L-2013 Luxembourg

English Language Centre
65 Avenue Gaston Diderich,
Luxembourg 1420

MALAYSIA

British Council Language Centre
P O Box 595, 10770 Penang

MEXICO

Anglo Mexican Cultural Institutes
Antonio Caso 127, Mexico 4, D.F.

Institute Anglo-Mexicano de Cultura AC
Felipe Villanueva No 52,
Colonia Guadalupe Inn,
01020 DF

Institute Anglo-Mexicano de Cultura AC
APDO 12755, Guadalajara, Jalisco

NEW ZEALAND

FIELSNZ
PO Box 2577,
Auckland

NZEIL
PO Box 10500,
Wellington

NORWAY

LMS Modern Language Association
of Norway
Jonas Liesvei, 1B
1412 Sofiemyr.

OMAN

The British Council
P O Box 7090, Muttrah

PERU

Newton College
Apartado 18-0873,
Miraflores, Lima 18

PORTUGAL

APPI
Associaco Portuguese de
Professores de Ingles
Apartado 2885, 1122 Lisbon

Institute Britanico Em Portugal
Rua Cecilio de Sousa 65
1294 Lisbon Codex

International House
Rua Marques Sa Da Bandiera
1000 Lisbon

SINGAPORE

Art Language Centre
7th & 8th Floors, Tanglin Shopping Centre
Tanglin, 1024

SOUTH AFRICA

English Language Educational Trust
74 Aliwal Street, Durban 40

SPAIN

Academia de Idiomas Lacunza
Urbieta 14-1, San Sebastian 20006

APAC Associaco de Professors
D'Angles de Catalunya
Apartado 2287, 08080 Barcelona

Association de Professors de Ingles
de Galicia
Apartado de Correo 1078
Santiago de Compostela

British Council
Calle Almagro 5, 28010 Madrid

British Language Centre
Bravo Murillo 377/2, 28020 Madrid

International House
Zurbano 8, Madrid 4

International House
Trafalgar 14 Entlo, Barcelona 08010

International House
Escuela Industrial 12, Sabadell,
Barcelona

International House
Pascual y Genis 16,
46002 Valencia

International House
Paseo de Mallorca 36,
Palma de Mallorca 07012

Stanton School of English
Montera 24 2 Piso,
28013 Madrid

TESOL Spain
Universidad de Cordoba,
Departmento de Ingles, Cordoba 10678

York House Language Centre
Mutaner 479, 08021 Barcelona

SRI LANKA

Colombo International School
28 Gregory's Road, Colombo 7

SWEDEN

Kursverksamheten Vid
Lunds Universitet
Regementsgatan 4, 21142 Malmo

Kursverksamheten Vid
Stockholms Universitet
P O Box 7845, 10398 Stockholm

LMS Lars Ake Kall
Wallingaten 12, S111 60 Stockholm

SWITZERLAND

Benedict - Schools
P O Box 300, CH1000, Lausanne 9

Ecole Lemania
3 Chemin de Preville, 1001 Lausanne

ELCRA Bell
English Language Consultants & Resource Associates SA
12 Chemin des Colombettes,
1202 Geneva

ETAS (English Teachers' Association
Switzerland)
Bolsternstrasse 22, 8483 Kollbrun

inlingua
Weisenhuasplatz 28, 3011 Berne

Klubschule Migros
Oberer Graben 35, 9000 St. Gallen

Volkshochschule des Kantons Zurich
Limmatquai 62, 8001 Zurich

TURKEY

British Council
9 Kirlangic Sokak, Gaziosmanpasa,
06700 Ankara

British Council
Ors Turistik Is Merkezi Istiklal
Caddesi 251-253, Kat 2,3,5, Beyoglu,
Istanbul 80060

Istanbul Turco-British Association
Suleyman Nazif Sokak 10
Nisantasi, 80220 Istanbul

School of Languages
Bogazici University
PK2 Bebek, Istanbul

UNITED ARAB EMIRATES

The British Council
P O Box 6523, Abu Dhabi

ECS Ltd.
PO Box 25018,
Abu Dhabi

UNITED STATES OF AMERICA

American Language Academy
2105 Grove Street, Berkeley,
California 94704

Berlitz International Inc
Research Park, 2923 Wall Street
Princeton NJ08540

ELS
5761-6 Buckingham Parkway
Culver City, CA 90230

English International
655 Sutter Street (Suite 500),
San Francisco, Ca 94102

ERIC
Centre for Applied Linguistics
118 22nd Street NL, Washington DC

Eurocentres
101 North Union Street, Suite 3000
Alexandria, Virginia VA 22314

International Language Institute
1601 Connecticut Avenue N.W.
Washington DC 20009

International Educator (The)
International Educators Institute
PO Box 103, West Bridgewater
MA 02379

Inlingua School of Languages
551 Fifth Avenue,
New York, NY 10176

International School of Languages
P O Box 6188, 958 W. Pico Boulevard
90212 Beverley Hills, CA

Monterey Institute of International
Studies
425 Van Buren Street, Monterey
California 93940

Peace Corps
1990 K St NW, Washington DC 20526

St. Giles College Educational Trust
2280 Powell Street,
94133 San Francisco, CA

School For International Training
Brattleboro, Vermont 05301

TESOL
1600 Cameron Street, Suite 300,
Alexandria, Virginia 22314-2705

Adelphi University
Harvey Hall, Room 130,
Garden City,
New York 11530

University of Alabama
Department of English, Morgan Hall
PO Box 870244, Tuscaloosa
Alabama 35487-0244

The American University
Asbury Building, Room 326,
4400 Massachusetts Avenue N.W.,
Washington, DC 20016-8045

University of Arizona
Department of English
Modern Languages Room 458
Tucson, Arizona 85721

Arizona State University
Language and Literature Building,
Room B504, Tempe,
Arizona 85287-0302

Azusa Pacific University
901 East Alosta Avenue, Azusa,
California 91702-7000

Ball State University
Department of English
Muncie, Indiana 47306

Biola University
Marshburn Hall, 13800 Biola Avenue,
La Mirada, California 90639-0001

Boston University
TESOL Program, School of Education,
605 Commonwealth Avenue
Boston, Mass. 02215

University of California at Davis
Titus Hall, Room 130, Davis,
California 95616

University of California at Los Angeles
Dept.of TESL and Applied Linguistics
3300 Rolfe Hall, 405 Hilgard Avenue
Los Angeles, California. 90024

California State University, Dominguez
Hills
Carson, California 90747

California State University, Fresno
Leon S. Peters Building, Room 383,
5245 North Backer Avenue,
Fresno, California 93740-0092

California State University, Fullerton
Humanities Building, Room 835C,
Fullerton, California 92634

California State University, Long Beach
1250 Bellflower Boulevard,
Long Beach, California 90840-2403

California State University, Northridge
Sierra North 318, Northridge,
California 91330

California State University, Sacramento
6000 J Street, Sacramento,
California 95819-2694

University of Colorado
Admissions Committee Chair
Linguistics-Box 295
Boulder, Colorado 80309-0295

University of Delaware
Department of Educational Studies,
206 Willard Hall, Newark,
Delaware 19716

East Carolina University
GCB 2201, Greenville,
North Carolina 27858-4353

Eastern Michigan University
Foreign Languages and Bilingual Studies
219 Alexander, Ypsilanti,
Michigan 48197

University of Florida
112 Anderson Hall, Gainesville,
Florida 32611

Florida International University
School of Education, DM 291
Tamiami Trail, Miami,
Florida 33199

Fordham University at Lincoln
Center
Room 1025,
113 West 60th Street,
New York, NY 10023

George Mason University
Department of English,
Fairfax, Virginia 22030

Georgetown University
School of Languages and Linguistics
Washington D.C. 20057

University of Georgia
Aderhold 125, Athens, Georgia 30602

Georgia State University
Atlanta, Georgia 30302-4018

Harvard University
54 Dunster Street, Cambridge,
Mass 02138

University of Hawaii at Manoa
Moore Hall 570,
1890 East-West Road,
Honolulu, Hawaii 96822

Hofstra University,
236 Gallon Wing, Mason Hall,
Hempstead, New York 11550

University of Houston,
University Park, Department of English
Houston, Texas 77004

Hunter College of the CUNY
Department of Curriculum and Teaching
West Building Room 1025
695 Park Avenue Box 568, New York,
New York 10021

University of Idaho
Dept. of English, Moscow, Idaho 83843

University of Illinois at Chicago
Department of Linguistics, Box 4348
Chicago, Illinois 60680

Illinois State University
Normal, Illinois 61761

Indiana University
Department of Linguistics
Lindley Hall 401, Bloomington,
Indiana 47405

Inter American University of Puerto
Rico, San German Campus
Call Box 5100, San German,
Puerto Rico 00683

Inter American University of Puerto
Rico, Metropolitan Campus
PO Box 1293, San Juan,
Puerto Rico 00919-1293

University of Iowa
Iowa City, Iowa 52242

Iowa State University
Department of English
203 Ross Hall, Ames,
Iowa 50011

University of Kansas
427 Blake Hall, Lawrence,
Kansas 66045-2140

Logman Publishing Group
10 Bank Street
White Plains
NY 10606-1951

University of Miami
222 Merrick Building,
PO Box 248065,
Coral Gables, Florida 33124

Michigan State University
Center for International Programs
East Lansing,
Michigan 48824-1035

University of Minnesota
1425 University Avenue Southeast,
Minneapolis, Minnesota 55455

University of Mississippi,
School of Education,
Room 152b, University,
Mississippi 38677

Monterey Institute of International
Studies
425 Van Buren Street,
Monterey, California 93940

Nazareth College
4245 East Avenue, Rochester,
New York 14618

University of Nevada, Reno
Reno, Nevada 89557-0031

University of New Mexico
Mesa Visa Hall 3090
Albuquerque,
New Mexico 87131

College of New Rochelle
Chidwick 103, Castle Place,
New Rochelle,
New York 10805-2308

New York University
TESOL, 829 Shrimkin Hall
50 West 4th Street,
New York, NY 10003

State University of New York at
Albany
TESOL Program, Albany,
New York 12222

State University of New York at
Buffalo
Dept. of Learning & Instruction
593 Christopher Baldy Hall
Buffalo, New York 14260

State University of New York at Stony
Brook
Dept. of Linguistics, Stony Brook,
New York 11794-4376

Northern Arizona University
Box 6032, Flagstaff,
Arizona 86011-6032

University of Northern Iowa
Baker Hall 155, Cedar Falls,
Iowa 50614-0502

Notre Dame College
2321 Elm Street, Manchester,
New Hampshire 03104

Nova University
3301 College Avenue,
Fort Lauderdale, Florida 33314

Old Dominion University
Norfolk, Virginia 23529-0078

University of the Pacific
School of Education,
3601 Pacific Avenue, Stockton,
California 95211

Pennsylvania State University
305 Sparks Building, University Park,
Pennsylvania 16802

Portland State University
PO Box 751, Portland,
Oregon 97207-0751

University of Puerto Rico
Rio Pedras, Puerto Rico 00931

Rhode Island College
Mann 043,
600 Mount Pleasant Avenue,
Providence,
Rhode Island 02908

Saint Michael's College
Center for International Programs,
Winooski Park,
Colchester,
Vermont 05439

University of San Francisco
School of Education,
2130 Fulton,
San Francisco,
California 94117

San Francisco State University
Department of English
1600 Holloway Avenue
San Francisco,
California 94132

San Jose State University
San Jose, California 95192

Seton Hall University
400 South Orange Avenue,
South Orange,
New Jersey 07079

University of South Carolina
Linguistics Program
Columbia,
South Carolina 29208

University of South Florida
International Language Institute
LIB 618,
4202 Fowlder Avenue
Tampa,
Florida 33620

Southeast Missouri State University
Grauel Language Arts Building,
Room 208B,
Cape Girardeau,
Missouri 63701

University of Southern California
Dept. of Linguistics,
Los Angeles,
California 90089-1693

Southern Illinois University at
Carbondale
Faner 3236,
Carbondale, Illinois 62901

University of Southern Maine
400 Bailey Hall,
Gorham,
Maine 04038

University of Southern Mississippi
George Hurst Building, Room 110,
Southern Station
Box 5038,
Hattiesburg,
Mississippi 39406

Syracuse University
316 H.B. Crouse,
Syracuse, NY 13244-9489

Teachers College of Columbia
University
525 West 120 Street,
New York,
NY 10027

Temple University
Ritter Hall, Broad and Montgomery,
Philadelphia, Pennsylvania 19122

University of Texas at Arlington
Box 19559,
Arlington, Texas 76019

University of Texas at Austin
Education Building 528,
Austin,
Texas 78712

University of Texas at San Antonio
6900 North Loop, 1604W,
San Antonio,
Texas 78259

University of Texas Pan American
Edinburg,
Texas 78539

University of Toledo
University Hall 5040,
Toledo,
Ohio 43606-3390

United States International University
Daley Hall of Science,
Room 307,
10455 Pomerado Road,
Poway,
California 92131

University of Utah
OSH 341,
Salt Lake City,
Utah 84112

University of Washington
English Graduate Office, GN-30,
Seattle, Washington 98195

Washington State University
Pullman,
Washington 99164-5020

West Chester University
Main Hall 550,
West Chester,
Pennsylvania 19383

Western Kentucky University
Bowling Green,
Kentucky 42101

University of Wisconsin-Madison
Department of English
5134 Helen C. White Hall
600 North Park Street
Madison,
Wisconsin 5370

University of Wisconsin-Milwaukee
Enderis Hall,
Room 355,
PO Box 413,
Milwaukee,
Wisconsin 53201

USIA Information Agency
English Language Teaching Division
301 4th Street South West
Washington DC 20547

Worldteach
Phillips Brooks House
Harvard University
Cambridge,
Mass 02138

Wright State University
438 Millet Hall,
Colonel Glenn Highway,
Dayton,
Ohio 45435

Index of Advertisers

INDEX

A

B

C

D

E

F

G

H

I

J

K